DARING TO DEFY
Port Talbot's War Resistance 1914–1918

Also by Philip Adams

A most industrious town: Briton Ferry and its people 1814–2014 (2014)
Not in Our Name: War dissent in a Welsh town (2015)

About the author
Philip Adams started his working life, which was all spent in various manufacturing industries, in Port Talbot steelworks. After retirement he has written books like this one, about people, places and events in south Wales. He lives in Shropshire, which still allows him to engage with historical societies in Neath-Port Talbot, where he grew up.

About the cover and title-page illustration
'I remember well how we thought we were so grown up'
Acrylic painting, 56.3 x 47.7 cm

The painting depicted is by David Carpanini, once of the Afan Valley. It captures the environment from which he and many of those described in this book emerged. He also described his work in words in *Art Review* (1998), saying:
'... it is in the valleys and former mining communities of south Wales, scarred by industry but home for a resolute people that I have found the trigger for my creative imagination. The close-knit and often claustrophobic social infrastructure is a fundamental part of my own background and I have attempted to use the natural drama of this location to explore aspects of the human condition such as fear, isolation, loneliness, brutality, dignity, pride and hope.'
'Fear, isolation, loneliness, brutality, dignity, pride and hope' is also an apt description of the human condition of those who dared to defy.

DARING TO DEFY

Port Talbot's War Resistance
1914–1918

PHILIP ADAMS

Published by Philip Adams
144 Corve Street, Ludlow, Shropshire SY8 2PG, UK
www.britonferrybooks.uk

First published 2016

Copyright © Philip Adams 2016

The moral right of the author has been asserted

All rights reserved. No part of this publication may be reproduced, stored in a retrieval system, or transmitted in any form or transmitted by any means, electronic, electrostatic, magnetic tape, mechanical, photocopying, recording, or otherwise, without prior permission of the authors of the works herein.

British Library Cataloguing in Publication Data. A catalogue record for this book is available from the British Library.

ISBN 978 0 9930671 2 9

Designed by Internet@TSP, Ludlow, Shropshire
Typeset in Bitstream Charter and PT Sans

Printed in UK by Printdomain Ltd, Thurnscoe, South Yorkshire

Contents

Chapter		Page
	Foreword	7
	Abbreviations	10
One	An introduction to Port Talbot	11
Two	Conscription and the tribunals	24
Three	The conscientious objector	46
Four	The Port Talbot objectors:	52
	Non-combatants	54
	Schemers	62
	Workers of national importance	99
	Tortured and tormented	108
	Absolutists	119
	Outcomes unknown	127
Five	Local support	140
Six	National support	163
Seven	Conclusions	189
Eight	Appendices	198

1. Timeline
2. Conscientious objector motivations
3. Tribunal members
4. Prisons and work centres
5. Significant events in Port Talbot concerning the war
6. Henry Davies' trial
7. Albert Rankin's prison notebook
8. Bibliography

		Page
9.	Definitions and tribunal language	
10.	Letter from Northallerton Prison	
11.	Statistics – homes, religion, employment	

Acknowledgements	*222*
Index	*224*

Note on spelling

The author has avoided Anglicised spelling of place names in favour of the Welsh place names, for example *Aberafan* replaces Aberavon and *Cwmafan* replaces Cwmavon. Readers may still need to use the Anglicised versions as search terms in certain cases.

Foreword

AS THIS FOREWORD is being written the townspeople, the workers in Port Talbot steelworks and many others are concerned about the works' future. It is now in doubt due to a combination of factors such as world over-supply of steel and the costs of production at Port Talbot. This is happening just as the United Kingdom has voted to leave the European Union and has a new Prime Minister. Current events are, therefore, providing an anxious time, and not only for those whose livelihoods depend on the steelworks.

However, two events that took place a hundred years ago, dim and distant though that era might now seem, are still worthy of reviewing today as well as the decisions in Mumbai on the future of the steelworks. The first event was that preliminary work was begun for the re-construction of that very Steelworks. The second, concurrent event, with the first Battle of the Somme imminent, was the introduction of conscription to the army in Great Britain. One aspect of the latter event has barely been recorded, until now. In March 2016, at an international conference held at Leeds University on the subject of 'Resistance to War', the names of Port Talbot and Briton Ferry were publicly acknowledged, together, as a main centre of opposition to conscription and war.

This acknowledgement was made by Cyril Pearce of Leeds University, whose creation, the *National Register of Conscientious Objectors* is now the authoritative database of objection to conscription in Britain in World War One. Detailed evidence to support Pearce's claim, with regards Briton Ferry, had already been publicly recorded in the 2015 book, *Not in Our Name: War Dissent in a Welsh Town*, but no comparable book existed about resistance in Port Talbot.

Therefore, the intention of this volume is to develop a largely empirical record of the experiences of those who resisted war and conscription from the communities of Port Talbot and the Afan valley, and to give some background to the context in which they did it. It is, therefore, a companion work to *Not in Our Name* and, to understand events in the Port Talbot area, there is considerable merit in considering their contents together.

Two other pertinent events that occurred during the preparation of this book[1] might be added to this foreword: firstly, world heavyweight boxing champion Muhammad Ali died in June 2016. Secondly, the Chilcot report of the Committee investigating the UK's invasion and occupation of Iraq in 2003 was published in July. One hundred years earlier, virtually to the day, the first of Port Talbot's conscientious objectors were at the Aberafan Military Service tribunal, determined to make their stance. Ali's celebrity status is renowned worldwide, but the Port Talbot objectors' names, such as the Bamford and Jones brothers, and John Wellington are hardly known today, even in their own communities. However, just like Ali, the Port Talbot objectors were arrested and found guilty of 'draft' evasion charges. They stood for the same things Ali stood for, and it is entirely fitting to link them to both Ali and the lessons to be drawn from the Iraq report. Unlike Ali, however, Port Talbot's objectors spent a large part of their next four years in prison.

This book will also link them with supporting figures who strove for peace and internationalism in the early twentieth century. Taken together, those who appear in this book, whether because of their religious, political or philosophical motivation, were advocates who took forward the cause of human rights.

---

[1] In 1966, two years after winning the heavyweight title, Ali antagonised the white establishment in the USA by refusing to be conscripted into the military for the Vietnam War, citing his religious beliefs and opposition to war. Ali was also stripped of his boxing titles. The U.S. Supreme Court overturned his conviction in 1971. Ali's actions as a conscientious objector to the war made him an icon for the younger generation.

Author's Note

THIS BOOK HAS been written with several readerships in mind. It is worth considering which chapters are of most relevance to you before starting on a cover-to-cover read. You will then be able to focus on the areas of greatest interest.

Chapter One is primarily for readers who are new to the history and geography of the Port Talbot area.

Chapters Two and Three will be of greatest interest to those who have a particular interest in the workings of the Military Service Tribunal system and its effects in Port Talbot.

Chapter Four is aimed, firstly, at people who live, have lived, or have ancestors in the districts of Port Talbot. Secondly, as it is essentially a research record, the chapter aims to provide a source for updating, adding to and possibly correction by family members, family historians and researchers.

Chapters Five, Six and Seven will be of interest to all readers, with Chapters Five and Six being of special interest for local and labour historians.

For academic readers, appropriate references are made to sources. For general readers, explanatory footnotes are provided where necessary at the end of each chapter.

The author has written this book, along with its companion volume on Briton Ferry, with the intention of eliciting further information from readers, especially with regards Chapters Four and Five in which the local situation is covered. This is both to complete any gaps in the current work and to confirm or augment the contents of the National Pearce Register of Conscientious Objectors. *The author welcomes correspondence from anyone with relevant information and assures them that it will be treated sympathetically and confidentially.*

Abbreviations

CO	Conscientious objector
DoRA	Defence of the Realm Act
FAU	Friends' Ambulance Unit
FoR	Fellowship of Reconciliation
GWR	Great Western Railway
ILP	Independent Labour Party
NCAC	National Council against Conscription
NCCL	National Council for Civil Liberties
NCF	No Conscription Fellowship
NFWW	National Federation of Women's Workers
NUWSS	National Union of Women's Suffrage
MSA	Military Service Act
PPU	Peace Pledge Union
PTHS	Port Talbot Historical Society
RAMC	Royal Army Medical Corps
SDF	Social Democratic Federation
TUC	Trades Union Congress
UDC	Union of Democratic Control
UDC	Urban District Council
WEA	Workers' Educational Association
WSPU	Women's Social and Political Union

Chapter One:
An introduction to Port Talbot

'If that industrial revolution that still hangs in Port Talbot's air had never occurred then this place would have remained a market town on the Severn shore. Aberafan – a settlement addled by sand at the mouth of the Afan. But C. R. M. Talbot put an end to all that.' [2]

THE MAIN PURPOSE of this chapter is to explain the location and names of the districts of Port Talbot for those who are not acquainted with the area. The second purpose is to provide some background to the social, industrial and political environment in which opposition to conscription and war took place in Port Talbot during the First World War period.

Port Talbot's districts

Port Talbot lies at the eastern end of Swansea Bay on a narrow coastal strip along the Bristol Channel. The River Afan flows into the bay at right angles to the coast.

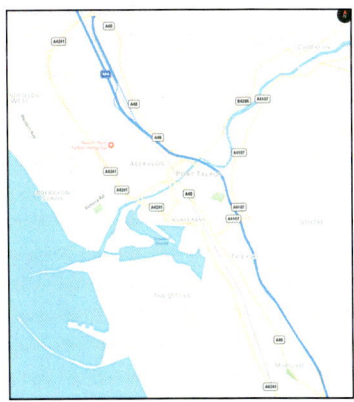

Port Talbot 2016

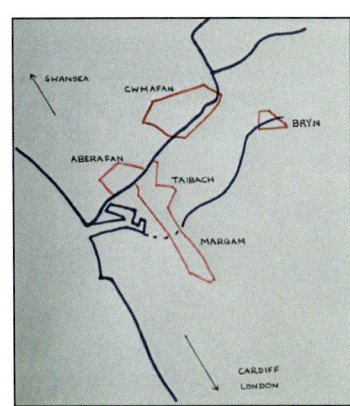

Port Talbot 1916

11

On the north side of the river lies Aberafan, with Taibach and Margam on the south side respectively. Upstream, at right angles to the coast in the Afan valley and its tributaries lie seven more communities: Abergwynfi, Blaengwynfi, Bryn, Cwmafan, Cymmer, Glyncorrwg and Pontrhydyfen. Here the river flows between the sharply rising hills of Foel Fynyddau, Penrhys and Nant-y-Bar on one side and Mynydd Margam and Penhydd on the other.

The population of this agglomeration, which excludes modern day Sandfields and Baglan has varied during the twentieth century. The population of the expanded Port Talbot in 2011 was 37,276, whereas a century earlier it was approximately 28,500.

The name Port Talbot first appeared in 1837 as the name of the new docks to be built on the east side of the River Afan by the Talbot family. It was originally applied to the urbanised area between the rivers Ffrwdwyllt and Afan[3]. Modern Port Talbot town is an agglomeration town created by the merging of the villages of Aberafan, Taibach and Margam. The *Borough of Port Talbot* was created in late 1921 to merge Aberafan Borough Council and Margam Urban District Council into Port Talbot and to incorporate the latter as part of Glamorgan County. The names 'Port Talbot' and 'Aberafan', are almost, but not quite, interchangeable. Today both Port Talbot and Aberafan are, technically, mere electoral wards within the county Borough of Neath-Port Talbot.

To confuse matters even further, the principal rugby club in the town is called 'Aberafan' and is located in Port Talbot whereas the soccer club 'Port Talbot' is found in Aberafan. Other historical changes to Parliamentary constituency, ecclesiastical boundaries and birth registration districts prevent a simple identification of administrative areas being made, for example, the Parliamentary constituency boundary. Aberafan constituency, which was created in 1918, has seen changes to its boundaries, with Briton Ferry, for example, being moved into Neath constituency from the 1930s to the 1980s. The 2016 Parliamentary constituency review proposes that the River Afan will form the boundary between the new Neath and Aberafan and Ogmore and Port Talbot constituencies.

It is now customary to use the Welsh spelling for most place names, for example 'Cwmafan', not 'Cwmavon' and 'Aberafan', not 'Aberafan', though the parliamentary constituency and the rugby club still uses the anglicised spelling.

Baglan, to the west, was an administrative addition brought about by boundary changes, whereas Sandfields, to the south, was built in the 1950s to house those working at the expanding steelworks. The modern postal district of SA13 conveniently corresponds with the 1916 administration for Port Talbot, with SA12 also corresponding with the later additions of Baglan and Sandfields. At the local government re-organisation of 2 April 1996 Neath-Port Talbot County Borough Council was created. Many local people did not expect this, anticipating that Neath and Port Talbot districts would become separate unitary authorities.

Cwmafan in the early 20th century

Port Talbot's industrial development before 1914

Although a copper-works had already existed at Taibach, it was the introduction of steam power there in 1804 that underpinned the development of blast furnaces and tinworks at Cwmafan and Margam at the start of the nineteenth century. By the end of the century however, iron and steelmaking dominated copper smelting. Bar, black-plate and tinworks were built in Cwmafan and Taibach and copper rolling moved from Taibach to Cwmafan. Collieries had existed at Margam from the seventeenth century at Brombil and nearby Morfa as well as in the Afan Valley. These supplied the metal works with coal to provide energy for the steam-powered machinery.

C. R. M. Talbot, MP for Glamorgan for sixty years from 1830, had seen the scope for ironworking at Port Talbot and opened an ironworks in 1831. His daughter realised the potential that a railway and port would offer and

13

she successfully developed both to attract trade away from Cardiff and Swansea's docks.

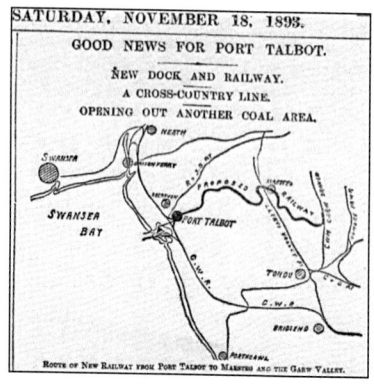

The docks received coal from the Garw, Rhondda and Llynfi Valleys once the port was certified by the Admiralty for the shipment of coal under its contracts. It was in the coal, railway and iron and steel industries of the district that most of the people described in this book worked. Coal exports were particularly important for the docks at the time of the First World War with exports increasing more than tenfold, from 253,006 tonnes in 1899 to 2,622,354 in 1916.

With the arrival of the South Wales Railway, of which C. R. M. Talbot was once Chairman, the town's infrastructure began to take its final shape, except, of course for the M4 whose arrival, did not materialise until over one hundred years later. Two further railways followed: the industrial Port Talbot Railway and then the Rhondda and Swansea Bay Company in 1897. That year the Port Talbot Company Ltd became the *Port Talbot Railway and Docks Company*. It issued a booklet to encourage the use of the railway and docks[4] which said:

> 'The prime cause, beyond the phenomenal demand for south Wales coal that has particularly led to the development of the port, is its favourable geographical position, both landward and seaward. On the former it has the advantage of being actually in the coalfield (its rivals, Cardiff and Barry, being eight and ten miles distant from the outcrop, a fact materially reducing railway tolls. The same consideration of saving, so important in the highly competitive markets of today applies equally upon its landward side, it being a tide nearer the sea than the eastern ports.'

The creation of a modern dock was one of the two main factors that encouraged the emergence of a modern steel industry in Port Talbot during the early years of the twentieth century. Cwmafan had become 'a marginal site with declining locational advantages'[5] for iron and steelmaking because of its distance from overseas sources of ore.

14

Port Talbot Docks 2016

The Port Talbot Steel Company was formed in 1906 to make rail and plate for the rail and, later, the shipping industry. The second factor, which provided a huge boost for capital investment and demand for its products, was the creation of the Ministry of Munitions in 1915, which saw government-subsidised expansion in the shape of the construction of new furnaces and a light plate mill.

C. R. M. Talbot

Publicity booklet for the new port (A.B.P.)

15

Copper Row (L) and 8 Woodland Row, Cwmafan (R) *(Port Talbot Historical Society)*

Housing and Public Health from 1875

Early settlement during the mid-nineteenth century, in places such as Cwmafan, saw miners' and copper workers' houses built as isolated rows, and often along the hillsides. That changed when the metal working companies built their own houses for their workers. At Cwmafan, for example, the copper smelters decided to build a settlement on flat land. Later settlements from the 1850s were more likely to be arranged in the simple form of a street grid. The grid consisted of four-roomed houses without cross-streets, with churches or chapels, schools and shops to be found on the intersections of the streets. Such settlement was 'dour and utilitarian ... to a design of forbidden appearance, using moulded blocks of black copper slag to form the surrounds of windows and doorways'.[6] Air and water pollution was profuse. Within the streets residents would have the benefit of grocers' stores and beer houses, within, or on the corners of, the terraces. Several chapels were usual within such a settlement as were mixed National schools.

The Parishes of Margam and Aberafan took advantage of the Local Government Act of 1858 to appoint a local Board of Health in 1864 whilst the Artisans Dwellings Act of 1875 strengthened previous acts.

All local authorities were forced to appoint Medical Officers of Health who could prosecute people who sold food or drink unfit for human consumption. The councils were also required to provide refuse collection. Town councils also began to provide public parks and most passed by-laws, which laid down minimum standards for *new* houses. Furthermore, in the 1860s and 1870s sewers were dug in large towns and, in the 1870s, water supplies were created. As a result of these measures towns were much healthier and cleaner by the end of the nineteenth century than at the beginning. Margam Local Board, for example, was concerned to take precautionary measures against a cholera outbreak and resolved to fund a temporary Assistant Inspector of Nuisances.[7]

The Artisans Dwelling Act gave councils the power to demolish slums, but large scale slum clearance did not begin till the twentieth century. Nevertheless, in the second half of the nineteenth century, living standards rose. Gradually houses grew larger. In the late nineteenth century *two-up, two-downs* were common. These were houses with two bedrooms, a kitchen and *front room* which shared three walls with adjacent houses. Many skilled workers lived in houses with three bedrooms. Some workers used *building clubs* to secure homes at their own initiative and expense. Often these were organised at chapels.

At the same time some housing was made available to workers by the employing companies as a matter of self-interest. Yet even at the end of the century there were some poor families still living in just one room. Under the 1894 Local Government Act the Board then became the responsibility of Margam and Aberafan District Councils until 1922 when the town was absorbed into Port Talbot. Municipal housing was arriving, but was not yet widespread. With the support of local building societies, much private building of quality-terraced houses was carried out in the first decade or so of the twentieth century in Aberafan and Taibach. This was the type of environment in which many of Port Talbot's soldiers and objectors lived at the start of World War One.

Education

Much education in the area had historically been developed to meet the needs of industry because the requirement was obvious to industrialists. In Cwmafan, Oakwood and Cwmafan schools had been started in the 1840s as works schools, but with the workers meeting their costs. Although their amenities were criticised by school inspectors in the 'blue books' the curriculum and teaching was regarded as fine, including letter writing and accounting methods. These schools were neither Anglican nor Nonconformist. The names 'Margam Tinworks school' and 'Margam Copperworks school' (renamed Eastern in 1902) give obvious clues as to their industrial origins. Indeed, a driving force behind the 1870 Education Act was Britain's industrialists' recognition of the need for education to enable the country to remain competitive in the world of manufacturing.

Board schools were started in the 1990s   Glan Afan School

Other schools were associated with religion. During the 1880s the nonconformists in Port Talbot reacted against the Anglican and Roman Catholic Church's monopoly of education in their 'National' schools until they finally secured the creation of an Aberafan School Board in 1893, as required by the 1870 Education Act. The board then administered both 'British' and 'National' schools. It had previously encouraged the establishment of what were known in Port Talbot as 'Unsectarian' schools which had been set up in chapel vestries. After the Welsh Intermediate Education Act of 1899 the Glan Afan 'County' school was established to bridge the gap between elementary school and university college.

Politics in Port Talbot

One person whose Chartist activities can be linked with the socialist objectors of the First World War is 'Dic Penderyn' of Aberafan. Richard Lewis, as he was named at birth, had a decent primary education in an Aberafan chapel before moving to Merthyr to work as a miner. He fought for workers' industrial and political rights, but in the Merthyr disturbances of 1831 he was charged with stabbing a soldier with a bayonet. There were grave doubts as to his guilt but little doubt that the hard-line Home Secretary, Lord Melbourne, wanted someone to die to set an example. Lewis was the scapegoat. Despite the entreaties of the Quaker Ironmaster from Neath, Joseph Tregelles Price, Lewis was hung outside Cardiff Gaol. Eighty years' later several of Port Talbot's conscientious objectors would be jailed there, too. Lewis' death strengthened civil rights; the objectors' activities strengthened human rights.

As the nineteenth century came to a close, working class representation in political office became a great concern for many in Port Talbot. Some

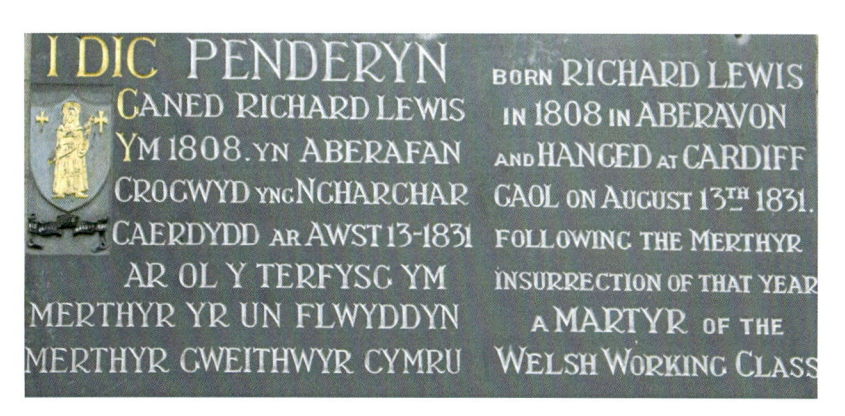

> ! DIC PENDERYN
> CANED RICHARD LEWIS
> YM 1808. YN ABERAFAN
> CROGWYD YNG NGHARCHAR
> CAERDYDD AR AWST 13-1831
> AR OL Y TERFYSG YM
> MERTHYR YR UN FLWYDDYN
> MERTHYR GWEITHWYR CYMRU
>
> BORN RICHARD LEWIS
> IN 1808 IN ABERAVON
> AND HANGED AT CARDIFF
> GAOL ON AUGUST 13TH 1831.
> FOLLOWING THE MERTHYR
> INSURRECTION OF THAT YEAR
> A MARTYR OF THE
> WELSH WORKING CLASS

Memorial plaque to Dic Penderyn – Merthyr Town Hall

who sought the election of working men and their advocates to Parliament saw the Liberal Party as the way of achieving this aim. A number of so-called 'Lib-Lab' candidates were subsequently elected Members of Parliament by this alliance of trade unions and radical intellectuals working within the Liberal Party. However, the idea of working with the middle class Liberal Party to achieve working class representation in parliament was losing acceptance in Port Talbot, especially after the formation of the ILP in 1893. Keir Hardie, a pacifist, became its Chairman and leader. In 1900 he became the first Labour MP in Britain and remained the sole Labour MP until World War One. When war came most of its members in the Labour Party executive, as well as most of the Labour MPs in Parliament lent their support to the recruiting campaign for the war. Only the ILP held out against the war. By this time Port Talbot had become a stronghold for the ILP, which insisted on standing by its long-held ethical objections to militarism. 'But the strangest thing about Port Talbot, nothing much was done there as far as ILP work was concerned. You'd have it in Taibach, but the great place was Cwmafan.'[8] Indeed, as a result, Cwmafan earned the appellation 'Little Moscow'.

Although, in the new Aberafan parliamentary election of 1918, Major Jack Edwards the coalition Liberal, was successful when challenged by Swansea's Robert Williams, from 1922 Ramsay MacDonald would become Labour MP for the constituency with Unionist Sydney Byass trailing in his wake. Port Talbot's socialists had finally rejected the idea of workers making common cause with the Liberals in exchange for what were regarded as scraps of charity from them.

View eastwards of Taibach and Margam in 2016

Later industrial changes

Before and during the first World War many men came to Port Talbot's steelworks from Clydeside, the Midlands and, especially, Tyneside.[9] Margam steelworks started production in 1918 under Baldwin's, and later Richard Thomas and Baldwin's ownership until the Steel Company of Wales was formed in 1951. Despite subsequent private and public ownership changes today's configuration is largely that originally envisaged by the Steel Company of Wales.

The significance of the Steel Company of Wales was that it was created by the intentional closure of many small sheet and tinplate producers, particularly those in areas of west Glamorgan such as Taibach and Cwmafan, in the decade after World War Two. The creation of this integrated centre of activity concentrated both employment and steel production on this single site. Sandfields housing estate was built on the western side of the town in the 1950s to meet the increased housing demand.

The coal industry's history was quite different. In 1914 south Wales coal production was at its peak, with its ports exporting record tonnages; but appearances were deceptive: oil firing of ships had been advocated since the start of the century. Demand dropped in the 1920s and 1930s and the private coal owners' efforts to maintain profitability led to wage restrictions, unemployment and hard times in the Afan Valley pit villages. Post-war nationalisation improved working conditions, but not the overall decline in demand for coal, as railways in Britain moved to diesel and electric motive power. In the 1980s, political forces, as much as economics, saw the beginning of the end of pits throughout south Wales. In the twenty-first century the Afan Valley has 'moved from mining to mountain biking'.

Religion in Port Talbot

The building of chapels which were integral to the lives of workers in the nineteenth century has already been mentioned. The important religious revival in Wales in 1904 can be studied elsewhere, but it is clear that there were widely differing views of the phenomenon.

'Dark and damp chapels it is held, bred little more than pious hypocrites who, usually clad in joyless Bible-black were ruled over by grizzled demagogue-like preachers.'[10] This was one perception of the effect of the 1904–5 national religious revival in Wales. Another was that 'Far from being isolated from the world, cut off by a language few outside of their borders could begin to penetrate, Welsh nonconformity had a generous world view that could at times be global in scope.' Nonetheless the movement kept the Churches of Wales filled for many years to come. In the Afan valley one young man offered this prayer:

Cwmafan – All Saints Church *(PTHS)*

Grange Street Congregational, Port Talbot

'Lord forgive me and my old friend for neglecting other services of Thy House for so long at a time, and for going up to the mountain to play cards, pitch and toss, and drink beer on Sunday. Now I give my heart to Thee, and I give my life. Lord, bless me and keep me.'[11]

Therefore, on account of the national religious revival, it is no surprise that the communities of Port Talbot were replete with dozens of churches and chapels of various denominations; Calvinistic Methodist; Church in Wales; English and Welsh Baptist; Evangelical; Gospel; Independent; Methodist; Pentecostal; Presbyterian; Roman Catholic; Seventh Day Adventist and Wesleyan. Hansen[12] considered that 'churches and chapels were the focal points of life, and the centres of culture, attendance being such that we saw branches, extensions, new buildings, mission rooms and school rooms continually being erected. Large numbers of people attended church or chapel three times on a Sunday.' If 'Aneurin Bevan considered that Sunday schools helped mould the character of the miner by cultivating the gift of expression'[13], then surely the same could be said for the steel, tinplate and railway workers of Port Talbot. Each Church and each member would have their particular views on war and conscription. Those which had a generous world view would, together with the ILP socialists, provide the opposition to conscription and war throughout south Wales.

It was not true to say, however, that 'In the nineteenth and early twentieth centuries the Welsh nonconformist tradition had ensured that militarism and war were denounced from the pulpit at every opportunity'.[14] In Wales, for every Rev T. E. Nicholas of Glais, who was against war, there was a Rev. John Williams of Brynsiencyn who preached war.

Summary

This chapter has provided a brief description of the Port Talbot of 1914 upon which war and later conscription would be imposed. It has also shown how that era's industrial, social and cultural configuration began to change from its nineteenth-century profile into that which exists today. The following Chapter will pick up events from the beginning of the twentieth century to examine the move towards conscription and the adverse reaction to conscription and war by elements of the Port Talbot populace in the years from 1914 to 1919.

Notes for Chapter One

[2] Peter Finch in Lynne Rees, *Real Port Talbot* (Bridgend, 2013)
[3] Arthur Rees, Port Talbot Historical Society: *Some street and place names of the Port Talbot district* (Port Talbot, 2004)
[4] *Description of the new Welsh coal port: Port Talbot.* West Glamorgan Archives/Port Talbot Historical Society
[5] Stephen Parry, *History of the Steel Industry in the Port Talbot Area 1900–1988*. Ph D thesis, University of Leeds (Leeds 2011)
[6] Jeremy Lowe, *Welsh Industrial Workers Housing 1775–1875*. National Museum of Wales (Cardiff, 1985)
[7] *South Wales Daily News*, 13 September 1892.
[8] David Egan and Richard Lewis, South Wales Miners' Library, Len Williams of Briton Ferry in a transcription of audio tape AUD/282 (Swansea, 1974)
[9] J. Ivor Hansen, *Portrait of a Welsh Town* (Edinburgh, 1968)
[10] Dr David Ceri Jones, in *Welsh History Month* (13 October 1915)
[11] J. Vyrnwy Morgan, *The Welsh Revival, 1904–5* (1909)
[12] J. Ivor Hansen, *Outline of a Welsh Town* (Port Talbot, 1971)
[13] Hywel Francis and Dai Smith, *A history of the South Wales Miners Federation in the twentieth century* (London, 1980)
[14] Robin Barlow, 2014, *Wales and World War One* (Llandysul, 2014)

Chapter Two:
Conscription, the tribunal system and prison

I know of no machine, judicial or other by which you can measure a man's conscience in the same way that you can measure the contents of a vessel, solid or liquid.

Lord Lansdowne

THIS CHAPTER EXPLAINS why the international situation at the start of the twentieth century led to conscription in Britain, how it was gradually introduced, and the mechanics that were used to administer it, namely the military tribunal system. Conscription was introduced to ensure that the army could be adequately manned when volunteering alone could not replenish battlefield losses. The tribunals were established to ensure that conscription was carried out fairly and in compliance with parliamentary criteria. Both were introduced during World War One, through the Military Service Acts. 'Conscription' can be defined as 'compulsory enlistment for state service, especially military service', but the term 'conscription' can also apply to compulsory industrial enlistment or to other professions and services.

International situation

At the start of the twentieth century, politicians in Europe had operated within an international system of complicated alliances and antiquated domestic political structures. Such alliances and treaties determined which parties would be defended by which. The national political structures determined the amount of democratic control that existed over the armed forces within the alliances. In 1914 Germany, Austria-Hungary and Italy were in a Triple Alliance by which each of the parties would be defended by the others, if attacked. Russia and France had also concluded a pact to resist

'Historial de la Grande Guerre, Peronne'

any aggression by the Triple Alliance. Associated with the Russia-France pact was the Entente Cordiale, an Anglo-French understanding on mutual security.

In their domestic politics all the major regimes were undemocratic in the sense that no executive government was accountable to a legislature elected by universal suffrage. Political power was, therefore, exercised by a small group drawn from the upper middle class and the aristocracy, without a plausible system to check and balance the legislative and executive branches of government. In addition, political leaders were under internal threat from minority nationalities within their borders and from an emerging industrial proletariat dedicated to securing economic, political and social rights for ordinary working people.

The regimes in both pacts had been gradually building up their armaments for at least a decade before the outbreak of war. In particular this had taken the form of a naval *arms race* between Britain and Germany in which the German Kaiser wanted a navy that could challenge Britain throughout its vast empire. The complexities of the European alliance system thus converted a localised conflict in the Balkans into a general European war; and subsequently the economic interests of imperialists then converted the European war into a World War. It can be seen that industrialisation facilitated an arms race and also provided the means to make war.

The 'need' for conscription

Britain was the only Great Power without universal military service (conscription) although pressure for its introduction had grown through the early years of the 20th Century. The National Service League, which was founded in 1906, was exercised by the fact that in 1914 Germany had 2.2 million soldiers against Britain's 711,000. Consequently, it is not surprising that five consecutive conscription bills were tabled in Parliament in the years preceding 1914.

Nevertheless, at the beginning of the war political opposition to universal military service also remained strong. The governing Liberal Party opposed the idea, as did large sections of the Labour Party and even some Conservatives. Even after the outbreak of war in August 1914, the Cabinet unanimously dismissed Winston Churchill's proposal for compulsory military service. Foreign secretary Sir Edward Grey described the British policy should be to pursue *a European policy without keeping up a great army*.

In the absence of conscription between 1914 and 1916, pressure was exerted to enlist voluntarily. The TUC and Labour, but not the ILP, supported recruitment in 1914 and justified it on the basis that it was preferable to conscription. Official pressure came in the form of propaganda such as Kitchener's posters to appeal to men's patriotic duty. Often incentives were offered by employers to keep volunteers' jobs open on their return from service. Women proffered white feathers to men who were not in uniform in order to try to shame them into joining the armed forces, as were postcards of the time. As the numbers of dead and wounded grew, this pressure increased.

The introduction of conscription

The first step towards military conscription was taken in August 1915 in the form of the *National Registration Act*. The reason advanced for national registration was that it would provide the government with the necessary information to establish whether war could be conducted with volunteers. The Act established that some five million men were found not to be serving in the Army, of which some 1.8 million were fit, not in important industries, and might be available to serve, should it be necessary. *Trade Unionist* sounded a cautionary note:[15]

The Conscientious Objector *(www.worldwar1postcards.com)*

'This week the national registration forms are being distributed and in many a home in the land it is a cause of anxiety ... it is a matter of deep concern for all trade unionists ... it is feared that registration is the forerunner of compulsory military service, and for the period of the war, industrial service; and one can imagine no greater menace to the fundamental principles of democracy than that.'

In reality this Act was the thin end of a wedge, one which quickly developed into the *Derby Scheme*, the second step towards conscription. Those deemed to be available by recruiting officers were required to attest to their willingness to serve should they be called upon to do so. The effect of this was to say: 'If you do not join voluntarily now, you'll be forced to join within a few months.' The scheme envisaged calling up conscripts by age group and by placement into occupational categories according to a Board of Trade assessment of the recruits' availability and usefulness. The Derby Scheme introduced the idea of tribunals in order to enable *employers* to appeal for exemption, or against the occupational groups into which those attesting had been placed. The groups were:

1. Essential civilian work
2. Trades and professions from which a *few* could be spared
3. Where a large proportion could be spared
4. Unnecessary occupation – all could be spared

The Derby Tribunals were more to do with recruitment for the army than for administering justice for potential recruits. The possibility of conscription, instead of voluntary enlistment, became more and more likely. The declining number of volunteers enlisting in 1915 was dropping to such an extent that it seemed a threat to the war effort. Prime Minister Asquith had originally said that the National Registration Act was not a prelude to conscription, but it was.

The Military Service Act 1916 and the tribunal system

The Military Service Act continued the system of tribunals used in the Derby scheme, but this time to deal with those whose wish was to be exempted from military service. Their reasons for objecting to service would be heard, whatever they were. The 1,805 local tribunals in Britain corresponded with local government districts and the sixty-eight Appeal tribunals with counties. Tribunals comprised a panel of five to twenty-five members. From the first week of February 1916, Recruiting Offices sent Form W3236 to all men of military service age, asking them to enlist, or to provide a certificate of exemption from the Local Tribunals which had been set up in February.

Men were called up according to the age class into which they fell. Class 1 consisted of those born in 1897. These men would be called up at nineteen years of age, Class 2 in 1896 and so on, up to class 23, for those born in 1875.

In Aberafan, a special meeting of the Town Council was held[16] over which the Mayor presided to read out a circular from Walter Long, the President of the Local Government Board. Long emphasised the 'serious and delicate' nature of the work of the tribunals and continued:

> 'It is left to the discretion of the local authority to appoint persons from within or without their own body, and I venture to urge strongly that they should not hesitate to select persons who are not members of the authority wherever this is desirable.'

"And what work are you doing of National Importance?"
"Why, I'm rearin' eight children an' helping to make airyplanes!"

The Tribunal *(www.worldwar1postcards.com)*

Anyone failing to enlist or provide a medical certificate[17] was to be regarded as a deserter. Under the Act, those aged between eighteen and forty-five were obliged to serve in the army unless they were married, widowed with children, serving in the Royal Navy, a Minister of Religion, or working in a reserved occupation. From May 1916, married men became obliged to enlist and, by 1918, this had become the case for all men up to fifty-one years of age.

The tribunals

Men, or employers, who objected to the call-up for any reason had to attend a local Military Service Tribunal, unless they or their employer had previously obtained a certificate of exemption. The grounds for exemption were: already doing work in the national interest, serious hardship, health or infirmity or conscientious objection. Tribunals might grant absolute, conditional or temporary exemption, but rarely did they grant absolute. Exemption could be granted from any military service, or from combatant service only. Tribunals were uncertain of the position with regards giving absolute exemption for conscientious objection. Conditional exemption was usually that a man did essential war work instead and temporary exemption was usually to give a man time to sort out his business or family affairs before joining up.

There were rights of appeal to a County Appeal Tribunal and, finally, to the Central Appeal Tribunal.

The Military Service Act specified that an appellant could make a statement and call witnesses. In fact, most cases were summarily dismissed by the tribunal and the men handed over to the military. In Port Talbot, Henry Davies' confidence and standing in the community meant he, sometimes, got a full hearing when representing objectors. Fellow members of the Independent Labour Party, or the No Conscription Fellowship, frequently took full transcripts of the hearings. They regularly reported them to the *Pioneer* by way of 'Afaneer's' pen. Other newspapers also carried less detailed reports, often anonymised and, sometimes, with slight inaccuracies or omissions.

Two aspects of the tribunal process should be noted. Firstly, the strong presence and influence of the military representatives. Secondly, the speed at which cases were dealt with is remarkable. The time spent face-to-face on each case in the tribunal room could not have averaged more than fifteen minutes.

Local tribunals

The membership of the local tribunals is listed in Appendix Eight. Councillor Harry Davies (Taibach) proposed a list of nominees for Margam Tribunal to Margam Council[18] which included representatives from the Labour Representation Committee, and the Chambers of Trade and Commerce. Five was the recommended number of tribunal members at each sitting, with one nomination recommended to be from local organised labour. The tribunals had a heavy workload, as evidenced by the numbers from Cwmafan attending a Neath tribunal:

> 'The conscientious objector was strongly in evidence at the resumed sitting of the Neath Rural District Tribunal held on Thursday under the Presidency of Mr W. B. Trick, JP. In fact, there were no less than one hundred applicants of the type referred to, most of them hailing from the village of Cwmafan, near Port Talbot. The majority were, however, engaged in certified occupations. Altogether there were 130 appeals before the tribunal.'[19]

An example of the confusion that could arise with 'certified occupations' came from a nearby town with a similar employment pattern:

> 'During the hearing of the cases at the Briton Ferry tribunal on Thursday evening, four applicants who had appealed on conscientious grounds withdrew their objections when they came before the tribunal and each of these were afterwards exempted. They were in certified trades. Others who stuck to their conscientious objections were objected to for exemption, although also working in certified trades.' [20]

On 26 February 1916, the Margam Tribunal sat on a Saturday and three brothers objected on religious grounds.[21] A fourth brother had already been denied exemption. To another appellant, who pleaded 'conscience', the Chairman said, 'Go out and fight with your own brother, sons and other people's sons. Application refused. The appellant left the room, smiling.' Not all cases were that easy.

A prime example of political conscientious objection occurred in February 1916, when thirteen ILP appellants were represented by Mr Henry Davies of Cwmafan. The Chair was anxious that the appellants would accept non-combatant service, 'as some had done at Swansea', saying a clause had been added to the Military Service Act to enable this. He did not think he could grant absolute exemption. Major Buchanan, the Military Representative, tried to entice applicants to accept this by saying that the appellants would not necessarily have to take the military oath. The thirteen were: Arthur Mullington, Lancelot Thomas Waters, William Grane, Christopher R. Scott, Daniel H. Phillips, J. Llewelyn, Joseph N. Davies, John Heycock, Albert R. Evans, David Mort, William Mainwaring, William Arthur Thomas and Edward Heycock.

They all refused to accept non-combatant service under any conditions and were 'prepared to take the consequences'.

Sometimes the tribunals, intentionally or otherwise, misunderstood how the Military Service Act should be administered. When four men asked for forms to apply for exemption to the clerk of the Cwmafan tribunal, they were refused by the Mayor, who was also tribunal chair, on the grounds they had not attested. Mr W. C. Anderson, MP for Sheffield, had to ask a question in Parliament of the President of the Local Government Board, responsible for the administration of the tribunal, for the forms to be supplied.

Port Talbot's Municipal Buildings c.1916 *(PTHS)*
(The courthouse was above the shopping arcade on the ground floor)

There was no wonder that trouble occurred at times in the tribunals. In July 1916 'uproar' was experienced when a member of the public, Mr R. Llewelyn, protested 'against the suppression of meetings at Taibach and other parts of the District'.[22] The Military Representative, Captain Preston, had to be restrained when he said: 'You are not fit to wipe the shoes of the men who are fighting for you' … 'I have two sons fighting for men such as you.' The Chair threatened to close the meeting, but at the request of Harry Davies, he allowed Mr Llewelyn to proceed before, finally, closing the meeting amid disorder. Mr Preston was later relieved of his role after making some unacceptable comments at a Swansea tribunal.

Appeal

When the Glamorgan Appeal Tribunal was held at Port Talbot in March[23] the Clerk wanted the Tribunal room to be cleared, despite an appellant's desire to be heard in public. The Chair explained that some of the appellants, not conscientious objectors, wished to be heard in private, but he gave way to holding it in public providing there was no disturbance or hindrance. It was, in the event, held in public with no disturbance. Seven other conscience appeals were held that day along with several other non-conscience appeals. Sometimes the Tribunals seemed to make up their own rules. 'At the Aberafan Tribunal on 17 June, in accordance with a decision arrived at between that committee and the Margam Tribunal, all conditional exemptions would in future be granted subject to the applicants joining the Volunteer Training Corps'.[24]

An example of religious objection to conscription was John Wellington's application. Wellington's application for exemption was heard at Margam Tribunal. When asked if he would undertake non-combatant service by the Chairman, Mayor Percy Jacobs, Wellington said: 'Noncombatant service is part of the military machine. I am prepared to do anything to bring the war to an end. I am fighting for these aims now in the church.'

Most objections were neither religious nor conscientious:

'At an Appeal Tribunal sitting at Port Talbot[25], a Margam farmer appealed for exemption for his son, who had only been allowed a month by the local tribunal. He had another son at home as ploughman, and an old man of seventy years of age assisted in the farm which comprised 240 acres of land and 240 sheep and eighty-five cattle. He had no daughters and no female workers. He was exempted until 30 August.

The military representative appealed against a number of decisions by local tribunals. A meat salesman, aged nineteen,

Percy Jacob
Aberafan Tribunal Chair

Edward Lowther
Margam Tribunal Chair

33

had been given until July. This was reduced to a week as an unattested man.

A Co-operative bread van man had been exempted till 30 August. The period was reduced by a month.

A licensed victualler had had nine months' exemption, but the military representative's appeal failed because the man had since been rejected by the Medical Board.

The exemption given to a Seven Sisters greengrocer was upheld.

In the case of a caretaker's son, the military representative said there were three unattested brothers. The father worked at a copper works, was a local preacher and a Co-operative Society and Friendly Society official. Exemption reduced to one month. A butcher and farmer from Taibach appealed on the grounds that if he was compelled to join he would have to close down. His mother had looked after the business until she died, and, added the applicant, "it is a job to get a woman like my mother". "I am glad to hear you say that," said the Chairman. He was exempted until 28 August.

A cold rolls assistant superintendent[26] contended that the local tribunal had not given the consideration to his appeal on conscientious grounds. It was pointed out that this appeal was put in too late, but the applicant was allowed to state his grounds. He said he was opposed to war. Asked if he belonged to any religious body, applicant replied "Only the Church of England". He also belonged to the ILP. The appeal was dismissed.

A baker, whose wife managed a millinery business, also appealed in vain on domestic grounds.

Two bakers who appealed for employees were granted a month for their men.'

Therefore, the majority of cases heard by tribunals, by far, were applications for exemption for domestic and business reasons, rather than for religious, political and philosophical beliefs. It can now be seen why it was the conscientious objection cases that provided most difficulties for the tribunals.

Kinmel Park and Cardiff Barracks

Kinmel Park Military Training Camp near Rhyl in north Wales was one of the key reception camps to which conscientious objectors would be sent after their appeal for exemption had failed. The hope of the authorities was that objectors might still succumb to military control, but invariably their expectations were not met. Therefore, the camp needed to be well-prepared to deal with objectors (still technically disobedient soldiers) who again refused to obey orders. Courts-martial were held regularly to issue standardised, but severe, sentences.

Kinmel Park Camp's main purpose was to train soldiers for military service. It was also used for injured soldiers to convalesce and to detain conscientious objectors temporarily. The conscientious objectors were sent there from an area west of a line from Blackburn, Lancashire, to Newport, Monmouthshire. The camp was known in the locality of Rhyl as 'Kill'em Park'. Kinmel Camp was actually twenty camps, with approximately twenty huts in each, on a site which had no physical barriers to separate it from the surrounding countryside. It housed some 15,000 soldiers and at any one time catered for some seventy conscientious objectors who had refused to obey military orders. Robert Graves and J. B. Priestley were two notable soldiers who were sent there. However, the full history of the Camp went largely neglected until the publication in 2014 of Robert H. Griffiths' *The Story of Kinmel Park*.

Prior to publication, attention on the camp's history had mainly focused on descriptions of the riots that had occurred there in March 1919. The Camp was then being used to repatriate Canadian soldiers but delays in

Kinmel Park Camp

35

doing so, coupled with deficient conditions, led to riots in which five people were killed, twenty-three wounded and seventy-eight arrested. Griffiths has rectified this and devoted a chapter to the Camp's use for accommodating conscientious objectors. Many young soldiers and conscientious objectors lived in insanitary and over-crowded conditions at the Camp. There were many deaths and suicides: it had been built when the prospect of a short war seemed realistic and, given this aspiration, the wooden barracks unsurprisingly provided only rudimentary facilities.

In April 1916, newspaper reports appeared of the first objectors being sent to Kinmel and being court-martialled and sentenced to two years' imprisonment with hard labour for disobedience. These were men who had lost their appeals at local Military Service Tribunals. Several from Port Talbot, as well as elsewhere in Wales, arrived at Kinmel Camp during the summer of 1916. Conscientious objectors were considered to be soldiers and expected to obey military orders at the camp. If they did not wear army uniform, refused to parade, or sign an enlistment form they would be referred to a Central Tribunal at Wormwood Scrubs and then – almost certainly – be sent to a prison.

In May 1916, a batch of seven Newport conscientious objectors arrived. Amongst them was Albert Rudall, an ILP and NCF member. Rudall died in 1918, aged thirty, as a result of the sustained harsh treatment and deprivation he received in Kinmel and elsewhere. He was one of five Welsh conscientious objectors to die in the work centres: H. Benyon of Swansea, G. H. Dardis of Risca, and Messrs J. Evans and Statton of Cardiff were the others.

Not all of Port Talbot's conscientious objectors were sent to Kinmel:

Cardiff Barracks

several avoided the north Wales camp and were sent to Cardiff or Barry Barracks. Many, however, found the conditions at Kinmel and the other camps so bad that they absconded.

At both Cardiff and Kinmel, most conscientious objectors simply refused to accept any military discipline and would be court-martialled as a result, whether or not they were allowed to appeal to the Central Tribunal, and would, almost certainly be sent to prison.

The court-martial

The court-martial's remit was to 'administer justice according to the Army Act'. A typical court-martial was that of Dan Morris[27] of Cwmafan. Such proceedings were carried out to a predictable formula and result. His charge sheet read as follows:

'The accused, no 35940 Private Dan Morris, 20th Battalion the Welsh Regiment, a soldier in the regular forces is charged with – when on active service – disobeying a lawful command given personally by his superior officer (in the execution of his office) in that he, at Kinmel Park, on the 23rd day of August 1916, when personally ordered by Second Lieutenant H. Pughe, 2nd Battalion the Welsh Regiment, to put on khaki refused saying: "I refuse, I am a conscientious objector."' This is signed by the Colonel commanding the 20th Battalion.

Two witnesses appeared for the military authorities, and the summary of their evidence read as follows: The first witness, Second Lieutenant H. Pughe stated: 'At Kinmel Park at 9.45 am on the 23 August, 1916, I was present at the quartermaster stores when I ordered the accused to put on khaki. He refused, stating: 'I refuse, I am a conscientious objector.' The second witness, Quartermaster Sergeant Edgar Lewys Thomas, stated: 'At Kinmel Park at 9.45 am on the 23 August 1916, I was present at the quartermaster stores when the accused was ordered by Second Lieutenant H. Pughe to put on khaki. He refused; and on being asked what his objection was, he replied: 'I am a conscientious objector'.

Both he and Aneurin Morgan of Cwmafan were sentenced with two years' hard labour, commuted to 112 days

More information on Dan Morris can be found in Chapter Four.

37

Wormwood Scrubs

Wormwood Scrubs

Wormwood Scrubs prison in west London was completed as a permanent prison in 1891 with its bricks being made in situ by some of the prisoners. In World War One 'the Scrubs' was where the Central Military Tribunals took place. The 'Scrubs' comprised four blocks, each of which had individual cells for 320 prisoners. Objectors were segregated from criminals housed in the other blocks.

The prison acted as a feeder location from where most unsuccessful appellants against conscription were re-allocated to other prisons or work centres as members of Army Reserve Class W. Some were retained at Wormwood Scrubs, in its capacity as a civil prison for various sentences. A list of prisons and work camps indicating those to which Port Talbot men were assigned can be seen in Appendix Four.

The Central Tribunal and outcomes for objectors

The outcomes for Port Talbot's objectors varied in accordance with what each individual was prepared to accept and with what any tribunal was prepared to offer. Generally, the local tribunals started by simply refusing exemption completely, or in Port Talbot's case, offering an opportunity for service in the Non-combatant Corps. Most were refused the total exemption applied for at appeal and were court-martialled, pending a final hearing at the Central Tribunal. Unlike the local and appeal tribunals, this tribunal comprised legal professionals under Lord Salisbury's chairmanship. Despite this, even the Central Tribunal itself failed to interpret the Military Service Act correctly. Even after a second Act to clarify an ambiguity in the first with regards absolute exemption for *conscientious* objectors, the Central

Tribunal got things wrong. The effects of the Central Tribunal's misinterpretation were important for many of Port Talbot's objectors:

- Its reluctance to grant absolute exemption. None from Port Talbot were so exempted
- Its frequent refusal to recognise socialists as genuine conscientious objectors, unless supported by religious faith. A number of Port Talbot objectors could not cite religious belief to support their cases.
- The assumption that eighteen and nineteen-year-olds were too young to have a settled opinion on the morality of participation in war. Port Talbot had five or six of this age.

It is worth noting that one Welsh objector, who was at Knutsford with Port Talbot's Jenkin William James, George Ll. Maitland Davies, not only breached the terms of his local tribunal's conditions, his intransigent, absolutist stance saw his case referred by the chair of the Central Tribunal to the War Cabinet itself.

Reason for application being accepted

The possible outcomes for applicants for exemption, conscientious and otherwise were:

Category   Reason for application being accepted

A	On the grounds that it is expedient in the national interests that the man should, instead of being employed in military service, be engaged in other work in which he is habitually engaged.
B	On the grounds that it is expedient in the national interests that the man should, instead of being employed in military service, be engaged in other work in which he wishes to be engaged.
C	If he is being educated or trained for any work, on the ground that it is expedient in the national interests that, instead of being employed in military service, he should continue to be so educated or trained.

D   On the ground that serious hardship would ensure if the man were called up for Army service, owing to his exceptional financial or business obligations or domestic position.
E   On the ground of ill-health or infirmity.
F   On the ground of a conscientious objection to the undertaking of combatant service.
G   On the ground that the principal and usual occupation of the man is one of those included in the list of occupations certified by Government Departments for exemption. 'Badged'.

Anyone assigned to Category A would be permitted to remain in their normal employment. Teachers were an occupation which might be assigned to Category A, but the placement of teacher-objectors within this category often led to heated disputes in south Wales and elsewhere. The example of Aneurin Morgan of Cwmafan in Chapter Four is such a case.

Those categorised as B would work in a place of their choice, subject to the approval of the tribunal and its advisers. Category C, D and E are self-explanatory. Tribunals were reluctant to place objectors into Category F. In Port Talbot the tribunals tried to persuade objectors to accept Non-combatant status instead of Category F. When the objectors refused that, the local tribunals were still reluctant to offer any form of exemption. Category G refers to 'starred' occupations where the employer applied for exemption because of the essential work being done for the war effort by the employee in question. The employee was then issued with a card, to provide evidence of this.

Garnet Waters' war service badge
(Mrs M. Day)

Daily life in prison

The prisons, into which objectors were placed-are listed in Appendix Four. They were described by George M. Ll. Davies as 'dehumanising for prisoners and warders alike'[28]. Despite the attempts in the 1898 Prisons Act for these institutions to replace unproductive labour punishment (penal servitude) with reform of the inmates through education and purposeful activities, the changes had not really taken effect by 1916. Penal servitude was replaced with 'hard labour' and 'the prison system was ill-equipped to deal with prisoners incarcerated only for reasons of their own consciences'.[29] Hard labour meant 'silence and separation' – seventeen hours per day in a cell on one's own with no communication. Exercise and attendance at chapel was permitted. After a month prisoners could work with others and, after twelve months, talking in pairs and reading books was allowed.

The typical daily routine for conscientious objectors has been described by Boulton:[30]

Time	Activity	Detail
5.30–6.00	Paraded to lavatories	Wash and empty cell pails. Scrub walls and furniture. Fold bedding to regulation pattern
6.00–6.30	Breakfast	One pint of porridge without milk
6.30–7.15	45 minutes controlled exercise	
7.15–12.00	Work	
12.00–13.00	Lunch	Typical: half pound potatoes; six ounces of bread; ten ounces of haricots; two ounces crude fat bacon
13.00–16.15	Work	
	Supper	One pint of porridge; a half a pound of bread. Cocoa was offered after four months of sentence had been served, or for good work until 1918.

The effect of a hard labour sentence

With hard labour	No hard labour
Board, blanket, pillow	Mattress, blanket, pillow
Mattress after one month	Mattress, blanket, pillow
Ten hours' daytime solitary confinement in own cell doing tasks	Not solitary confinement

No speaking	Only task-related conversation
After one month prisoners could work outside the cell door or in an assigned place elsewhere with other prisoners	Daily work with others outside cell
Forty minutes' silent exercise	Forty minutes' silent exercise
Write and receive one letter a month when approved	Writing materials issued
One visit every three months	Visits possible with permission

Emrys Hughes[31] described the prison uniform as: 'Green flannels with red stripes, striped cotton shirts, thick socks and dark grey clothes, stamped with white arrows and small caps'. During the evenings reading was permitted and on Sundays the men were allowed to attend a religious service within the prison. The personal property allowed were spectacles, four pictures and two books. Letters were censored. A half-hour visit was allowed every few months and this meant that wives or girl-friends may have had to travel hundreds of miles to visit. A quick weekly bath was permitted and underclothes were changed every two weeks.

In 1917 a number of concessions were granted to those men who had served over twelve months of their sentence. They were allowed to associate and communicate during exercise and walk in groups of two or three of their own choosing. Two exercise periods were timetabled. Prisoners could borrow four library books at a time and were allowed to wear their own, civilian clothes. Should they have so wished, they could have hired a fellow prisoner to clean their cell, but they never embraced this option.

Earlier in the book the pro-war propaganda postcards depicting the COs in an unfavourable light was discussed. The anti-war campaigners also produced prints and postcards for fundraising. The 1917 print on page 44 by an anti-war supporter is aimed at painting a more accurate picture for the public of what life was really like for conscientious objectors in prison.

The tribunal process is shown on this and the facing page as a flow chart.

The tribunal route from Port Talbot

(Prospective conscript takes Form W3236 to attend recruiting office. If no exemption certificate):

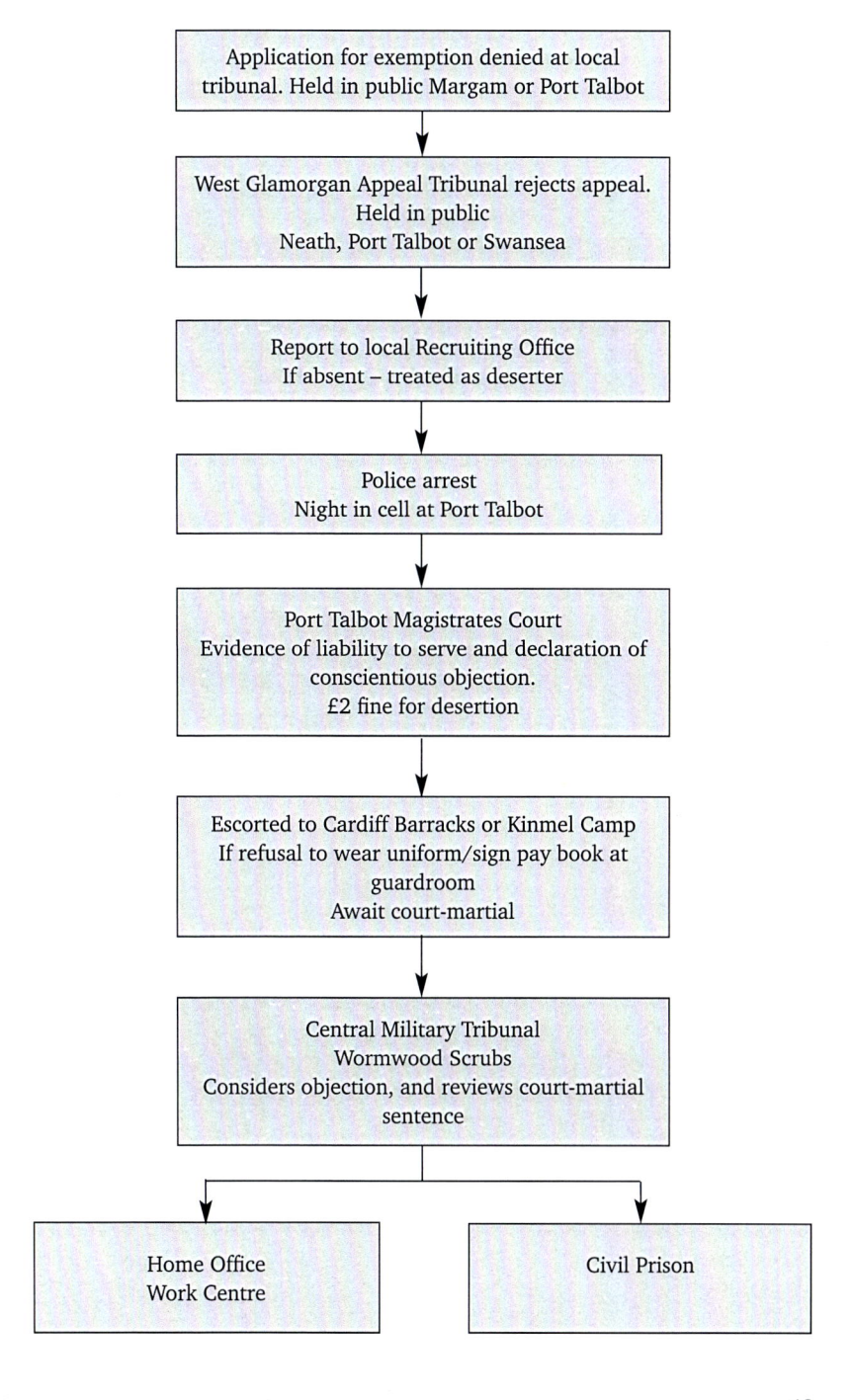

```
┌─────────────────────────────────────────┐
│  Application for exemption denied at local │
│  tribunal. Held in public Margam or Port Talbot │
└─────────────────────────────────────────┘
                    ▼
┌─────────────────────────────────────────┐
│  West Glamorgan Appeal Tribunal rejects appeal. │
│              Held in public              │
│       Neath, Port Talbot or Swansea      │
└─────────────────────────────────────────┘
                    ▼
┌─────────────────────────────────────────┐
│       Report to local Recruiting Office  │
│          If absent – treated as deserter │
└─────────────────────────────────────────┘
                    ▼
┌─────────────────────────────────────────┐
│               Police arrest              │
│         Night in cell at Port Talbot     │
└─────────────────────────────────────────┘
                    ▼
┌─────────────────────────────────────────┐
│         Port Talbot Magistrates Court    │
│  Evidence of liability to serve and declaration of │
│           conscientious objection.       │
│              £2 fine for desertion       │
└─────────────────────────────────────────┘
                    ▼
┌─────────────────────────────────────────┐
│  Escorted to Cardiff Barracks or Kinmel Camp │
│   If refusal to wear uniform/sign pay book at │
│                 guardroom                │
│             Await court-martial          │
└─────────────────────────────────────────┘
                    ▼
┌─────────────────────────────────────────┐
│         Central Military Tribunal        │
│              Wormwood Scrubs             │
│  Considers objection, and reviews court-martial │
│                 sentence                 │
└─────────────────────────────────────────┘
              ▼              ▼
┌──────────────────┐   ┌──────────────────┐
│   Home Office    │   │   Civil Prison   │
│   Work Centre    │   │                  │
└──────────────────┘   └──────────────────┘
```

43

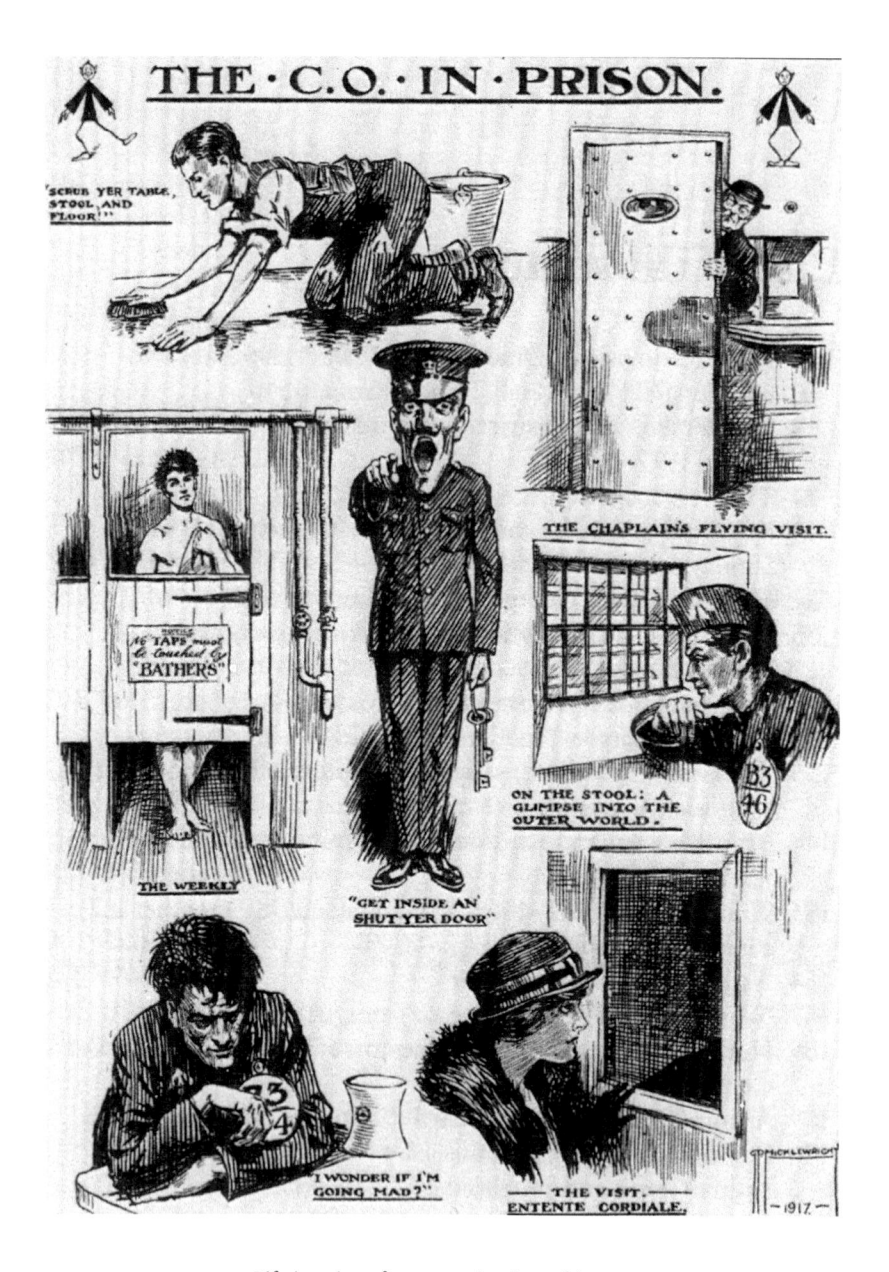

Life in prison for a conscientious objector

Summary

This chapter showed that the need for conscription in Britain had its origins in the deterioration of the system of European alliances at the start of the twentieth century. The resulting instability led to a war in which the huge losses sustained demanded substantial recruitment for the army. The tribunal system created by the Military Service Act of 1916 was the mechanism used to ensure fairness in the system of recruitment. The chapter examined the criteria used by the tribunals to decide who should be exempted from service and what sort of exemption was appropriate and fair. Finally, it looked at the general outcomes for those who were refused full exemption, but persisted in their application for it, on grounds of conscience.

The next chapter will define conscientious objection and its origins, and portray some widely held stereotypes of objectors.

Notes for Chapter Two

[15] *Pioneer*, 14 August 1915
[16] *Glamorgan Gazette*, 11 February 1916
[17] The *Herald of Wales* reported on 20 May 1916 that a Cwmafan conscientious objector applicant was exempted on medical and not conscience grounds.
[18] *Glamorgan Gazette*, 18 February 1916
[19] *Glamorgan Gazette*, 24 March 1916
[20] *South Wales Weekly Post*, 25 March 1916
[21] *Cambria Daily Leader*, 6 March 1916
[22] *Llais Llafur*, 15 July 1916
[23] *Glamorgan Gazette*, 31 March 1916
[24] *Herald of Wales and Monmouthshire Recorder*, 24 June 1916
[25] Alderman Hopkin Morgan, J.P. (Neath) presided
[26] This was certainly William 'Willie' Rees
[27] *Pioneer*, 2 September 1916
[28] Quoted in Jenni Llewelyn, 'Pilgrim of Peace: A life of George M. Ll. Davies Pacifist, Conscientious Objector and Peace-maker' (Ceredigion, 2016)
[29] Quoted in Llewelyn, as before
[30] See the entry under 'Albert Rankin' for the daily diet at Penderyn Work Centre
[31] Emrys Hughes was an Aberdare absolutist objector who was court-martialled five times. His two years' sentence was served at Devizes, Shepton Mallet, Redcar and Caernarfon. Released in April 1919 he was the first objector to become an MP.

Chapter Three:
The Conscientious Objectors and their objections

Will Thorne:[32] *'Can you define Conscientious Objection?'*
Prime Minister Asquith: *'I tried to do it last week and I will try again'*
Will Thorne: *'You will have a job'*

Introduction

This chapter will consider the origins of conscientious objection, the reasons for it, how its meaning was defined in World War One, and the characteristics of objectors as portrayed in a number of contemporaneous stereotypes.

The origin of modern conscientious objection

To most people today, conscientious objection refers to opposition to conscription and war. At the end of the nineteenth century, however, it referred to a person's resistance to medical vaccination and not to conscription for military service. Prior to conscription being introduced in 1916, the war was fought by volunteers and a smaller number of professional soldiers, but as loss of life mounted it became apparent that volunteering alone would not suffice. The introduction of conscription gave rise to another form of conscientious objection: to compulsory military service.

Defining conscientious objection

This raises a set of questions right away: How do you define conscientious objection? What were the objectors objecting to? Was it taking a human life? Was it war, or conscription? Was it militarism? Was it the denial by the state of an individual's freedom of choice? Was it an objection against fighting all wars, or this particular war? Were the objectors' objections political, religious or philosophical? Interpretation of the word 'conscientious' was difficult for many tribunals. This problem was conflated with the nature of the exemption to be granted, whether total, temporary or partial. Many tribunals said it was not possible to grant total exemption from any form of military service on the grounds of conscience.

The grounds for objection, however, can generally be categorised as religious, political and philosophical. Their differences are not always clear cut and are not mutually exclusive. Generally, people understand that one's religious beliefs may prohibit one joining the army to take life, politically that wars were regarded by many as undesirable because they set the working class of one country against that of another, or that it was politically illiberal to force people to join the army. Finally, that it was just morally wrong to take human life.

What made a conscientious objector? Was it when someone declared that to be the case to a tribunal? Was it only when the Central Tribunal decided that the objector was genuine? And if the tribunal did decide, did it depend on whether or not the objector accepted alternative service or continued as an absolutist? Did it depend on the degree of exemption awarded? For example, if someone served in the Non-combatant Corps were they a true conscientious objector?

Writers have attempted to describe a spectrum of resistance to militarism and war in terms of the degree of refusal to follow military discipline, or to perform alternative tasks prescribed by the state, following call-up. At one end of this spectrum lie those who accepted call-up without making any application for exemption. Even with this category of conscript soldiers some would turn against war once they saw from their own experiences what it entailed. At the other end of the spectrum were those who applied for exemption on grounds of conscience and refused absolutely to accept military authority or alternative service of any kind throughout the war and spent most of the war in prison.

Between these extremes were those who refused to kill but were prepared to participate in humane activities on the battlefield. The Friends Ambulance Unit was one example that preceded conscription and the Non-combatant Corps another example which followed conscription. Also, between these extremes were those who were not prepared to accept military discipline but would undertake tasks that did not directly contribute to the war, for example those who were prepared to undertake work of national importance in Home Office work centres or civil prisons.

Some 950 conscientious objectors are known to have come from Wales during the First World War, of whom over seventy were from the Port Talbot area. In order to account for this population it is necessary to explain the criteria used in this book for counting someone as a 'conscientious objector'. It is:

> 'anyone who appeared before a military service tribunal at any level and claimed to the tribunal to be a conscientious objector, or is likely to have been so considered had that person not already joined an organisation such as the Friends Ambulance Unit prior to the introduction of conscription'.

This definition covers all types of objectors, whether they went through the tribunal process or not. It does not count anyone who objected to conscription and war because they fell outside the criteria for conscription, such as age, or who later opposed conscription and war after opting to serve in the army, or being conscripted.

The dialogue between Prime Minister Asquith and trade union leader Will Thorne quoted at the head of this chapter was an early indication of the serious problems that the concept of conscientious objection would bring once conscription was introduced. Port Talbot was no exception to this experience. Prior to conscription, objection, on whatever grounds, remained a hidden matter and a latent problem. With the stage-by-stage introduction of conscription, however, it became patently obvious that problems could, and would, arise.

Definition of the word 'conscientious' was itself difficult. This problem was conflated with the nature of the exemption from conscription to be granted, whether it was for conscientious or other applicants and whether that exemption was to be total, temporary or partial. For example, many tribunals said it was not possible to grant total exemption from any form of military service on the grounds of conscience.

Some, who might otherwise have had objections to military service, had already been placed in 'starred' occupations prior to conscription and were never, 'combed out' to appear before a tribunal. The same applied to many who voluntarily joined such bodies as the Friends Ambulance Unit prior to conscription. These are yet further complications in defining and counting the numbers of conscientious objectors.

Nevertheless, a comprehensive record of World War One conscientious objectors in Great Britain has been compiled as the Pearce Register, which lists approximately 19,500 objectors. The register records how the objections were classified by the tribunal system and the objectors' responses to its decisions, but it does not record other individuals who opposed conscription where they were ineligible for it.

Stereotyping conscientious objectors

Lois Bibbings[33] identified several characterisations of objectors throughout the country.

A common view was that conscientious objectors were to be despised and rejected; that they were hated figures and were treated as outcasts because the war was popular. This view was often depicted on government propaganda postcards.

Another view, parallel to this, was 'Of cowards, shirkers and unmen'. This was a view of the 'unmanly', the antithesis of the brave, altruistic and vigorous soldier. In this view the conscientious objectors were viewed as selfish, indolent, cowardly and un-British.

A third depiction aimed to associate conscientious objectors with deviance, degeneracy, decadence and criminality. The deviance was in terms of race and gender, but criminality was particularly emphasised as a characteristic through the objectors' imprisonment.

The fourth portrayal was of the conscientious objector as a 'national danger' and a 'threat to the country'. Far from the unmanly attributes described in the second depiction, here he is a menace and a peril that might bring down the nation.

A fifth trait is that conscientious objectors were actually upstanding and honourable citizens. They were not outcasts but were supported and admired for standing up for their beliefs. In this case a comparison with those who evaded conscription through cowardice and self-preservation is instructive.

The final attribution is more powerful than that of being mere upstanding citizens. In fact, conscientious objectors can be seen as patriots and heroes, whereas the disillusioned soldier fails sometimes to live up to his image.

Yr Alltudion Cymraeg: The Welsh Exiles
A Group of Welsh Objectors at Knutsford (1917)-
(Some of the men in this picture from Gorseinon and Ystradgynlais have been identified. So has Jenkin William James of Pontrhydyfen (third from right in front row). Do readers recognise anyone else from Port Talbot? They are in Knutsford Prison)

A Christian stereotype and the Defence of the Realm

The interaction of religious conscientious objection with the Defence of the Realm Act resulted in a variant of Bibbing's fifth type, where objectors held firmly to their beliefs. This was the stereotype of the Christian martyr.

The Defence of the Realm Act and gave the government wide-ranging powers.[34] One of these powers concerned those discouraging conscription, and those whose activities were considered to interfere with military recruitment or training, to be imprisoned without trial. The Act stated that 'No person shall by word of mouth or in writing spread reports likely to cause disaffection or alarm amongst any of His Majesty's forces or among the civilian population'.

Ten persons were executed under the Act for *intent to assist the enemy*. Nothing so drastic happened to anyone from Port Talbot, but there were several arrests and important court cases involving those who were found guilty of offences under the Act. These cases arose from the possession and distribution of three separate NCF leaflets.

One of these, the Maximilian leaflet, provides us with the Christian portrayal of the objector but it was claimed by the authorities to be a direct incitement to contravene the Act. As the leaflet indirectly characterised all objectors as being akin to Christ and the early Christians, it was suggested that banning its distribution would, effectively, be like banning the Bible. The defence offered on behalf of the Port Talbot NCF was that the leaflets were merely pointing out the penalties that would be incurred by those who resisted conscription. They were not discouraging them from being recruited. Although it was illegal to incite defiance of the Act, public advocacy for repeal was perfectly legal.

Whilst the first duty of the state is its defence, its second duty, is justice within the realm. It is worth considering whether the Defence of the Realm Act delivered on either count for Port Talbot's conscientious objectors.

Summary

The important questions discussed in this Chapter were: the definition of conscientious objection; its origins, the motivation for objecting, and the stereotypical perceptions of objectors' behaviour as human beings. It is now time to answer more specific questions regarding their treatment at tribunals and the sentencing outcomes that the seventy-odd Port Talbot men experienced.

The main questions to be asked will be:
Were the objectors acting alone?
What ages were they?
What religion were they?
What were their politics?
Were the objectors single or married?
Which part of the Port Talbot area were they from?
What jobs did they do?
How did the tribunals treat them?
What happened to them afterwards?
These are the matters that will be examined in the next chapter.

Notes for Chapter Three

[32] A trade unionist in the forerunner of GMB Union who was involved in 1889 London dock strike and who supported the war.
[33] Lois Bibbings, 'Telling tales about men: conceptions of conscientious objectors to military service during the First World War, (Manchester, 2011)
[34] For example: to enable the requisitioning of buildings and land supposedly essential for the war effort. This act introduced new licensing hours, rationing, censorship, British Standard Time and control of the mines and railways.

51

Chapter Four:
The Port Talbot Objectors

*Despite all wars, within this narrow cell
The blessed sacrament we'd celebrate*[35]

T. E. Nicholas

Introduction

OVER 70 OF THE 950 OBJECTORS from Wales came from the Port Talbot area. This is a large number in comparison with big cities such as Salford and Manchester, which recorded 100 and 300 respectively.[36] The Port Talbot figure also puts into perspective the claim made for Dundee by Duncan 'that, with seventy COs, Dundee and District has produced more COs than any other comparable part of the country'. Dundee, however, is not comparable: its objectors were drawn from a much bigger eligible population than Port Talbot.[36a]

The purpose of this chapter is to record as fully as possible the Port Talbot objectors' backgrounds, experiences at tribunals, and the outcomes of their sentences.

Few of the Welsh objectors, or their supporters, are as well known throughout Wales as Emrys Hughes, Morgan Jones and George Ll. M. Davies[37]. Perhaps this is because all three were absolutist objectors who all became members of Parliament. Whilst the likes of Davies have biographies which include reviews of their objections to war and conscription, little has been written about the Port Talbot objectors either as a whole or as individuals.

A conventional classification of objectors is their particular response to war and to conscription. Three general categories will be used in this chapter to categorise the Port Talbot men. They are:

- Those who chose or accepted non-combatant status of some kind, such as the Friends' Ambulance Unit or the Non-combatant Corps.
- Those who accepted an alternative to the army such as the Home Office Scheme in which they did civilian work with no military control. These 'schemers' or 'alternativists' can be divided into those who went to Home Office Work Centres and those who returned to 'normal' work of some kind.
- Those who absolutely objected to any form of activity that could be related to conscription or furthering of the war effort. These were known as 'absolutists'.

The quantity of records made of their responses varies because there are many gaps. It is hoped to be able to fill at least some of them from new sources such as family archives and anecdotal information which is not yet in the public domain. The repetition between entries in this chapter is intentional, however, so that each person's record can be consulted with minimal reference elsewhere.

Those recorded here still may not represent the entire population of objectors from Port Talbot. There are no memorials to the Port Talbot objectors, tribunal records are incomplete and newspaper coverage was neither exhaustive, nor, in some instances, entirely accurate. Some names may, therefore, still be missing from the list, but further research may provide answers.

Non-combatant badge and RAMC card
(www.worldwar1postcards.com)

The Non-Combatants

This group of objectors comprised those who wore a military uniform but would not bear arms. Within the group there were two distinct elements: The Friends' Ambulance Unit (FAU) and the Non-combatant Corps (NCC). The former was set up in France at the outset of the war and its members were volunteers, mainly young, pacifist Quakers. The latter corps was formed in conjunction with the Military Service Act of 1916. Its 3,400 members were those who were opposed to conscription but were prepared to accept a tribunal's offer of non-combatant duties. This corps was an army unit which was subject to military discipline whose tasks were mainly physical labour: building, cleaning, loading and unloading anything, except munitions. They were denigrated as the 'no courage corps'. The Welsh Students Company of the Royal Army Medical Corps was a branch of the Corps.

Of the six non-combatant objectors from Port Talbot, none were in the Friends Ambulance Unit but one was an early volunteer for the RAMC. He is unusual, not in that he joined prior to the introduction of tribunals, but because he was court-martialled. It is interesting, however, to consider the way the RAMC is positively portrayed bearing the wounded in the picture on page 53, with the NCC member's negative portrayal in the postcard on page 55, where he is seen sweeping-up. The remainder of the Port Talbot's objectors who were only exempted from combat service made their beliefs known through the Tribunal system.

Those included in this section are:
David John Jones
Thomas David Powell
Idwal Gwyn Rees
William 'Willie' Rees
John Penry Thomas
William Arthur Thomas

Their experiences were not accurately reflected in the propaganda of the time. Contemporary postcards, for example, by implying that their duties were low risk suggested cowardice, whereas they were often at greater military risk than many. They also had the additional pressures of social disapproval and mis-treatment.

It is instructive to compare the following case, raised by King, an MP, with that of Port Talbot objectors Aneurin Morgan, Lemuel Samuel and Jack Woolcock, which Philip Snowden MP was to raise in Parliament a few

The objector portrayed as cowardly *(www.worldwar1postcards.com)*

months later. In the same sitting as King's, Snowden raised the case of Cwmafan's David John Jones, asking whether a medical student like Jones who was attached to the Officers' Training Non-combatant Corps would be permitted to substitute some other voluntary work of national importance.

Mr King asked the Under-secretary of State for War 'whether men in the Corps had refused to handle shells, rifles and other military supplies and whether their court-martials had resulted in hard labour, fifty-six days of field punishment No. 1 and whether it is in accordance with Regulations that they were tied up three nights out of four; whether they were, contrary to Regulations, dragged round the square and thrown on the ground, picked up, and again thrown down and kicked; whether soldiers who watched these proceedings made their disgust apparent; where these men now are; whether in December, 1917, fourteen men, being Seventh Day Adventists, were court-martialled at Abancourt for refusing to do military work on the Sabbath; whether they received sentences of nine months' hard labour; and whether any of these men are now in Wormwood Scrubs Prison or at Knutsford Work Centre?'

The questions raised by King and Snowden were essentially rhetorical: simply asking the question would raise public awareness of the issues and would ensure that the authorities took corrective action, or provide information.

Rev. David John Jones (1887–1970)

Baptist David John Jones was born in 1887, at Ynysafon, Cwmafan, but emigrated with his widowed miner father to Pennsylvania, USA, before returning to Wales to study theology at Bala-Bangor College. When war came he joined the Welsh Students Company of the Royal Army Medical Corps. This 260-strong company was a special company formed by the War Office, mainly for ordained ministers and theology students in Wales. It was created for those who wished to serve their country, but were opposed to bearing arms on religious grounds. Its formation was instigated by Brigadier-General Owen Thomas and Rev. John Williams of Brynsiencyn, the senior chaplain to Welsh soldiers.

Rev. David John Jones' modest memorial stone in Oddfellows Cemetery *(Find My Past)*

The Company were trained at Llandrindod Wells and Hillsborough Barracks in Sheffield before leaving, via Kinmel Camp, for France in December 1915. In all, Jones was with the RAMC Welsh Students' Company for three years and two months and was subject to military discipline even though he would not be required to fight or take life. The NCF and the Quakers repudiated this compromise arrangement of wearing a uniform without bearing arms, considering the unit to be part of the military machine.

Although Jones did not have to engage with the tribunal system, like many fellow conscientious objectors, he did appear at a court-martial. This unusual situation demands an explanation. It seems that Jones became disenchanted with some of the orders he was given in the Medical Corps and became subject to special military jurisdiction at a court-martial. A compromise was reached because Jones continued in the Company.

In 1919, he entered the University College of North Wales at Bangor. On graduation he first became Baptist Minister for Capel Judah at Dolgellau and then in Chester and Nanticoke, Pennsylvania between 1929 and 1957. Jones died in 1970 and is buried at Schuykill, Pennsylvania.

Thomas David Powell (1891–1936)

Powell was born in King Street, Aberdare. He worked as a carpenter in the building trade and it is likely that he was drawn to live in Port Talbot by the attraction of decent housing and employment.

We first hear of him as a conscientious objector at the Glamorgan Appeal Tribunal at Margam on 28 March 1916. This was the 'class' appeal of thirteen objectors, in which the tribunal chair expressed the opinion that he was only allowed to offer exemption from combatant service. Henry Davies represented the group with his usual skills of advocacy and pointed out that the Chair's opinion was incorrect. Powell's appeal, like the twelve others, still for total exemption, was refused.[39] Despite the combative and persuasive oratory of Henry Davies, Powell alone accepted the entreaties of Mayor Jacob, the Tribunal Chair, to accept exemption from combatant service only. No more is known. It is highly likely that Powell's skills as a carpenter would have been used for some form of building work in an army barracks or similar establishment.

Idwal Gwyn Rees (1895–1964)

Idwal Gwyn Rees hailed from Castle Street, Aberafan. His father, William, was a waterman with Aberafan Borough Council, brother, David Alfred Rees, was an outfitter in the town; brother William was a check weigh-man at the Mansel Tinplate Works and brother Evan Thomas Rees was following a teaching career in a local elementary school.

Idwal Gwyn was an Anglican student at Bangor Normal College undergoing teacher training when he was asked to report to the local recruiting office. At the Aberafan Military Service Tribunal on 26 February 1916, unmarried, he was exempted from combatant service only. He was dissatisfied with limited exemption. When requested, he failed to report to barracks on 29 September and was arrested at his home by PC Vernon.[40] He appeared at the police court before W. J. Williams and Moses Thomas, saying that he 'was not amenable to the Act'. As an absentee he was fined £2 and remanded to await a police escort to Cardiff army barracks.

Accordingly, on 18 October 1916, he was removed to the Non-combatant Corps (Western) at Cardiff. He refused to comply with military discipline, declining to sign army papers. This resulted in him being sent to Kinmel Camp on 30 October. Further non-compliance led a court-martial

57

which resulted in a sentence of 112 days' hard labour. At the Central Military Tribunal on 24 November he was reckoned to be a Class A, genuine, conscientious objector. This meant his case could be referred to the Brace Committee which had the power to offer him work at a work centre as an alternative to prison. On 11 December he was released from Wormwood Scrubs to fulfil work of national importance, as a member of Army Reserve W. This was to be done at Llanddeusant in the Black Mountain of Carmarthenshire and later at Carmarthen Civil Prison.

In the Autumn of 1925 Rees married Sarah Jones. They lived in Springfield Terrace, Aberafan. He died on 6 April 1964 and is buried in Baglan Church, Port Talbot.

William 'Willie' Rees (1891–1956)

Rees lived in Castle Street, Aberafan. His occupation has been recorded as both a 'Cold Rolls Superintendent' and as the Assistant Manager of a tinplate works. The works concerned had been deemed a 'controlled establishment' and Rees' occupation, which had been 'badged', had recently been de-badged making him eligible for enlistment.

His application for exemption on religious grounds was refused by the local tribunal, held at Aberafan Police Court. Rees' case was the first to be heard, followed by four others, including his brother and John Selwyn Jones, his near neighbour. Police Sergeant Jones stated that three notices had been served on Rees, who claimed through his representative, Mr Henry Davies of the ILP, that where certified occupations had been removed from the list, a period of two months should elapse before further attendance at a tribunal was expected. Further, it was argued, that as Rees was working in a 'controlled establishment', it was logical that he was doing work of national importance and should have been exempted on those very grounds.

However, the tribunal chair seemed to consider that a successful appeal, from his point of view, would be to get appellants to accept non-combatant status. The applicants did not want it, but that is what was decided for Rees and Jones. After the tribunal, on 3 March, Rees wrote to the *Glamorgan Gazette* to complain of reports that their applications were reported as 'contemptible' and 'disgusting', saying that they 'actually met with the approval of a considerable number of the public present ... and even the tribunal, in refusing our application, recognised our sincerity.'

From 13 April Rees, a single man, was thus deemed to be an absentee from the Non-combatant Corps (NCC), awaiting an arrest which was duly actioned on 25 May. At the court, all the defendants were fined forty shillings for being absentees and handed over, with Rees and Jones escorted to the NCC (2nd Western) at Kinmel. On 25 July Rees was court-martialled there for refusal to sign army enlistment papers and received a punishment of two years' hard labour. This was to be served at Walton Prison, Liverpool where he would remain to await any appeal he might be allowed to make. John Selwyn Jones accompanied him to Walton. At Wormwood Scrubs, the tribunal decided that NCC status was inappropriate for him and allowed him to join the Home Office Scheme from November. The sentence was served at Llanon Reservoir and Llanddeusant waterworks.

It is worth noting that T. E. Harvey MP took an interest in Rees's case. As a Quaker, Harvey was placed in a difficult personal position by Britain's declaration of war in August 1914. Quakers traditionally took the view that all war is incompatible with the spirit and teachings of Christ. Harvey remained one of the small band of Liberals, at that time still including Norman Angell and E. D. Morel, who had grave doubts about the war. He and another Liberal Quaker MP, Arnold Stephenson Rowntree, helped to draft the section of the later Military Service Act that provided for the possibility of conscientious objectors doing work of national importance as a condition of exemption from service in the army. He also served as a member of the Pelham Committee (formally, the Committee on Work of National Importance), the body charged in March 1916 with trying to find suitable civilian occupations for conscientious objectors prepared to undertake the work of national importance he had helped to be written into the Military Service Act.

John Penry Thomas (1881–1946)

Llandovery-born Thomas was the son of a Cardiff docks stevedore and a music teacher who lived in the Canton district of Cardiff. Thomas was encouraged to study, and consequently he became head teacher of a local elementary school. He lived near St Athan in the Vale of Glamorgan before moving to the Port Talbot area on obtaining a position in the area.

In August 1910, he married Winifred Mary Mainwaring of Colwinston at Baglan Church. The couple lived at Gwalia Stores, a bakery and grocery outlet on Port Talbot High Street, when he was called up. Thomas' objection to military service had a religious foundation: he was a Congregationalist. When offered non-combatant status and due to join the NCC at Cardiff on 11 September 1916, he failed to report. This resulted in his arrest as an absentee on 3 October and an escort to Kinmel to be assigned to the 4th Western training reserve battalion. In February 1917 Thomas was drafted into another NCC unit at Shirehampton to the north-west of Bristol.

On 1 March 1919 he was still attached to an NCC unit, the 3rd Southern, with his official demobilisation being 31 December 1919. He only shared six more years with Winifred because she died in 1926 to be buried at Groes Chapel, Margam. John Penry returned to live at Gileston, in the Vale of Glamorgan, where he died in December 1946.

William Arthur Thomas (1882–1953)

Whitland-born Thomas of 41 Tanygroes Street was an ILP member who worked as a postman. Thomas was recently married when he applied for exemption from service.[41] His case was heard at Margam on 14 March 1916 when he was offered to join No 2 Non-combatant Corps at Kinmel. He accepted, no doubt realising that an appeal might be possible which might gain him fuller exemption. Glamorgan Appeal Tribunal on 28 March 1916[42] upheld the Margam decision. Conscription had only been introduced on 2 March 1916 and the Non-combatant Corps later that month. This may explain why he was sent to Kinmel before being offered Non-combatant status. Thomas' early enlistment would mean that, by the time he was demobilised, on 26 November 1919, he would have spent almost five years away from his family in both Great Britain and Ireland and been subject to military discipline during all of that time.

The fact that Idwal Gwynne Rees and William Rees also decided to leave the NCC suggests that inappropriate pressure may have been exerted on them at tribunal to elect for non-combatant service; it is equally possible that the decision to accept the tribunal's offer was freely made and that it was within the NCC that things became disagreeable. D. J. Jones also had misgivings about the Corps.

And, although J. P. Thomas was still attached to an NCC unit at the war's end, he, too, clearly had serious doubts about his choice. Of the six non-combatant service cases above, the only case that went to plan in the eyes of the authorities was that of William A. Thomas.

(Above) William Thomas' enrolment paper
(Find My Past)

(Left) William Thomas' home in Tanygroes Street

The 'Schemers': the Devil's own brigade

In an entry in Bransby Griffiths' notebook, M. Jones of West Bromwich, a fellow inmate at Penderyn, alluded to his fellow schemers as 'The Devil's own brigade'. They were anything but.

Army order X ... and the Home Office Scheme

Army order X of 25 May 1917 required objectors to be sent from military prison to the nearest civil prison pending a review of their cases by the Brace Committee if requested at the Central Tribunal. If the review found his case to be genuine, an objector would remain in a civil prison to do work of national importance, or in a work camp, in either case under the Home Office Scheme as a member of Army Reserve, Class W. Unfortunately, Army order X order was not retroactive and this arrangement left hundreds of objectors in military prisons or guardrooms.

The Home Office Scheme (HOS) created Work Centres throughout the country in under-used prisons or as countryside work camps. It was aimed at avoiding the brutality that objectors had experienced from the army, or whilst in criminal prison. The schemers were civilian-controlled and paid by the police but many still regarded themselves as political prisoners. With the *Absolutists* they bore the brunt of the persecutions. The NCF view was that those in this reserve were still part of the military machine and liable to recall. Objectors were based in used prisons, asylums and workhouses and worked outdoors or indoors depending on the location. Typical outdoor work was timber cutting, road making; drain-laying; rail maintenance and agriculture. Indoor work was often mailbag fabrication; brush and basket-making and rope-making. Those covered in this section are:

Percival Albert Berryman
David Davies of Denbigh
Joseph Davies
Leyshon Davies
Robert J. Davies
Albert Rankin Evans
Isaac John Evans
Robert Evans
Nicholas Arthur Gill

William Grane
Edward Heycock
John I. E. Heycock
Ivor Hopkins
Robert Evan Hughes
Thomas Henry Hughes
Jenkin William James
J. E. Jones
Lewis Emlyn Jones

Vaughan Jones
William Ivor Jones
The Jones brothers of Pantdu
  Evan Jones
  Robert Jones
  Rees Jones
  John Jones
William (Gwilym) Lewis
Joseph Llewelyn
Richard Mainwaring
Thomas Arthur Mainwaring

William J. Mainwaring
Thomas John Mills
Arthur Mullington
David William Older
Daniel H. Phillips
David John Phillips
Albert Owen Rankin
George Rees
John Wellington
Lancelot Thomas Waters

Percival Albert Berryman (1897–1982)

Berryman was from near Perranporth in Cornwall, a market gardener like his father. As a teenager and single man he decided, as did many others, to cross the Bristol Channel to Port Talbot to seek a new life. It is not known whether he had any religious or political affiliations before arriving in Wales but soon after arriving he joined the ILP and became a Great Western Railway (GWR) employee.

It is assumed that his main motive for objecting to conscription was political, but there may have been other reasons, too, when he became one of the first to appear before Margam Tribunal, along with several other railway workers. His application for exemption was rejected, so he appealed to the Glamorgan Tribunal on 28 March 1916.[43] Along with Nicholas Arthur Gill, he claimed exemption on the grounds that he was already doing work of national importance. The case was postponed to consider their position but the Appeal Tribunal later upheld the original decision that their work could not be so classified.

It is worth stating that several men found themselves in almost a reverse position to Berryman. Those were the men already in certified trades who withdrew their objections, relying on their employment classification to exempt themselves from service, rather than to make an application on the grounds of conscience. As the war progressed and the army's losses mounted, the criteria for classification for certified employment was tightened up so that men who had been 'badged' when in civilian occupations could be 'combed out'. This process led to much resistance amongst the trade unions because they feared industrial conscription would be its sequel. It also led to many re-applications for exemption after combing-out took place, and more work for the tribunals.

The most likely path taken by Berryman, after the appeal and military processing was over, would have been, like Gill, to join the Home Office Scheme. Further evidence is needed to confirm or refute this, however. On 16 August 1919 Berryman married Rhoda Ellen Walters, from Marsh Street. He died in the Autumn of 1982, aged eighty-five.

David Davies of Denbigh (1894–

This is one of the two David Davies known to be a conscientious objector in Port Talbot. He came to the town from Trefnant, near Denbigh. Davies was arrested on 26 June 1916 and tried at Denbigh Police Court for being absent when called up to the army. His tribunal history remains a blank until his arrest was recorded and he received the usual forty shilling fine for being an absentee from the army. He was then remitted to Kinmel Camp after being held temporarily at Wrexham. At Kinmel he was assigned to the 23 Works Brigade of the Cheshire Regiment. 'Private' Davies continued to ignore army orders, including not reporting for his posting to Liverpool on 5 February 1917. This disobedience could only have one outcome. That was to be a court-martial at Kinmel on 8 July 1917, at which he received a sentence of two years' hard labour to be served at Walton Prison, Liverpool.

The sentence was subject to any appeal he was allowed to make at the Central Tribunal. It duly resulted in his being offered alternative service in the Home Office Scheme. He accepted, but it was not the end of difficulties for him and the authorities, however. He was directed to Llanddeusant Waterworks in the Black Mountain area of Carmarthenshire. This was the work camp where Willie and Idwal Rees of Port Talbot had been stationed for their intransigence some time earlier. Troubles arose at the camp because of the conditions experienced at this remote, bleak site: hard labour, terrible weather and a poor diet. In military terms the mass abscondment that took place would have been called a mutiny; Davies was implicated.

Joseph Davies (1885–1926)

Joseph M. Davies was from Park Row, Cwmafan. After leaving school he became a furnaceman in a tinplate works and lived in Afan Street, Felindre.

Davies, who had become an ILP member, was called up for service in the early days of conscription but failed to attend for enrolment. Rather than appear at the recruiting office, he decided instead to await arrest, and have his application heard, and, predictably, rejected by Margam Tribunal.

This led to an appearance before Glamorgan Appeal Tribunal on 28 March 1916.[44] It upheld the Margam decision, despite the entreaties on the applicant's behalf by Henry Davies. Joseph Davies avoided the recruiting office once again for nearly two months until he was re-arrested as an absentee on 25 May 1916. An escort to Cardiff barracks followed the arrest for him to appear before a court-martial on 6 June. The court decreed a sentence of six months' hard labour, but the actual length of sentence would depend on how quickly his appeal was heard. It turned out that he had served over two months of it at Dartmoor before the Central Tribunal required his presence at Wormwood Scrubs on 25 August 1916. The Tribunal deemed him to be a genuine objector who should be offered the chance to serve under the Home Office Scheme. He served it at Warwick and Princetown Work Centre, Dartmoor.[45]

Leyshon Davies (1886–1953)

Davies, a Carmarthenshire man from Llwynhendy, lived during the pre-war years at 71 Green Park Street, Aberafan in a large household of four adults and six young children, all under fifteen year of age. No doubt part of Davies earnings as a tinman was a welcome contribution to the family's household expenses.

He was a member of the Plymouth Brethren, a nonconformist Christian movement which originated from Anglicanism and made a testimony to peace in the early years after the movement's foundation. The Brethren are regarded as one of the 'historic peace churches' because of their shared rejection of participation in war. The curious thing about his case is that, despite being a member of the Brethren, which would almost certainly gain him total exemption from service, he decided to forego an application on religious grounds and used the tribunal system in May 1917, to voice his strong opposition to conscription and war.[46]

Consequently, it was not long before he found himself at a court-martial. He was now the disobedient Private Davies, a notional member of the 3rd Welsh Regiment at Kinmel Camp. He was ushered to Wormwood Scrubs on 22 May to serve the one year's hard labour decreed at the court-martial.

When the Central Military Tribunal's opinion was made known in July, Davies was, unsurprisingly, decreed to be a Class A, genuine, objector. That qualified him to accept an offer to participate in the scheme to do work of national importance in a Home Office Work Centre, or to be consigned to prison. He accepted the scheme and was posted to Work Centre on Dartmoor from May until July 1917.

It is believed that he married Katherine Hammond in 1920.

Robert J. Davies (1894–1971)

The NCF recorded Robert Davies' home as Sea View Cottage in Baglan and his occupation, at twenty-three years of age, as a tinplate bundler. The *Herald of Wales*[47] described him as a 'platelayer', which is a railway job. This latter description presumably indicated a steelworker in Port Talbot plate mill, rather than a railway worker. Given the importance of steel plate for armoured applications, it is surprising that Davies was not 'badged' by his employer, but the latter may have had reason not to badge him. Nonetheless, after failing to report to the recruitment centre, he was arrested and appeared at Neath Magistrates Court in October 1916. He told the bench that he 'considered himself as doing work of national importance … and … who was a greater asset at work and out of the army.' Nevertheless, he was fined forty shillings for desertion and awaited a military escort to one of the Welsh barracks at Kinmel, or Cardiff.

He was court-martialled at the army training centre to which he had been allocated on 11 November 1916, and then, undoubtedly, received a sentence of hard labour pending an appeal to the Central Tribunal at Wormwood Scrubs. The tribunal regarded Davies as suitable to join the Home Office Scheme if he wished. He accepted and thereafter was assigned to prisons and work centres at Warwick, Dartmoor, Wakefield, Shrewsbury and, finally, Talgarth where he worked to lay water pipes for the new sanatorium.

Joseph Brett was a fellow objector at Talgarth who kept an album to record his fellow objectors' movements. That album, along with NCF records, is how Robert Davies' final movements, but not the date of his release as an objector, are known. Davies married Margaret Walsh in 1933 to bring up daughter Joan at 2 Ty'r Halen, Baglan. Davies continued as a steelworker. He died locally in 1971.

Albert Rankin Evans (1888–1964)

Albert Evans was from St Clears in Carmarthenshire. At twenty-one he married Katie Edwards of Tanygroes Cottages, Aberafan. He obtained work as a locomotive attendant in a local tinplate works and became a member of the ILP and, possibly, an NCF member.

At the introduction of conscription, the twenty-eight-year-old had no children but applied for exemption, most likely on the grounds of political conscience. The date of his original Margam tribunal is not known, but as with many Port Talbot objectors, his call-up and application for exemption was quite early considering that his appeal was heard at the Glamorgan Tribunal on 28 March 1916.[48] At the appeal he was represented, along with twelve others, by Henry Davies. It, too, was refused when Evans rejected the offer of non-combatant service but it is most probable, given the solidarity shown by the 'Port Talbot thirteen', that his destiny followed a similar path to the others during the years of war. It is quite certain that he found himself in prisons or work centres at various locations in Britain for the remainder of the war and, possibly, into 1919.

Thereafter nothing is known of him for the next twenty years or so until Evans was recorded as a foreman in the tinplate works. He and Kate brought up their family at Margam Road after the war.

Isaac John Evans (1896–1958)

Llanelli-born Isaac John Evans was from Carlos Street, Port Talbot. He worked as a coal miner in Cwmafan and had married Blodwen Evans in 1913. After the refusal of his application for exemption at the local and appeal tribunals, he failed to appear at the recruitment office. He then found himself arrested by Police Sergeant Evans as an absentee[49] from the army and remanded, declaring himself to be 'a conscientious objector'. At Port Talbot Magistrates Court, he was fined the usual £2 and awaited an escort to an army induction centre. For south Wales conscripts it was usual for the induction to be held at either Cardiff Barracks or Kinmel Camp, near Rhyl. These events suggest that Evans had rejected any offer of alternative service such as the Non-combatant Corps, had he been so offered. Even at this point (July 1918) twenty-two-year-old Evans could have accepted military discipline.

However, by the time of his tribunals, the government had tightened the criteria for conscription, including both married men and reducing the number of 'essential' war occupations. The 'comb out' of men from less essential occupations was instigated a second time in 1918 to replenish losses of army personnel on various fronts. It seems that Evans was 'combed out' at such a late time that he was not likely to have been released from work centre or prison for anything up to another year. Whatever happened to Evans, his wartime experience was unlikely to have ended at the November armistice.

He did not return to the pits, becoming a tin-worker after the war and living at Depot Road, Cwmafan. Evans death was recorded in Merthyr Tydfil district in 1958.

Robert Evans (1888–1968)

As a single man Robert Evans lived in London Road, Cwmafan. Evans was a furnace-man in a tinplate works and attended a Congregationalist chapel. It is reasonable to assume that his religious beliefs were the main foundation of his objection to conscription.

Details of the local tribunal which heard his case are unknown, but his fate followed the usual pattern. His case is traceable from the time of his arrest as an absentee and trial at Port Talbot police court. The court found him guilty of being an absentee from HM Forces, fined him forty shillings and referred him under escort to Cardiff barracks on 23 April 1917. There he was unsuccessfully persuaded to accept military discipline in the usual way, failing to obey any order given. The consequence in such a case is to sent to Kinmel for a full army induction. This duly took place on 1 May at Kinmel Camp where he again refused to sign papers to join the 58th Training Battalion of the Army Reserve W. Private Evans received a sentence of two years' hard labour, commuted to one year 253 days, one of the severest of the hard labour sentences. Fortunately he was sent to Wormwood Scrubs on 3 May to await a review of his case by the Central Military Tribunal. On 29 June 1917 he was pronounced as a 'class A, genuine conscientious objector'. Surprisingly there is nothing to show that the tribunal had sought references from his Chapel, or elsewhere. On 12 July, he was removed to Princetown Work Centre on Dartmoor.

After his release he married Margaret Davies in 1922 and was still a furnaceman, living at Cunard Terrace in 1939.

Nicholas Arthur Gill (1896–1957)

Arthur Gill was baptised in Truro in 1896 and lived with his grandparents who were general dealers in Clement Street, Truro. He worked as an errand boy.

By 1914 Arthur had moved to the Port Talbot area. It was to be a permanent move. He soon joined the ILP and applied for exemption from military service but was refused at Margam Tribunal. At Glamorgan Appeal Tribunal on 28 March 1916 he was again refused.[50] Gill, who was a GWR locomotive engineer, and his colleague, Percy Berryman, another Cornishman, claimed that they were already doing work of national importance. Gill said he would not hold himself responsible for 'inflicting death', then refused non-combatant service in the form of hospital work. When asked why not he simply said that 'I should not care for it'. None of this was sufficient to support his claim, so the Appeal Tribunal upheld the Margam decision.

The next steps are not recorded but most cases followed a similar pattern, so it can be assumed that Berryman would have been arrested, fined, and remanded at Port Talbot Police Station to await a military chaperone to Cardiff Barracks. Further dissidence in response to military commands led to the inevitable court-martial on 24 June 1916. This event resulted in a ruling of 112 days' hard labour to be served at Cardiff Prison. Some two months were served before Gill's appeal was heard by the Central Tribunal on 28 August at Wormwood Scrubs. Its finding was that he was a genuine, Class A objector that should be subject to the direction of the Brace Committee. That he was offered the Home Office Scheme was likely. If he accepted the offer he would be sent to a work centre or to one of the prisons, which had been emptied during the course of the war. The choice that Gill made remains to be determined. After the war Gill married Mary A. Scourfield of Maesteg and lived in Port Talbot.

William Grane (b. 1885)

The William Grane who was reported as the Port Talbot conscientious objector is believed to be Dublin-born William Albert Grane. He boarded in Llandebie whilst he worked at the nearby Cilyrychen Limestone Quarry. The quarry may have occasionally supplied the furnaces at Port Talbot, and provided Grane with contacts in the steel town.

Grane somehow found his way to Port Talbot from Llandebie where he, along with Lemuel Samuel, became an ILP and NCF member and an early applicant for exemption at Margam Tribunal. Like almost every other applicant on conscientious grounds, his application was refused, as was his appeal at Glamorgan Appeal Tribunal on 28 March 1916.[51] At this same appeal twelve other ILP members were represented by Henry Davies, who had to assert himself to be heard. Yet, for some reason, Grane was the only objector who was questioned by tribunal members.

There this narrative ends, but it is certain that Grane would have had to make similar choices to those made by other objectors. Short of a drastic event, such as his premature death, or an unanticipated decision to join the colours, Grane would have had to decide the degree of co-operation or resistance he would offer to the military authorities as he went through the tribunal system. It is certain that he and his twelve colleagues-in-appeal, as ILP members, would have been well-supported and advised but would, nevertheless, have been moved several times between various prisons and work centres to complete their sentences. After Grane had left the limeworks it was manned by German prisoners-of-war so it was unlikely that he would have returned there to perform work of national importance?

Edward Heycock (1880–1938)

The well-known Port Talbot local historian, A. Leslie Evans,[52] recognised that 'Over the past two centuries members of the Heycock family have been prominent in the Taibach scene', referring to the debt owed by Llewelyn Heycock, Chair of Glamorgan County Council in 1962-63, and an elder at Bethany English Presbyterian Church, for 'the stimulus he received from his uncle, Ed Heycock … a pioneer in the local labour movement'. Llewelyn, born in Alma Terrace in 1905 was the eldest of William Heycock's six sons. There was no mention by Evans of Ed's conscientious objection so it is time to take Edward's biography a little further.

Edward was the son of his namesake father, and tin roller, and Margaret Heycock of 37 Park Street, Taibach. He was one of eleven children. During his work at a local railway station he became attracted to the ILP and later the NCF and was described as 'a burly railway engineer.' Edward was the senior son and twelve years older than brother, John, who also decided to apply for exemption from conscription on conscientious grounds. It is likely that he was partly motivated on religious grounds, too.

At Margam tribunal[53] Heycock criticised the conduct of the tribunal, raising his voice to ask 'is it possible for a conscientious objector to receive justice at the hands of this tribunal? It doesn't look like it for they have quick despatch here tonight'. Heycock went on to say that if he 'was a coward he could have secured all the exemption he wanted by taking 2s 9d from the state, and relying on being indispensable to his employers'. When the Chairman pointed out that Heycock's locomotive pulled coal trains which aided the war effort and the destruction of life, Heycock replied sharply: 'I drag coal along the line to warm the little children in Italy, but I am not responsible for the exorbitant prices charged by the dealers.' When tribunal member Hallowes commented that the war was 'to put down militarism' he received a sharp response from Heycock: 'You said the same thing about the Boer War. It was Kruger that time; it is the Kaiser this time.' A fellow tribunal member, Mr Routledge, moved that his application be dismissed.

At the Glamorgan Appeal Tribunal on 28 March 1916 his appeal against the decision of Margam Tribunal of 7 March not to grant him exemption was refused.[54]

The remaining events in Heycock's war years will have to be determined from, as yet, undiscovered sources. After the war, Ed Heycock continued to be active in local trade unionism and politics, becoming Labour Mayor of Port Talbot in 1927–8 ... 'a genial man of great depth of character (who) became a popular figure in local politics, being admired for his sound judgement.'[55]

John I. E. Heycock (1892–1959)

John I. E. Heycock was born on 18 November 1892 and baptised at the Chapel of Ease in Margam. He lived variously at Tanygroes, Park Street in Taibach and Tudor Street in Port Talbot after marrying Margaret Williams. John is likely to have become an ILP member before his marriage when he worked as a railway fireman, and it is possible that either the party's close affinity with the NCF, or his religious beliefs, or both, encouraged him to join the fellowship, too.

There is little doubt that the result of his political attitude towards conscription and war was an application for exemption early in 1916 on conscientious grounds. The lack of a transcript of any kind from the local Margam Tribunal means that an assessment of the balance of his objection between religious and political reasons cannot be made. The application was nonetheless rejected, as was his appeal at Glamorgan Appeal Tribunal on 28 March. The absence of tribunal records for his case means that the remaining

71

events in his war years will have to be determined, if possible, from other sources. He was working as a locomotive driver through the inter-war years.

Ivor J. Hopkins (1891–1941)

Ivor Hopkins was born at Chapel Cottages but lived during his teenage years at Graig y Tewgoed, Cwmafan. He married Agnes Williams in 1913 and the twenty-six-year-old was a coalminer when conscription came into force.

Fortunately, a partial record of Hopkins' local tribunal at Margam was reported.[56] The newspaper's description of events as a 'dramatic incident' was quite detailed: Hopkins' application was not heard until 9 pm because his case was, presumably, preceded by many others. In any case, Hopkins had already read out a written statement in support of his application when Henry Davies asked to continue to speak on his behalf. Lowther, the Tribunal Chair, seems to have grudgingly granted Davies permission to speak, warning him that it should not be a long one, simply saying: 'You must not make a speech'.

At that point Davies interjected and insisted on saying that 'every claim had been disallowed in a perfunctory manner that suggested pre-judgement of the case without a knowledge of the facts'.... Lowther had admitted that he could not define 'conscience' when challenged to do so by Davies. This interjection by Davies was to express his dissatisfaction with the general conduct of the tribunal, rather than a specific comment about Hopkins' particular case. Davies summarised his position by saying 'we shall make an appeal to a tribunal that has some knowledge of it.' After such a divisive dialogue it was hardly surprising that Hopkins' case was rejected.

The rejection of his application in this way propelled Hopkins into making a fruitless appeal. As a result, Hopkins refused to report at the recruitment office until he was arrested 25 May 1916, as an absentee. The Port Talbot Court fined him and remanded him pending an escort to Cardiff Barracks to join the Army Reserve. His continued antagonism towards military instructions resulted in a court-martial at Cardiff on 6 June 1916. The upshot of his disobedience was a sentence of six months' hard labour, commuted to two months, to be served in Cardiff Civil Prison and subject to a further appeal.

On 25 August his case was considered by the Central Tribunal at Wormwood Scrubs. It deemed Hopkins to be a Class A objector who should be offered alternative service under the advice of the Brace Committee in the Home Office Scheme. Hopkins accepted this and was transferred to Princetown Work Centre at Dartmoor on 28 August. His remaining history is unknown but he could have spent almost three more years as Private Hopkins within various work centres and prisons.

Robert Evan Hughes (1893–1926)

Robert Evan Hughes was born in Ffestiniog, Merionethshire, one of the three children of Maggie and Robert Hughes, a pit sinker. Robert Evan came to live at Pwll-y-Glaw, Cwmafan and work as a coal miner. His mother brought the family to Cwmafan without her husband. That young brother Harry Hughes was born in the USA suggests an itinerant lifestyle was led by the family. Several other mining and quarrying families are known to have migrated from north Wales to Cwmafan and indeed to the USA at this time.

Hughes married Annie Davies in 1913, but the next we hear of Robert Evan was the twenty-three-year-old's arrest on 25 April 1916, and handover[57] to the military. This was soon after the introduction of conscription on 2 March. For him to have been arrested on this date the following events would had to have taken place within the preceding fifty-four days:

1. no certificate of exemption from his employer issued
2. the receipt of form W3236 calling him up to the recruitment centre.
3. the centre's response to his non-attendance
4. sufficient time for an arrest warrant to be authorised and effected
5. attendance and rejection of application at a local tribunal
6. attendance and rejection of application at an appeal tribunal

By any measure this was a remarkably efficient sequence of events by all concerned and one must ask why? It is quite easy to understand why, with ILP or NCF help, applications for exemption on conscience grounds could have been made quickly. It is more difficult to understand the authorities' alacrity, especially when Hughes' occupation is considered as being important for the war effort.

Was there some intervention by his disaffected father? Perhaps to influence the employer, or the recruiting authority? In the absence of further information, one can only speculate about the events that preceded his arrest, and one can only speculate about Hughes' future path. Did he accept non-combatant status, or was he offered alternative work at his own pit, or elsewhere, under the Home Office Scheme? Or were his convictions so strong that he became an absolutist? Readers of this book may have the answers to such questions.

Hughes' itinerant lifestyle did not continue after the war had ended. He died locally at the age of thirty-three.

Thomas Henry Hughes (1888–1959)

Hughes was from Ty'r Owen Row in Cwmafan. He became a County elementary schoolteacher when quite young before he married Caroline in 1909. In April 1917, the twenty-nine-year-old Congregationalist was fined £2 by Port Talbot Magistrates as an absentee under the Military Service Act. Captain W. E. Rees represented the Military Authorities.[58] He was remanded until handed over to be escorted to Kinmel Training Camp. Hughes had declared himself to be a conscientious objector and when asked if he had anything more to say remarked: 'It is a waste of time'. Clearly, Hughes' opinion was that the war was pointless.

He was court-martialled at Kinmel as a member of the 58th Training Reserve Battalion for refusing to accept military authority and received a sentence of two years' hard labour to be served at Wormwood Scrubs. Hughes' final appeal to the Central Tribunal was heard on 23 June. By this time, he had served the most vicious part of his sentence, which had been commuted to 112 days. Presumably the Tribunal accepted that his religious objection was genuine and, accordingly, offered him the route of joining the Home Office Scheme. His acceptance resulted in his removal from the Scrubs to Dartmoor's Princetown Work Centre.

Hughes later became a Head Teacher and he and his family settled at Crown Street in Port Talbot.

Jenkin William James (1893-1944)

James was born in Margam and lived at Oakwood, Pontrhydyfen, before his parents moved down the valley to settle their growing family at Park Row, Cwmafan. He was the eldest of William and Mary Ann James seven children. They were brought up as Calvinistic Methodists. By eighteen years of age James had become a local Council school teacher and had both a science degree and a teaching diploma by the outbreak of war.

At the time the authorities were attempting to conscript him he was working as a science teacher in a secondary school, near Caernarfon, north Wales. Jones's application for exemption was heard on 7 March 1916, at Margam. It was motivated by religious belief but was, nevertheless, unsuccessful, as was the appeal. He showed no inclination to enlist and eventually his presence was required at the Aberafan County Police Court[59] to answer to a charge of being an absentee from the army. James plainly told the court that he was a conscientious objector. Captain Walter Rees, representing the authorities, said the 'schoolteacher had given the military no end of trouble' and asked for a heavy penalty. Was the 'trouble' simply that James was working away from his Port Talbot home, or had he deliberately tried to evade the police? As a visible public figure who worked in a school it could hardly have been the latter. James had been classified as category B1 at Swansea; unless he was medical category A he would not be immediately called up. In 1917 he was called up with the choice of being conscripted to the army or the coal mines. He decided that even the latter would be supporting the war so he was arrested for being an absentee.

Jenkin William James

Mr Charles Jones declared him guilty, imposed a heavier-than-normal fine of £5 and remanded him, awaiting an escort to the army reception centre for the 66th Training battalion at Cardiff. There he would be expected to be inducted and trained for service. The army's expectation and James' behaviour failed to coincide, with the result that the twenty-four-year old's court-martial was heard at Cardiff on 24 September 1917. He was dealt a sentence of 112 days' hard labour. Of these he had served sixty-five days at Wormwood Scrubs, before his final appeal to the Central Tribunal was to be heard. He was kept in solitary confinement for twenty-three hours a day for thirty days. Fellow inmates, who were Quakers, gave him what support they could.

The mailbag group at Knutsford, 23 April 1918

During that period, from 27 September he had no idea what his future would be. However, on 6 November his minister from Jerusalem Chapel, J. Morgan Jones, responded to the Tribunal's request for references. It decided by the Central Tribunal on 19 November that he was a genuine objector who should be offered the possibility of joining the Home Office Scheme. He accepted it and started to serve his next sentence at Knutsford Work Centre from 30 November 1917. Irish political prisoners from the 1916 Easter Rising had been consigned to Knutsford the previous year, prior to their transfer to Frongoch internment camp in Merioneth, labelled by one writer as 'The University of Revolutions'.

At Knutsford there were instances, however, in which the conscientious objectors were the subject of derision, harassment and thuggery by local inhabitants and the press. After several disturbances Governor Hunt – by reputation an intelligent and humane authority figure – decided to intervene in order to protect his charges. 'The Government was more concerned with isolating objectors from the public than punishing them ... (and) clearly wished to deny the objectors, many of whom were articulate and influential people, the opportunity of converting people to pacifism.'[60]

The COs were mindful of Hunt's considerate behaviour, showing their gratitude by presenting him with a parchment scroll, written in round-hand pen.

> 'As a mark of the high regard and respect in which we, the men who have been employed at Knutsford Works Centre hold you may we ask your acceptance of this address?
>
> We feel that we speak for all those who have passed through this centre when we say how fully we have appreciated your skilful management of affairs: your unfailing patience; your tact in preserving harmony among men of such varying temperaments and ideas, and the keen concern which you have always had for the general welfare of the community committed to your charge.
>
> We shall not forget these things; and in presenting you with this small token of our esteem, we should like, if we may, to wish both for yourself and family many years of happiness and prosperity.'

In May 1918, there was great 'rejoicing in the neighbourhood' of Knutsford because conscientious objectors with good conduct were released for employment or sent to Dartmoor. It is not known whether James was still in the 'good' Knutsford cadre, or whether he was in the Dartmoor group to be further detained. However, anecdotal family information suggests he was sent to Dartmoor where he was engaged in stone-breaking with a character called 'Mick the murderer'. James taught him maths and Mick helped James fulfil his quota of broken stones.

James was released in January 1919, on condition that he worked at Pontrhydyfen Colliery, despite still being in poor health. This condition was lifted on 14 June 1919, enabling him to seek work as a teacher. He found it hard to even get interviews, despite being greatly respected and supported both by his chapel and the residents of Pontrhydfen. In December, J. Morgan Jones, the Minister of Jerusalem chapel presented him with a Bible on behalf of the people of Pontrhydfen.

Jenkins married in 1935 and he returned with his wife returned to Merionethshire. Co-incidentally their home at Gwenallt, Bala, was not very far from the site of Frongoch internment camp. After holding several posts in the Caernarfon area, he finally became Head of Bala Boys' Grammar School.

One of his four children, daughter Catherine James of Dolgellau, has recorded his life in a short video clip about his life as an objector in Pontrhydfen. It is called 'Imprisoned for his Conscience' and can be accessed at *vimeo.com/88405556* .

The Jones brothers of Pantdu

Evan K. Jones (1889-1950)

The name Evan Jones was commonplace throughout Wales at the turn of the twentieth century and its prevalence in Cwmafan was no exception. The Rev. E. K. Jones of Wrexham, the Editor of 'Y Deyrnas'[61] who had visited Briton Ferry in 1918 as a prominent member of the anti-war movement in Wales bore the name, but the Evan Jones in question was the eldest son of David and Martha Anne of Kendon Row, Cwmafan. As the family grew to a household of twelve, several moves of home were required, first to Avon Hill House, then to Pantdu, Cwmafan. Whereas his father's work was to finish off the tinplate product, Evan and his brothers did heavier manual work, involving the rolling of steel into sheet prior to processing as tinplate. It is likely that, to ameliorate the conditions of this somewhat gruesome working environment Evan became a member of the ILP and then committed himself to the NCF.

Evan and his three brothers not only followed their father into the tinplate industry, they followed each other, too, through the tribunal system to oppose war and conscription. Evan was 27, when asked to report for military service and brothers Robert 26, Rees 24 and John 22. Evan's application for exemption was heard at Aberafan local tribunal[62] in July, 1916. When offered work of national importance he replied that he would 'only work for peace'[63]. It may have been the case that the Tribunal's intention was to 'badge' Jones in an essential occupation with his existing employer and that Jones declined this form of exemption. His reasoning for refusing to do this was because he considered this would help the military.

His application appears to have been rejected outright, but Jones was in no hurry to report to the recruiting office, or to make a further appeal. In fact, he did not appeal at all, so the only way the authorities could try to recruit him was to arrest him. They did so on 29 March 1917, and he appeared at Port Talbot Police Court two days later. He was found guilty of being an absentee from the army, fined forty shillings and handed over to 58 Training Battalion at Kinmel Camp. At Kinmel he still showed no appetite for signing up, or obeying any orders, so he was speedily put in front of a court-martial His sentence of two years' hard labour was magnanimously commuted to one year 253 days, to be served at Wormwood Scrubs. Whether he appealed to the Central Tribunal whilst there, or whether the Tribunal simply called for

A rollerman and behinder processing steel for tinplate

him is not known, but he certainly had his case heard by the Tribunal.

Due to the change of policy by the government, Jones was offered alternative service when he attended the Tribunal on 15 June 1917. It considered that Jones was a Class A, genuine objector who should be referred to the Brace Committee. It offered to assign him to a suitable work centre in an under-used prison or countryside work camp, where he would be expected to undertake such tasks as forestry work or waterworks construction. His exact movements thereafter are yet to be discovered: he could have accepted this alternative work, or he could have continued to offer absolute resistance to military authority.

Rees Jones (1892-

When Henry Davies appeared for Rees Jones, who was at work on the day of the local tribunal, he was questioned by tribunal members regarding Jones' attitude to the tribunal. They felt his stance was contradictory because he was supporting the war by working and should, instead have faced the tribunal.[64] In simple terms, the bench implied that he was not a genuine objector.

> *Henry Davies said:* 'Rees Jones cannot be responsible for the perversion of the fruits of his labour. It is his only means of securing food and clothing'.
>
> *Tribunal member F. B. Smith:* 'But he cannot eat a meal under present circumstances without the assistance of militarism ... it is

79

because of the war and the work of the British navy that Rees Jones is able to get something to eat'.
Henry Davies: 'I don't see that ... Mr Jones was able to eat before the war began'.
Loud cheering followed and Chair Jacobs threatened to clear the Court. Rees Jones' application was then dismissed.

Robert (b. 1890) and John Jones (b. 1894)

Later in the proceedings, Chair Jacobs said that the brothers had been 'fond of quotations from the Bible', so he would read them a few. He read: 'Shall your brothers go to war and shall he sit here?' Laughter followed when he was asked to quote Chapter and verse and failed to do so. A tribunal member, W. J. Williams, then handed the Mayor another text, which he read to the court: 'Greater love hath no man than this; that a man should lay down his life for his friends'.

John Jones responded by saying 'Yes, but that text has no relation to war. It was one of the sayings of Christ and it is upon the strength of his teachings that I base the whole of my objections. There is a difference between a man who dies for his faith and one who is endeavouring to kill another'.

Both Robert and John Jones' cases were dismissed.

J. E. Jones (1894–

22-year old J. E. Jones, was not one of the Pantdu brothers, but his case followed theirs. It was also on religious grounds and provided an interesting turn of events. Under the heading of 'A Genuine Case', the Glamorgan Gazette reported on the points so forcibly made by Jones on behalf of the Pantdu brothers. Jones pointed out that F. B. Smith had frequently asked why conscientious objectors 'had not thrown up their employment rather than countenance the war'. He added: 'Well, I am one who has done that. I was working in a controlled establishment and my employers told me that if I would sign the usual form they would procure me exemption on the ground that my work was in the national interest and I refused; so they discharged me.'

A man at the back of the court shouted 'Shame'. 'Order', said Chairman Jacobs, 'Constable, put that man out.' This tribunal had an NCF member,

James Price, who commented drily, 'well, this is at least a genuine case of conscientious objection'. The chair offered Jones the choice of 'non-combatant service, or case dismissed'.

Lewis Emlyn Jones (1896- 1983)

Lewis Emlyn Jones' family of six brothers and sisters and two step-sisters lived in Jersey Row, Cwmafan. He worked a riser in the tin-house of a local tinplate works and was single at the time of his attempted conscription.

In May 1916 Jones was refused exemption[65] at the first tribunal in which he had appeared with the Bamford brothers and David Davies. After losing his appeal, he failed to report to the recruitment office. After his preconceived and continued absence, Jones was eventually arrested by Sergeant Evans. Jones said: 'I am a conscientious objector; I have nothing to say'. He spent the early part of New Year's Day 1917, at Port Talbot Police Court where he was charged with being an absentee from HM Army by failing to report[66] as required, some six months earlier. His fine was forty-shillings. The next step to be taken by the state to convince Jones to perform military service was to escort him to Cardiff barracks where he would be expected to don an army uniform and sign his papers. A further refusal resulted in an escort to Kinmel Army camp in January 1917. At the inevitable court-martial, Jones received a sentence of two years' hard labour, commuted to 112 days.

On 11 January 1917, his sentence started in earnest at Wormwood Scrubs, where his appeal against the decision of the court-martial would be heard. In the event, the Central Tribunal regarded Jones as a candidate for the Home Office Scheme. He accepted its offer and became yet another member of Army Reserve W, and a soldier in name, but actually paid by the police. The NCF disapproved of the scheme because the COs in the scheme were reservists liable to recall to be part of the military machine.

Jones' passage through the scheme is unrecorded, but 'schemers' like him were based in used prisons, asylums and workhouses and were forced to work outdoors or indoors. Typical outdoor work was timber cutting, road making; drain-laying; rail maintenance and agriculture. Indoor work was often mailbag fabrication: brush and basket making and rope-making.

Lewis Jones married Eva Warner in 1919 and had a son, Graham W. Jones. Lewis returned to work as a tinplate annealer and died locally, aged eighty-seven.

Vaughan Jones (1893-1979)

Vaughan Jones's appeal was one of five cases heard at Margam[67] Appeal Tribunal. Jones was born at Deri but lived at 16 Caradoc Street, Port Talbot. Jones was a seaman when he informed the Appeal tribunal in May 1916, that he was 'away at sea' when he had failed to report to the recruiting office and would be going back to sea again the day after his appeal was heard. The Chairman simply said: 'No you will not'. His appeal, along with those heard at that time of Thomas John Mills, David Olden, John Selwyn Jones and William Rees was unsuccessful.

Jones neither went back to sea, nor did he report to the recruiting office. He had to be arrested on 25 June 1916. There is no record of Jones thereafter, unless his full identity can be confirmed as Wilfred V Jones, born 29 May 1893, of 14 Gethin Street, Port Talbot.

William Ivor Jones (1894-1973)

This is an intriguing, but incomplete, story of the brothers Jones of Jersey Row, Cwmafan, a family which must not be confused with the Jones brothers of Pantdu, four of whom were objectors.

William Ivor Jones, born in May 1893 was one of the four sons of David and Susannah Jones of 8 Jersey Row[68]. He had three brothers, a sister, a step-brother and two step-sisters in a household of ten. One brother, Lewis Emlyn, was also a conscientious objector. William Ivor, Secretary of Cwmafan ILP, worked as a behinder in the mills of a local tinplate works. He appeared before Neath Rural Tribunal in March 1916, at which Mr W. J. Trick, JP presided. Jones made his position clear: I am 'opposed to war and the taking of human life and refuse to violate my conscience.'

It was reported that over one hundred applicants were heard at that particular hearing, including four Cwmafan brothers, the Joneses of Pantdu, and with 'most of the rest from Cwmafan'.[69] It seems that the workload of the Port Talbot Tribunals, which served an industrial area, was so great at that time that many applicants had to be transferred to a less busy rural tribunal at Neath. It is already confirmed that William Ivor and Lewis Emlyn were objectors-in-conscience, but both Emrys Wynn Jones (b 1895) and Wilfred Llewelyn Jones (b 1899) were likely due for call-up from 1916 onwards. One of two unresolved cases in the Pearce Register (15829 and 15945) may be that of Emrys Wynn Jones. Both of the applicants involved appeared before the Central Tribunal in September 1916. As far as Wilfred Llewelyn Jones is concerned, case 16345 refers to a 'W.J./L. Jones'. This case involved a court-martial at the All Welsh Depot in Cardiff on 29 May 1918 and a sentence of six months' hard labour at the Scrubs but there is some doubt that this is Wilfred Llewelyn Jones.

As far as William Ivor's later life is concerned, he married Ann James in 1919, was employed by the GWR as a shunter and lived in Maesgwyn Street, Aberfan.

William (Gwilym) Lewis (1897–

William Lewis, was from Bwlch Farm, Cwmafan. The nineteen-year old was arrested in order to appear in court before Alderman J. M. Smith (Mayor of Aberafan) and Mr J. Gibb on Friday 14 June 1918, charged with being an absentee under the Military Service Act.[70] PC Cole gave evidence of arrest and Captain W. E. Rees represented the National Service Department. The defendant was reported as saying: 'I received my papers. I did not intend going.' He was fined £2 and remanded to await escort to Cardiff. He was court-martialled at Cardiff Barracks on 12 July for refusal to accept military orders. His sentence is not known but he did appeal to the Central Tribunal at Wormwood Scrubs for exemption on grounds of conscience. The tribunal heard his case on 4 September. Even though the November Armistice was approaching it should not be assumed that Lewis would be released automatically at the termination of hostilities. Whether he accepted the Home Office Scheme, or rejected any such offer and remained in prison, it is probable that Lewis was held in custody, like most of the younger conscientious objectors, until well into 1919. Lewis was single during his imprisonment, marrying Edith Rogers in 1920.

Joseph Llewelyn (1896-1961)

Joseph Llewelyn of 5 Gower Street, Taibach, was the second son of Mary and Rees Llewelyn, a Trade Union branch secretary, in a household of eleven people. Joseph was a scrap bundler in a tin-works where most family members worked. With such a background it is not surprising that Joseph became both an ILP and NCF member.

Considering that conscription only took effect from 2 March 1916, Llewelyn's application, and failure to secure exemption in such a short space of time, might suggest that the ILP or NCF branches may have encouraged eligible members to make early applications to learn how best to represent members on grounds of conscience, or otherwise. His early application received an early refusal, both at the Margam and Glamorgan Appeal Tribunals, being one of the cadre of thirteen ILP objectors represented by Henry Davies on that occasion. Following the court's decision on 28 March 1916, Llewelyn became a fugitive from the recruiters, but he was apprehended and arrested as an absentee on 25 May.

He was held at Cardiff prison and then Cardiff barracks on 10 June. There the army tried their best to get Llewelyn to sign his pay book, wear a uniform and drill. He refused, automatically triggering a court-martial. Normally this would attract a penalty of up to two years' hard labour, subject to an appeal to the Central Tribunal. As a result of his appeal, on 25 August 1916, the tribunal declared that he was a genuine, Class A objector whose case should be referred to the Brace[71] committee. They would advise the tribunal of suitable work of national importance for Llewelyn. It appears that he did not opt for such work and his next transfer was to prison. It is possible, therefore, that he should be classified as an 'Absolutist' rather than as a 'Schemer'.

Richard Mainwaring (1881–1955)

The Mainwaring brothers of Alma Terrace, Taibach must not be confused with either the Mainwarings of Cwm Brombil or those of Overman Row, a family which also included two brothers with the names Taliesin and William.

Richard, a coal miner, was the eldest son of Richard and Mary Mainwaring of Alma Terrace. He had three younger brothers and a sister. Mainwaring's application for exemption was heard on 7 March 1916, at Margam Tribunal which was held in the Council Offices, Taibach. It was unsuccessful, as was his later appeal. He did not report for service so he was arrested on 16 May 1916. This resulted in a police escort to the Welsh Regiment Depot in Cardiff and a speedy transfer to Kinmel Camp on 2 June to join the army reserve. Equally fast, Mainwaring was returned to Cardiff for some reason where he was, indeed, court-martialled on 6 June for disobedience. The ruling of the Court was that he was to receive six months' hard labour, commuted to four months.

It is worth examining the generosity of such a commutation. The first

Warwick Prison (Wikipedia)

part of any sentence saw the greatest hardships. Even though Mainwaring only spent the first twenty-three days of his sentence in Cardiff Prison before being called to the Central Tribunal at Wormwood Scrubs, on 29 June, he would have experienced the harshest conditions. These were ten hours' daytime solitary confinement, no speaking at all, and forty minutes' silent exercise. If he had been fortunate, he would have already written and received the one letter in and out allowed to hard labour prisoners during the first month. At the review of his case at the Central Tribunal, it was judged that Mainwaring should be offered the chance to join the Home Office Scheme. This would allow him to be in a less harsh custodial regime, albeit in Warwick Prison Work Centre. He was called to go there on 20 November 1916, but was unable to do so due to illness. Thereafter his story is still to be disclosed, but he was still unmarried living with his sister Catherine at Alma Terrace in 1939 when he worked as a coal merchant.

Thomas Arthur Mainwaring (1893–1926)

Prior to World War One, Mainwaring was a common name in the Port Talbot area, no more so than at Cwm Brombil, Margam. Thomas Arthur Mainwaring, who worked as a waggoner on a farm, was one of the Mainwarings brought up at Cwm Brombil Cottages by his widowed grandmother,

85

Gwenllian. She had been widowed in 1890s when her husband, Thomas, was killed along with eighty-six others, including young Noah Mainwaring, in an explosion at Morfa Pit.

When conscription came Thomas Arthur Mainwaring as well as Richard and William all showed their opposition by applying for exemption on grounds of conscience. Thomas Arthur was one of the group of Aberafan men arrested on 25 May 1916, as absentees.[72] It is not difficult to envisage the predictable pattern of events that led to his arrest, but is somewhat more problematic to forecast the events that followed. A realistic assumption might be that his continued objections took him at least as far as the Central Tribunal and that he was declared a genuine conscientious objector, but his employment would hardly have been regarded as essential to the war effort. Therefore, he was most likely referred to a Home Office work centre.

He married Mabel Dummer late in 1922 and died in the Autumn of 1926, aged 33. Whether the above events concerning his arrest and later contributed to his premature death is a matter of speculation.

William J. Mainwaring (1889–1945)

Born in Kenfig Hill, William J. Mainwaring lived at Overman Row, Morfa. He was the eldest of the seven children of Sam and Catherine Mainwaring. Their four eldest sons worked at Morfa Pit: William, Tal and David were underground haulage drivers and John was labouring.

Unsurprisingly for a haulier, William became an ILP member and in the early part of the war also joined the NCF. His grounds for applying for exemption are unknown, but political reasons are his most likely motivation. He was a single man when his call-up came but he declined to respond to it. At Margam Tribunal on 7 March 1916, his application was refused with the Appeal Tribunal unsurprisingly upholding the lower tribunal's decision three weeks later.

When Mainwaring failed to report for service he was arrested by PC Bryce. At court he was fined forty shillings and was afforded the usual police escort, in public via the railway station at Port Talbot, to Cardiff Barracks. He claimed, through E. G. Davies, who was defending him, that he had already lodged an appeal to the Central Tribunal.[73]

At the barracks he defied military instructions such as drilling, signing an army pay book or donning an army uniform. He certainly did not consider himself a member of the army reserve. To him, obedience would have been tantamount to regarding the military orders as legitimate. A court-martial at Cardiff inevitably followed from the fractious Cardiff events. On 26 July 1916, Mainwaring received two years' hard labour for his non-compliance. He was at Cardiff for barely two months when a final appeal was allowed. This was completed at Wormwood Scrubs on 18 September. Few were surprised that the tribunal declared him to be a genuine, class A conscientious objector.

Where he spent the rest of the war is unknown. There is nothing to suggest that he was offered the first option: to see out his sentence in a work centre, or to return to the pit to do work of national importance. If offered either of these, he may have refused anyway and carried on as an 'absolutist', spending the rest of the war, and well into 1919, in and out of civil prisons throughout Britain.

It is believed that he married Margaret Wayman in 1921 and settled at Groes. He died at fifty-five years of age, to be buried in Margam on 5 February 1945.

Thomas John Miles (1895–1945)

Miles was the son of a boot repairer from Tymaen Street, Cwmafan. Thomas, once worked in the family business, but was a collier and single when called up. His motivation for conscientious objection can only be hypothesised, but he appeared with Vaughan Jones, David Olden, John Selway Jones and William Rees at Aberafan tribunal held in the Police Court in March 1916. One newspaper headed their report on the tribunal as 'Batch of Absentees'.[74] In May his appeal was heard with four others and rejected.[75]

The next step in his objection is unclear. On balance he seems neither to have been 'badged' from the outset, or subsequently to have been returned to the pits by the Pelham Committee. This suggests he was offered a place on the Home Office Scheme, which he may well have rejected and been kept in prison.

In 1926, Miles married Mary James, a dressmaker of Park Row, Cwmafan and lived at David's Row, Mynydd Bychan. Their son, David, was born in 1928. Miles was still working underground when he died.

Arthur Mullington (1895–1998)

Arthur Mullington was one of eight children who lived at the family home in Carmarthen Row, Port Talbot. He joined the ILP when a colliery labourer in his teenage years and his application for exemption was most likely on socialist grounds.

Both his application to the local tribunal and his appeal to Margam Tribunal in March 1916 were rejected.[76] This was a tribunal in which the Chair, Mr F. W. Gibbins, said that he was anxious to see the thirteen ILP objectors accept non-combatant service wrongly claiming that he could offer nothing else. Henry Davies, who represented them, corrected him on this and all of them refused non-combatant service as a matter of principle. It is assumed that Mullington followed a similar path to others because nothing has been found to inform us otherwise of his fate during the war. It is hoped that his name will yet appear when the diaries of a fellow objector in prison or work centre are discovered. Until that should happen, his story thereafter starts in the next decade.

Mullington married Catherine E. Gardner and set up home in Alma Street, Maesteg, in 1920, to raise a family before boarding the 9,399-ton 'Euripides' for Sydney, Australia, in 1928. The family's ultimate destination was Georgetown, on the Tamar River in northern Tasmania. George died on 9 September 1998, aged 103. This makes him not only the longest surviving World War One conscientious objector from Port Talbot, but possibly from the whole of Great Britain.

The location of Georgetown, Tasmania

David William Older (1881–1926)

When Older lived with his family at St Pauls, in Bristol, he was a wood machinist. Employment in the expanding steel industry may explain the reason for his move to Port Talbot. However, his early history and motivations are uncertain until he came to view during the war.

At his Margam Appeal in May 1916[77], which was heard with four other conscientious objectors, he stated that he had been ill for three months following his application. The appeal was rejected and Older's next known appearance was when he was arrested on 25 May as an absentee and taken to Cardiff Barracks. Why he was still at the Barracks on 6 November 1916 is something of a mystery. The most likely scenario is that, during the intervening time, he was court-martialled. If so the normal sentence of six months' hard labour would have been spent. The most likely explanation is that he had served his sentence elsewhere and was returned to Cardiff pending an appeal which he may already have submitted to the Central Tribunal, the outcome remains unknown.

Older returned to Bristol after the war, where he died at a young age. One wonders whether this was as a result of the chronic ill-health that Older had experienced during the tribunal procedures. He was only forty-five at death, whereas his wife reached eighty-five when she, too, died in Bristol.

Daniel H. Phillips (1894–1956)

Uncertainty also surrounds the life of Daniel H. Phillips, of Water Street, Taibach, except for a cameo newspaper report, which confirms that he was a conscientious objector and an ILP member. Phillips was one child in a family of seven children. He worked as a mason's labourer on house building sites. His conscientious objection was first recorded at the Glamorgan Appeal Tribunal on 28 March 1916. He appeared along with twelve other Port Talbot men at the appeal, but it failed. It is believed that he married Mary H. Jenkins late in 1919.

David John Phillips (1885–1949)

Phillips was born in Bryn, Port Talbot and lived at 2 Hill Grove after his marriage to Margaret Daniel in 1909, but by the time of his submission to the authorities in 1917 they had moved to Curwen Terrace in North Cornelly.

He worked as a coalminer and his religion was Baptist. Nothing is known about any local or Appeal tribunal for him, but it would appear that he successfully evaded call-up and was, therefore, regarded as an absentee. It would also appear that there was a matter of religious principle involved in his actions, rather than family circumstances, because, as a coal miner, he would possibly have been exempted from conscription because of the national importance of his work.

On 13 April 1917, after giving himself up to the military in Cardiff, he was immediately sent to the 58 Training Battalion (58 TRB) at Kinmel. Despite giving himself up he refused to comply with military instructions and received a court-martial for his disobedience on 21 April. The outcome was a penalty of two years' hard labour, commuted to 112 days, to be served at Wormwood Scrubs, pending an appeal to the Central Military Tribunal. He was soon classified by the tribunal as eligible for the Home Office Scheme. The speed with which the Tribunal were able to come to a decision suggests that they did so without any need for references about Phillips' religious beliefs, which were, clearly, considered genuine. Phillips served eighty-one of his 112 days' sentence.

Afterwards his whereabouts as an objector are unrecorded publicly, but by 1939 he and his wife had returned to Hill Farm, Penhyddwaelod, Bryn. He was still a miner and she a county midwife.

Albert Owen Rankin (1892-1955)

Rankin was from Ystradgynlais, and first worked at a local colliery as an electric crane driver but, by the time he was due for conscription, he had moved to Port Talbot to work in the steelworks. He was a single man when his call-up papers arrived at 11 Eagle Street. Rankin was a Baptist, and it is

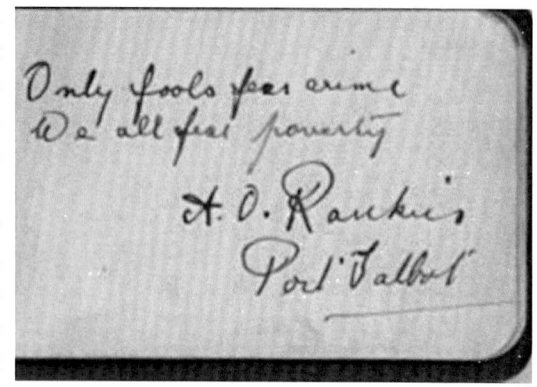

Rankin's notebook

expected that his faith played some part in his objection. He did not respond when called up and was therefore arrested by the police as an absentee for his case to be heard at Aberafan Police Court on 22 November 1916.

He told the bench that 'he recognised the law meant him to be a soldier, but he was 'determined that he would not join the army' and 'would not accept non-combatant service,[78] having been offered it at the appeal tribunal. 'I have been out of work for the past seven weeks, so that you see I am determined to resist the military authorities.' He was fined the usual forty shillings and consigned to the army's 60 Training Battalion at Cardiff Barracks. His refusal to comply with any military orders resulted in a rapid despatch to Kinmel Camp for a court-martial which was heard on 28 November. His sentence is not known, but he was remitted to Wormwood Scrubs on 1 December, no doubt with the expectation that he would be successful in mitigating the sentence he was about to serve.

The Central Tribunal were uncertain of his sincerity and wrote to his Chapel for references on 10 January 1917. They were forthcoming and accepted. Rankin could now be offered the possibility of the Home Office Scheme to do work of national importance. Accordingly, he was sent to Wakefield Prison on 20 March 1917 before being transferred to Penderyn Waterworks Work Centre in September, 1917. Both postings were quite eventful.

Wakefield (March–September 1917)

At Wakefield the 'absolutist' objectors had sound reason to suspect that alternative work might aid the war effort. One of the Wakefield practices that conscientious objectors found especially repugnant was that of being hired out to private employers to perform their usual tasks of making mailbags, mats or baskets. Rankin would later find similar arrangements at Penderyn Work Centre. They considered such practices would displace the incumbent workers, thereby freeing them up to serve in the army. One hundred and forty of the six hundred Wakefield inmates refused to co-operate with this practice, a stance that resulted in forty arrests and seven objectors being returned to prison.

Later, the Wakefield objectors were exposed to brutal attacks and thefts from elements of the local population, encouraged in their antagonism by a hostile and irresponsible press. It was alleged that up to three hundred objectors rioted at Wakefield in May 1918, but the reality was rather

A group of objectors at Wakefield
Can you identify anyone from the Port Talbot area? John Adams of Briton Ferry is on the extreme right of the front row.

different: they were actually being hounded by local residents, provoked into violent action after the residents' anti-pacifist views were whipped up by the rhetoric of an antagonistic local press.

Penderyn

In March 1918, sixty-one conscientious objectors were still placed at Penderyn Work Centre to build a waterworks on the site, working for Mountain Ash Council's contractors. In separate gangs, the objectors worked from 7.45 in the morning and finished late in the afternoon. The men elected a six-person committee to represent them. This had two purposes: first, to act as a communication channel to the outside world through the No Conscription Fellowship and, secondly, to represent the objectors' needs, such as diets, accommodation, terms of employment and working conditions.

The detainees fell into one of two groups: those from south Wales and those from elsewhere, from Devon, Glasgow London, Leicester, Leeds and Lancashire. The Men's Committee itself was mainly drawn from the Merthyr area. Under the Chairmanship of F. A. Jones, it included an Oxford MA,

Herbert A. Davies, also of Merthyr, as well as a cohort of manual workers. The committee sometimes had unique matters to deal with. On one occasion Davies, a local worthy, had referred to the objectors at the Aberdare Military Tribunal as a 'very undesirable lot of individuals, many of whom 'laughed and scoffed at willing soldiers and used a language which no religious person would use'. The Men's committee replied; in a letter to the *Merthyr Pioneer*, it corrected important facts about the allegations, including proof that Davies could not have heard the 'blood boiling' remarks.

The committee continued its most emphatic and dignified response:

> 'While we hold all war to be wrong and, therefore, consider the profession of the soldier to be unnecessary and its continuance an evil, we do not "laugh and scoff" at those who think otherwise and who are prepared to sacrifice their lives for their ideals.'

The committee were anxious to ensure that the men were properly fed to carry out the heavy manual work required in the construction of the waterworks. The camp's menu became news: some reports were claiming that the men were too well fed whilst others claimed they were underfed! So the *Merthyr Pioneer* published the standard diet and workday. The committee closely monitored both the diet and the working times.

Even that, however, was not the principal issue to which the committee had to turn its attention. Before Rankin's arrival, on 10 March 1917, it had been reported that eleven of the men objected to being employed by the private contractor because they had agreed to do work of national importance. They did not consider the work that they did as such work. Eleven were removed and replaced, allowing for the transfer of Rankin. The following week, the contractor informed Mountain Ash Council that the Black Gang had threatened to strike for an immediate increase in wages.

At the Armistice in 1918, the COs were clearly anticipating their demission from the Centre, as evidenced by the co-workers' inscriptions in Bransby Griffiths' notebook. Amongst quotations from Arnold, Bacon, Burns, Cervantes, Engels, Hugo, Milton and Wilde could be found obvious elation at the prospect of release from the camp. These quotations are reproduced as Appendix Seven. On release, Griffiths of Briton Ferry, walked the twenty-two-mile journey home. Perhaps Albert Rankin walked with him and then continued for the three miles to his Port Talbot home. Rankin subsequently married Janet Moore and lived thirty-three more years.

> *Porridge, cup of tea, coffee or cocoa*
>
> 07.45 Work.
> 09.00 Breakfast
> Work
> 13.00 Lunch
> Work
> 17.30 Dinner:
> *Soup*
> *6 ounces uncooked meat*
> *7.75 ounces potatoes*
> *7.75 ounces of swedes or 6.5 ounces of carrots or parsnips*
> *3 to 3.5 ounces (before cooking) of Butter beans, haricot beans*
>
> To be divided between 61 men at dinner:
>
> *– boiled pudding – either jam or apple, made as follows:*
> *9lb flour; 3 lbs dried fruit; 2 lb suet; rice sago or milk puddings*
> *3lbs of rice with milk*

George Rees (1895–1973)

George Rees was from Cwmafan Road, Aberafan, one of six children. He worked as a furnace-man in a tinplate works.

His arrest as an absentee was on 27 October 1916. After arrest, Rees was routed to Kinmel, from the local police court where he had been duly fined forty shillings and remanded. His recalcitrant response to the military orders at Kinmel led to the expected court-martial in November 1916, and an award of 112 days' hard labour to be endured at Wormwood Scrubs. On appeal, the Central Tribunal considered him to be a genuine objector and allowed him the choice of continued imprisonment, should he remain contumacious, or to follow their recommended option to work at a Home Office Centre.

He spent time from March to August 1917, at Landdeusant Waterworks where life for the objectors was not pleasant, even in spring or summertime. The construction site was located in wild Black Mountain country, five miles south-east of Llangadog, an area better known today for its growing population of red-kites.

Rees' full history, as with many other objectors, has proved difficult to trace completely. Indeed, even the army record offices had sometimes to write to families to check exactly where their objector-members had been deployed. The NCF often had far better knowledge of their whereabouts and kept families well-informed, but for Rees even the meticulously kept NCF sources have not revealed everything.

In 1921 Rees married Eily L. Price and brought up their family in New Street, Aberafan, with George continuing to work in the tinworks as a shearer. They were still living there at the start of World War II.

Lancelot Thomas Waters (1894–1971)

Lancelot Thomas was a son of Thomas and Grace Waters, of Pilton Green in Gower. The family ran a number of blacksmith's forges to service farms in the locality. Lancelot was the fourth of six sons and had a sister, Constance Grace.

The Watters family story is most compelling and Lancelot played his part in it. To appreciate Lancelot's part, it is worthwhile considering each of the Watters children in turn. His eldest brother was 'Massie'; that is Massena Garnet Waters who left home to become a locomotive driver at the Albion steelworks, Briton Ferry. He was an ILP member and soon became Chair of the town's NCF. In these roles he became involved in a famous legal case which became the subject of a question in Parliament. It concerned a prison sentence imposed by Neath Magistrates on Massie himself and a fellow NCF member, William Davies. The case had its parallel in Port Talbot.

The Waters brothers

The pair received a stretch of one month's imprisonment with hard labour for distributing a leaflet against recruiting, an action which was held to be a breach of the Defence of the Realm Act. A similar sequence of events occurred in Port Talbot. Apart from the issues arising from the police raid on the ILP premises in Briton Ferry where the leaflets were stored, this matter became one for Parliamentary discussion because of the different treatment the two received from their employers. After the case Davies was dismissed by the GWR, despite the fact that discussions about his employment continued peacefully, whereas Waters was allowed to continue work because of the threat of industrial action at the steelworks.

Hubert Victor Waters remained in Gower but became the centre of controversy because of allegations by the Waters family during his tribunal hearings that the Military Representative was prejudiced against them. Philip Snowden MP asked the President of the Local Government Board if he would have a special enquiry made into the action of the Gower Rural Tribunal in respect of his treatment. Snowden claimed that Waters was denied a fair hearing because the Military Representative on the Tribunal, Colonel Pearson, had a grudge against the Waters family. Pearson, who had also sat on Port Talbot tribunals, was removed. Waters' still had to go through the full tribunal process including incarceration at work camps in the Scottish Highlands and Wakefield Prison until he was finally allowed to work for his father in Gower.

Cecil David was younger than 'Hubert Victor'. After marriage, he settled at Maes-y-Cwrt Terrace in Port Talbot where he joined the Amalgamated Society of Railway Servants, working as a signalman, before moving to Briton Ferry. He became an NCF and ILP member, attending the National ILP Conference at Leeds in June 1917, with fellow Briton Ferry members, Ivor H. Thomas and Joe Branch.

Lancelot Thomas lived at 143 Tanygroes Street in Port Talbot and became active in both the NCF and the ILP, becoming its Chair in 1915. In early 1916 he applied for exemption from service on conscientious grounds but it was rejected at Margam tribunal. During the proceedings there was 'little evidence of sympathy for the objectors'. Tribunal members, Mr Richard Evans and John David, appealed for neutrality, saying their duty 'was not a pleasant one' and that the only desire they had was to do justice'. Waters asked for an explanation as to why his plea had been rejected. 'Because it is not sufficient,' said Edward Lowther, the Chairman, curtly. His appeal was made along with twelve other Port Talbot ILP members in March 1916. Despite the representation of the celebrated Henry Davies of Cwmafan, the Margam court's decision was upheld.

It is unfortunate that we have no further information about his future as an objector, but he was in correspondence with the *The Pioneer*[79] newspaper in April and May 1918. The correspondence was a criticism of Vernon Hartshorn[80] who had suggested that the Labour Conference's views about the suitability of its first candidate for the new Aberafan constituency were not those of the Conference at all, but the personal views of George Bramley, Bob Smillie and Philip Snowden.

Lancelot Waters married Gwladys Davies in 1923 and died in Colchester.

Abram Waters' experience paralleled that of some of the Port Talbot objectors. After he had accepted alternative service cutting wood at Weston Work Camp he came to believe that this was freeing a professional woodcutter to serve in the army, so he rejected the scheme. His defiance led him back in prison early in 1917.

The primary motivation of the Waters family as a whole to oppose conscription was clearly political, but it may have also had a religious element. The table below places Lancelot Thomas and his brothers in terms of seniority within the family.

Name	Activity	Location in 1916
Massena Garnet Waters	Defence of Realm Act violation	Briton Ferry
Hubert Victor Waters	Conscientious objector	Gower
Cecil David Waters	ILP and NCF activist	Briton Ferry
Lancelot Thomas Waters	**Conscientious objector**	**Port Talbot**
Abram George Waters	Conscientious objector	Gower
Bertram Christian Waters	Unknown	Gower

John Wellington (1878-1963)

The Taibach area of Port Talbot was well-populated with the surname 'Wellington' at the end of the nineteenth century and there were several large families with the name. It is no surprise, then, that four John Wellingtons lived in the area, including the John Wellington in question, an occupant of 68 High Street. His parents, had raised eight children, but as the household gradually diminished in number his parents 'downsized' to 16 Water Street to accommodate themselves, John and elder brother, Henry, a theology student. John worked as a tin sheet packer and was still single when war broke out.

Wellington's application for exemption at Margam tribunal was on religious grounds. When asked by the Chair, Mayor Percy Jacobs, if he would undertake non-combatant service, Wellington said: 'Non-combatant service is part of the military machine. I am prepared to do anything to bring the war to an end. I am fighting for these aims now in the Church.'[81]

> *The Chair:* 'Is there anything you can suggest to bring this about?'
> *Wellington:* 'I want you to respond to the dictates of my conscience. I feel that I cannot kill on any account; I am serving the Christ who stood alone in the garden of Gethsemane. To take life I cannot.'

Wellington was exempted from combatant service only, but he refused it, believing that wearing a uniform and performing non-combatant duties offered too much support to the war. He appealed the local tribunal's offer of partial exemption to the Glamorgan Appeal Tribunal. On 25 March 1916, Mr F. W. Gibbins of Neath, who presided said: 'I quite appreciate your views; but we have an unpleasant duty to perform. I would rather any job in the world than to judge between consciences.'[82]

After Wellington had again rejected the option of non-combatant service he received a call-up to report at the recruiting office. He did not respond when requested but, as he was deemed to be enlisted, was liable to prosecution for desertion. This led to police arrest with charges being put at Port Talbot Magistrates' Court on 17 May. He was fined the customary forty shillings as a deserter and awaited an escort to Kinmel military barracks.[83]

On 20 June, shortly after his arrival, he was court-martialled and sentenced to two years' hard labour following a refusal to wear an army uniform. When the opportunity arose to lodge an appeal he did so. The Central Tribunal accepted his reasons for not wishing to undertake non-combatant duties in army uniform. Now, as a genuine, class A, conscientious objector he would have the chance to do work of national importance under at a Home Office work centre. His movements under the scheme are not known but they may have been recorded in a diary of his, or that of a fellow conscientious objector, as his own signature was found in the diary of J. Nicholl Carter, a Quaker who helped objectors in the work centres. At 60 years of age Wellington still worked as a tinplate sorter and lived in Bath Street, Port Talbot.

Workers of National Importance

The Pelham Committee and Work of National Importance

The Pelham Committee was a Board of Trade appointed committee whose purpose was to advise Military Service Tribunals, when asked, on the types of work that were of *national importance* and were suitable for objectors as an alternative to military service. Such work included agriculture, forestry, food supply, shipping, transport, mining, education and public utility services. In Huddersfield, for example, two thirds of objectors stayed where they were to do this work and did not go to prison or work camps. Work of national importance was also evident at Port Talbot, but not to the degree evident in the Yorkshire town. Christadelphians were considered to be prime candidates for such work, as evidenced by the cases of the Bamfords. Several other men who were not Christadelphians, however, did similar work.

Many men who claimed exemption on the grounds of the national importance of their job had their claims rightly dismissed by the tribunals. Those who remained in their occupations to do work of national importance were either 'badged' by their employers as a result of official listing, or after a successful application by the employer to a tribunal. Some of the alternative 'work of national importance' in prisons and work camps was often regarded by those performing them as unimportant and pointless drudgery.

Those who did work of national importance were:
John Bamford   *William Grove*
Sidney Bamford   *Frederick James Lewis*
James Davies   *Daniel Rees Michael*
Sidney John Ford   *David John Stephens*

John Bamford (1891–1941)

The Bamfords were a Christadelphian family of two sons and three daughters from Somerset Place, Cwmafan. Both John and his brother Sidney were tinplate behinders, working at the local Copper Miners' Tinplate Company.

As a single man of twenty-five years of age, John was eligible for conscription but he applied for exemption from service on religious grounds. Providing he was medically fit, he would be enlisted in the Army, unless acceptable grounds of objection were submitted to the local Military Service Tribunal. He had a strong case: for most Christadelphians, the tribunals took the view that their belief was sufficient to grant absolute exemption. The Christadelphian belief is that there is 'compelling evidence from the Bible that God has plans for world peace'.[83] Objection to conscription and war, therefore, supports those plans. In John Bamford's case there were also pragmatic grounds: the employer could have requested conditional exemption on the basis that continuing his normal employment was in the national interest.

However, it appears that Bamford had a point to make about conscription. If he failed to attend he would be arrested by the army recruitment centre, unless his employer had, indeed, made an application for his exemption. He applied, for the local tribunal to decide on the merits of his case on 3 June 1916, along with his brother, John, Lewis Jones and David Davies.[85] This resulted in a refusal for full exemption and an appeal which also met with refusal. He was only offered conditional exemption if he was prepared to accept non-combatant status. This would have meant him wearing a uniform and assisting the army, but would not entail killing. Unfortunately, it would not 'contribute to world peace', so his refusal of non-combatant status resulted in his arrest and a court appearance in Port Talbot. He was fined and escorted to the army induction barracks at Kinmel Camp in north Wales.

There he was required to sign a pay book, wear a uniform and follow military discipline. It is clear that he refused to do so and that the outcome was a court-martial on 16 June 1916. He received a sentence of 112 days' hard labour to be served at Wormwood Scrubs. However, the Government was soon to decide that all cases of imprisoned objectors be reviewed as to their genuineness by a judge-led Central Tribunal at Wormwood Scrubs. As a result, Bamford, as a 'genuine objector' was allowed to do 'alternative service'. This meant alternative to both combatant service and imprisonment under a scheme known as the 'Home Office Scheme' (HOS). It was supposed to offer 'work of national importance' but it did not. It was a token: frequently it involved tedious and, often, useless tasks.

Bamford accepted and was sent to Princetown Work Centre on Dartmoor to serve his sentence. Soon, common sense prevailed, possibly because the committee running the scheme recognised that there was genuine work of national importance to be done in Cwmafan. Bamford was allowed home on leave in September 1916, to learn that he was being

Copper Miners' Tinplate Works c 1910 *(Port Talbot Historical Society)*

offered alternate service at the Copper Miners Tinplate Company, where he was previously employed. He accepted this, but he was still, technically, Private Bamford, a member of army Reserve. He married Ruth Francis in 1936 and died five years later.

Sidney Bamford (1893-1967)

Sidney Bamford was two years' younger than brother, John. Like John, he was a tinplate 'behinder' working at the local Copper Miners' Tinplate Company. As a single man of twenty-three years of age, Sidney, too, was eligible for conscription. Providing he was medically fit, he would be enlisted in the Army unless any acceptable grounds of objection were submitted to the Tribunal. However, it appears that Sidney Bamford, too, had a point to make about conscription. Whether his employer applied for exemption on the grounds that he did work of national importance is not known, nor are the details of his tribunals. Sidney applied for exemption to the local tribunal. It decided on the merits of both brothers' cases on 3 June 1916, along with Lewis Jones and David Davies and it resulted in a refusal as usual. Sidney was also asked if he would join the army as a non-combatant. He refused and this resulted in arrest and court-martial. At this point his brother's wartime experience went separate, but similar, ways to his as the tribunal process went through its remorseless administration.

After a court appearance in Port Talbot, Bamford was fined and escorted to the army barracks at Cardiff, and not to Kinmel. There he was required to sign a pay book, wear a uniform and follow military discipline. He refused to comply and his resolve led to a court-martial on 6 June 1916. His sentence of hard labour was to be served at Cardiff Civil Prison, but he still had the possibility of a further appeal on the genuineness of his case to Scrubs.

On 25 August 1916, the Central Tribunal sitting at Wormwood Scrubs, deemed him to be a Class A, genuine, objector and referred him to the Brace Committee to offer him 'alternative service' to imprisonment under the 'Home Office Scheme'. He accepted the offer and was, like brother John, first consigned to Princetown Work Camp on Dartmoor. Later he was relocated to Penderyn Waterworks, to where a fellow Port Talbot objector, Arthur Rankin, was also confined. Pragmatically, the tribunal afterwards permitted Bamford to do alternate service at the Copper Miners' Tinplate Company with brother John, where both were previously employed.

In October the Bamford brothers were presented with a gold pendant, a cigarette case and a purse of money at a reception held by friends to mark their return. The Copper Miners Tinplate Company continued in production until 1942. Sidney married Mary Letitia Potts in 1924. It seems that Sidney Bamford subsequently left the tinplate works to work as a farmer and, on 14 April 1936, he was one of eleven passengers who boarded the 'Sneaton' at Swansea, bound for Montreal.

James Davies

Davies was recorded in NCF records as a member living at 13 Margaret Street, Felindre, Aberafan. He was working as booking clerk for the Rhondda & Swansea Bay Railway Company when he appeared before Margam Tribunal in March 1916. His arrest resulted in 'incarceration with the Bamfords'.[86] The incarceration may have been confinement at Port Talbot police station after arrest, or later at an army barracks, or during a later internment in prison whilst the Central Tribunal was deciding his fate.

Davies was court-martialled at Cardiff six days after the Bamfords[87] on 12 June. He received four months' hard labour, commuted to one month for disobeying orders, subject to appeal at the Central Tribunal. This was heard on 29 June, and its decision was that he could be returned to his usual work. The parallel with the Bamfords is that they, too, returned to their usual workplace at the Copper Miners' Tinplate Company several months later.

Davies' case is interesting because the Central Tribunal decided, maybe after advice from the Pelham Committee, that his work as a booking clerk was of national importance. This needs explanation. He would have been classified as a Class A or Class B objector; if Class A, the tribunal would have directed him where his work would be; if Class B Davies could have requested his old job and would be granted it, should the tribunal agree.

Why would his work as a booking clerk be of national importance? The explanation is that Port Talbot's railways were very busy during the war catering for the transhipment of coal from the Afan and Rhondda Valleys to the docks at Swansea, Briton Ferry and Port Talbot. Further, work had started in 1916 on the re-construction of Port Talbot Steelworks. There was plenty to be done on Port Talbot's railways for both freight and passenger traffic. There was a considerable movement of soldiers and even conscientious objectors, which required experienced clerical support.

Aberafan Station (Rhondda and Swansea Bay line) *(Port Talbot Historical Society)*

Sidney John Ford (1894-1949)

Ford was a Truro-born GWR locomotive driver who applied for exemption to Margam Tribunal on 7 March 1916[88]. This is what happened there:

> *Chairman Lowther:* 'Do you have any relatives serving?'
> *Ford:* 'Yes sir, I have three brothers in the army and one has been killed.'
> *Lowther:* 'And you have the face to come here … and tell us you have conscientious objections after that!'
> Ford replied that his brothers were the keepers of their own consciences when people in the room began to cheer.
> *Tribunal member Hallowes:* It's a pity Ford had not adopted the same point of view as his brothers.

The application was refused by Chairman Lowther who 'courteously offered him non-combatant status'. The decision was upheld by Glamorgan Appeal Tribunal on 28 March[89]. At the tribunal Ford used similar phraseology to explain his stance as another ILP man, David Stephens; 'I am not prepared to do anything that would further the military aims of the country'. This statement, and his representation by Henry Davies, suggests that his motivation was mainly political. Ford was later arrested as an absentee, tried at Port Talbot Magistrates, fined and chaperoned to Cardiff Barracks. There he did nothing in the way of signing an army pay book or wearing an army uniform that would 'further the military aims of the country', so he had to present himself before a court-martial on 24 June 1916. The court's pronouncement was that he should serve 112 days' hard labour at Cardiff Civil Prison, subject to an appeal. The first one hundred days of such a sentence were meant to be the hardest. They usually were, and Ford served sixty-five of them before his case was considered by the Central Tribunal. Its decision at Wormwood Scrubs was very clear: Ford was a genuine Class A objector who should be offered the opportunity to perform alternative service of national importance, as decided by the Brace Committee.

Whether he accepted the offer is not known. If he did, he is likely to have moved from Home Office work centre to work centre. If he did not, and became an 'absolutist', he would most likely have had to experience the nauseating 'cat and mouse system'. Ford and was back in Truro in 1939.

William Grove (1889-1943)

Grove was born at Dyffryn Cottages but lived at Tydraw Cottages in the Penycae district of Port Talbot before the war when he became a locomotive fireman on the Port Talbot Railway. By the time conscription came in 1916 William had been promoted to an engine driver.[90] The fact that he appeared before a tribunal suggests one of two possibilities. Firstly, that his employer had not included him, or rather his job, on the list of essential occupations. Secondly that he had been so included but wished to make his anti-conscription stance known at a tribunal. Thus, at twenty-seven years of age, he was not exempted and got called-up. Other factors which might have intervened to put him on the list of essential occupations were his seniority in the engine sheds where he worked and whether or not he held trade union membership. Possibly the employer was not zealous enough in retaining Grove, effectively surrendering him to the army. Grove himself was obviously displeased enough about conscription to reject it and to make his stand at a tribunal.

Within a year or so, the battlefield losses in France and Belgium would see a tightening of the criteria for essential occupations, resulting in the prospect of industrial action by the rail unions. Their members had become seriously overworked by the demands of the excessive overtime required to man the railways when on a war footing. In such circumstances the most likely progression for Grove thereafter would be that he went to final appeal at the Central Tribunal and was offered work of national importance under the advice of the Pelham Committee. This would likely have been as an engine driver. Grove was still recorded as an engine driver in 1939, living on Penycae Road, but four years later he died at the age of fifty-four.

Frederick James Lewis (1889-1981)

Lewis, who was from Oakwood Row, Pontrhydyfen, became an Assistant Surveyor in a colliery after his schooldays. His application for exemption was refused at Margam. When he was unable to attend Glamorgan Appeal Tribunal on 28 March 1916, his case was deferred[91] but was certainly heard later because he was recorded as being in prison. The likely sequence of events is that he was refused again and escorted to a military reception centre, where any failure to obey orders would lead to a court-martial. The prison sentence is most likely to have been at this point: at Wormwood

Scrubs awaiting an appeal to the Central Tribunal. If it offered him the chance of the HOS and he refused, or he declined an offer to perform his usual work as an alternative to conscription, imprisonment would again follow, but not necessarily at Wormwood Scrubs.

He married Charlotte L. Tanner, a railway engineer's clerk in 1923, and afterwards the couple went to live, Cowbridge, where Lewis worked with a public works contractor.

Daniel Rees Michael (1881-1956)

Daniel Michael was born at Jersey Row, Cwmafan, the son of a copper weigher and the eldest of five children. He was living at Pantdu and working as an annealer at Copper Miners Tinplate Company with John and Sidney Bamford when his turn to be conscripted arrived

The motivation for Michael's conscientious objection and application for exemption is hard to determine. Nevertheless, his local application was unsuccessful until the Central Tribunal heard his case. He was referred to the Pelham Committee on 29 May 1916. During the six or seven intervening weeks the committee may well have sought references to assist in their decision. Finally, the committee declared on 12 July that there was work of national importance available with his employer. Whether the 'badged' work was in his normal occupation as an annealer is unknown. If it was, one wonders why his employer did not 'badge' him at the outset, but, had they done so, the conscientious objection that he wished to declare would not have been so publicly revealed.

David John Stephens (1898-1918)

David John, the son of Evan and Mary Stephens of Tymaen Street in Cwmafan left school to work in the pits in the years immediately before the war. Originally a hewer's helper, Stephens soon became the hewer and Jonathan, his younger brother by four years, the helper.

David Stephens declared himself to be a Calvinistic Methodist when he appeared before the local tribunal in early 1916. Even had he claimed exemption for religious reasons, it was ignored by the first tribunal, and ignored again at the end of March by the appeal tribunal[92]. Nor did his employer seem to have applied on his behalf, possibly because he was still building up experience in this important and dangerous work, and was not

Bryn Navigation Colliery

yet in employment that could be considered essential. Although the Tribunal's Chair offered non-combatant status or conditional exemption to other applicants, it was not offered to Stephens. The suitability of conditional exemption seemed to have been clear in this case but Stephens simply said that he refused 'to do anything to further the military machine'.

It is reasonable to suppose that Stephens did not report to the army recruitment office to sign up, thereby being regarded as an absentee. This was an offence which normally attracted a fine of forty shillings and up to two years' hard labour, with the confinement element of the sentence being subject to a possible appeal to the Central Tribunal.

Stephens had to await its decision at Wormwood Scrubs. The Tribunal finally seem to have taken Stephens' religious beliefs into account, possibly after asking for references from his chapel, because they considered him to be a class A, genuine, objector who should be offered the chance to do work of national importance. He accepted the offer but the work did not last long before tragedy struck. This newspaper report[93] takes over the story under the heading 'Brothers Buried':

> 'Two Cwmafan brothers, David John Stephens (24) and Jonathan Stephens (20), the sons of Mrs Evan Stephens of 31 Tymaen Street, Cwmafan, were killed by a roof fall while working in the same stall at the Bryn Navigation Colliery, Bryn, Port Talbot, on Friday. They were completely buried and their bodies were only recovered some time later.'

They, like millions of others, never saw the end of the war.

Conclusion

To find fewer than a dozen objectors assigned to work of national importance in a heavily industrialised area like Port Talbot may seem surprising. It should be remembered, however, that several men felt they would be hiding the true strength of their socialist or religious opposition to war and conscription by, effectively, recognising a Military Tribunal's power to conscript them to an industrial task. This point of view meant that many objectors would be found instead within the ranks of the 'schemers' or the 'absolutists'. The second reason for the small number of objectors categorised as essential workers was the increasingly stringent 'combing out' of workers as military losses increased during the course of the war.

Tortured and tormented

None of the objectors had an easy time. Whether they appeared before the tribunals and joined the Non-combatant Corps, whether they elected for the Home Office Scheme, whether they remained Absolute or whether they did work of national importance at their normal job, this was still the case. It could be said that, in each of these categories of objector, men suffered in accordance with the consequences of the choices they made, and most could foresee what the consequences would be. There were others, however, who suffered quite unforeseeable consequences in the form of physical torture and severe mental torment. These men's experiences will now be reviewed. They were:

David Davies   Aneurin Morgan
Dan Edwards   Thomas Henry Williams
Lemuel Emanuel   Jack Woolcock

David Davies (1892–

There is much to speculate about this coal miner, Methodist, ILP and NCF member from London Row, Cwmafan, the eldest son of Thomas and Margaret Davies. His tale as a conscientious objector starts in May 1916. After failing to report for military service with the Bamfords and Lewis Emlyn Jones,[94] all three were made to appear in front of Aberafan Bench after being arrested by Police Sergeant Jones. Davies' story continues into

July, with the newspaper report[95] headed 'Making a soldier'. It is a curious turn of events in just two months:

> 'Private David Davies of the 2nd Monmouthshires, stationed at Howbury Camp, Bedford, came home at the end of last week on six days' sick leave. Private Davies is a conscientious objector and was an active and interested member of the Cwmafan NCF. For three weeks prior to his arrest he was laid up with severe muscular rheumatism and the circumstances are worth relating. After he had risen from bed he was arrested – rather, he was invited to make his appearance at the court in Aberafan, in company with other conscientious objectors. He was in such a weak state during the proceedings at the Police court that he expressed a desire to be examined.
>
> Nevertheless, he was given the usual fine and escorted to Cardiff. At Cardiff he was medically examined by an army doctor who passed him for second class service and he was straightaway sent to Bedford Hospital.[96] This resulted in his clothes being sent home. He was in hospital for three weeks. Leaving there he was detained in camp for thirteen days and fed on milk. He has been away from home altogether for seven weeks so it is manifest that Private Davies was literally forced into the army.'

Why Davies was assigned to the 2nd Monmouthshires is difficult to explain. It became a Pioneer battalion at the time of his posting. This might suggest that he had accepted non-combatant status which he later rejected by disobeying orders and getting court-martialled. Other Port Talbot men did the same.

There are gaps in our knowledge of the events that followed, but from 1917 Davies was kept in and out of custody for the next two years or so. He was court-martialled when a member of the 4 (R) Welsh at Pembroke Dock on 15 January 1919 at which he received two years' hard labour. On 23 May 1919 (yes, 1919), he was finally released from Carmarthen Civil Prison, although scheduled to return to prison on 3 July. His treatment, like Clifford Allen's,[97] was under the 'cat and mouse act'. This procedure was first used on suffragettes but was later applied to some conscientious objectors. It involved objectors who went on hunger strike in prison. To avoid problems, the authorities would release prisoners when they had become

109

very weak, but would re-arrest them if they continued their defiance. At that point the cycle would start again, with the intention of breaking the prisoner's steadfastness.

At the time of Davies' Pembroke Dock court-martial, a fellow Methodist, Ivor Owen Thomas of Briton Ferry, was tried and received the same sentence, also to be served at Carmarthen Prison. Thomas went on to become MP for the Wrekin in 1945 but the final chapters of Davies's story await discovery.

Dan Edwards (1885–1968)

Dan Edwards was from Park Row, Cwmafan. Unlike his elder brothers, who were a platelayer and a coal miner, Dan's career was as a County school teacher. When the events described below took place, Dan was single and a member of both the ILP and the NCF.

Given the nature of Edwards' and his colleagues cases, it is unsurprising and unfortunate that a complete written record does not exist of the proceedings of all the tribunals that were held. Had they existed, we might have had the background and an explanation for the events below. Nonetheless, as Edwards was an ILP member, it can reasonably be assumed that at least a part of his motivation for exemption from conscription was political.

Edwards was summoned to Port Talbot County Police Court with Jack Woolcock in early July 1916, on charges of absenteeism from the army, having failed to appear at the local recruiting office when commanded. The outcome of their appearance was a fine of forty shillings and a military escort to the designated Army Barracks. Cardiff Barracks was a frequent destination from the courthouse in Port Talbot and, indeed, Edwards was remitted there.

There is nothing unusual in his story so far. Unaccountably, however, Edwards, and two fellow Port Talbot objectors, Jack Woolcock and Lemuel Emanuel were suddenly to be incarcerated at Buttrills Camp, in Barry. This normally served as an overspill barracks for Cardiff. but the brutal treatment they received there was quite unprecedented, abnormal and illegal. Indeed, it became the subject of a question in the House of Commons by Philip Snowden MP on 10 August 1916.

The events at Barry were described in local newspapers under the heading of 'Shocking treatment of Conscientious Objectors':[98]

'Dan Edwards, Jack Woolcock and Lemuel Samuel, the three Conscientious Objectors who were arrested some time ago have been discharged as being "indifferent" and medically unfit for service. They were detained at Cardiff Barracks for twelve days and then sent to Buttrills Camp, Barry Dock, where they were subjected to cruel treatments. On July 23 they were asked to submit to a medical examination for two reasons viz they had come from a smallpox area; to see if they were fit for punishment consequent on court-martial. On the Monday following they were allowed to work out under open escort; that went on for some time. They were again examined and within an hour from that they appeared before the Sergeant of the Company which they were placed in who told them that they were passed for service. They refused to wear khaki and were consequently escorted to the guard room. The next day they were brought before the Commanding Officer who sentenced them to 72 hours' detention and stated that he did not want to hear about "conscience".

On the same day they were ordered to break stones; this work they refused and were again brought before the Commanding Officer who extended the original sentence to 168 hours-to be extended again in the event of their resisting to do the work. They refused and were consequently subjected to the most cruel treatment.

The following treatment applies only to Dan Edwards, and Jack Woolcock: khaki was forced upon them in the bathrooms by the military police. They were forced to face a wooden board for eight days (for four hours each day with their toes and noses right up against the boards and not allowed to turn an any direction; and while in this position picks were tied around their shoulders during which period they were fed on 'skilly'. They were taken out for pack drill and dragged about in handcuffs, and when refusing to fall in step were kicked on the feet; marched through the camp bare-footed and their hair forcibly cut.

On 7 August they were taken to Cardiff in a weak state and ordered to be discharged by Colonel Cox as suffering from heart disease. They were again taken to Barry Dock and detained there until 10 August when they were sent home as ordered by Colonel Cox.

Their appearance is adequate proof of the punishments they have undergone.'

Their discharge took place on the same day that the question about them was asked in the House of Commons. There is little doubt, that it was his political activities in the ILP that provided him with the tools to become a trade unionist. In 1939 he lived in Tongwynlais, with wife Matilda and was the Divisional Secretary of the National Union of Teachers.

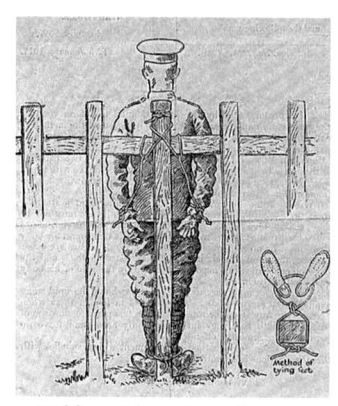

Field Punishment

It is not known whether the Field Punishment inflicted on the Port Talbot objectors was official, but it was a common punishment during World War One. A commanding officer, such as Cox, could award field punishment for up to 28 days, while a court-martial could award it for up to 90 days, either as Field Punishment Number One or Field Punishment Number Two.

Field punishment number one

Field Punishment Number One, consisted of the convicted man being placed in fetters and handcuffs or similar restraints and attached to a fixed object, such as a gun wheel or a fence post, for up to two hours per day. During the early part of World War One, the punishment was often applied with the arms stretched out and the legs tied together, giving rise to the nickname 'crucifixion'. This was applied for up to three days out of four, up to 21 days total. Conscientious objectors who had been conscripted to the army were treated the same as any other soldier, so when they consistently refused to obey orders they were usually given Field Punishment No. 1. Alfred Evans, who was sent to France, where he would be sentenced to death (later commuted) with 34 others, claimed that 'it was very uncomfortable, but certainly not humiliating'. Some conscientious objectors even saw Field Punishment 'as a badge of honour'.

Although the 1914 Manual of Military Law specifically stated that field punishment should not be applied in such a way as to cause physical harm, in practice abuses were commonplace. For example, the prisoner would deliberately be placed in stress positions, with his feet not fully touching the ground. In Field Punishment Number Two, the prisoner was placed in fetters and handcuffs but was not attached to a fixed object and was still able to march with his unit. This was a relatively tolerable punishment.

In both forms of field punishment, the soldier was also subjected to hard labour and loss of pay. Field Punishment Number One was eventually abolished in 1923, when attachment to a fixed object was forbidden by law.

Lemuel Emanuel (1889-1952)

Emanuel was from Llandebie, one of nine children. He followed his father's trade as a hairdresser and was quite peripatetic around south Wales, moving to Port Talbot at the time of his arrest. William Grane was another Conscientious Objector from Llandebie who had found his way to Port Talbot at that time. Both had common interests as NCF and ILP members.

Nothing is known about Emanuel's call-up or application for exemption, but he certainly failed to appear at the recruiting office as he was requested. He was duly arrested in July 1916, but owing to a shortage of magistrates his case was not immediately heard. A fellow lodger had offered to pay his bail, but this was refused and he was kept in the cells at Port Talbot police station until he was taken to Cardiff barracks.[99]

Emanuel was fortunate, for some reason, to miss the worst torture inflicted upon his colleagues, Dan Edwards and Jack Woolcock. Nevertheless, he had his hair forcibly shaved off, an act which was perhaps more insulting and vindictive to a professional hairdresser like Emanuel than to others. On 7 August all three were taken to Cardiff in a weak state and ordered to be discharged by Colonel Cox as suffering from heart disease. They were then taken to Barry Dock and detained until 10 August when they were sent home as ordered by Colonel Cox. On 28 August, 1916, Emanuel was court-martialled at 3 South Wales Borderers and received a six-month-sentence of hard labour.

A careful examination of the Imperial War Museum's claim that 'Severe physical brutality towards all conscientious objectors seems to be a First World War myth', will reveal that it is a misleading statement as far as Edwards, Woolcock and Emanuel are concerned. The statement is not untrue because the it is carefully qualified by the word 'all'.

In the 1930s Emanuel was still working as a hairdresser in Loughor and, in 1949, at sixty years of age, he married Lydia Morris before his death three years later.

Aneurin Morgan (1892-1953)

Aneurin Morgan, a hosier and travelling draper, was the last of six children to remain in the family home at Park Row, Cwmafan. Whilst still single, however, Morgan decided to change vocation to become an elementary school teacher. He does not seem to have had any particular religious or political attachment but decided, nonetheless, to object to conscription. He first appeared at Neath Rural Tribunal in March 1916, along with William Ifor Jones and his three Cwmafan conscientious-objector brothers. At first the tribunal chair, Mr Trick, teased Morgan because he was prepared to sell goods to soldiers' wives but was not willing to fight with the soldiers.

After the tribunal had granted Morgan two months' exemption to wind up his business affairs, he failed to respond to his call-up at the appointed date and was arrested as an absentee at by Police Sergeant Evans. The arrest took place at 08.30 am on 21 August 1916, prior to his appearance at Port Talbot Police Court. Morgan was fined forty shillings, and sent under escort on the 11.30 am train from Port Talbot station to Cardiff Barracks to enlist with the 20 Welch Regiment. His refusal to sign the army pay book culminated in his despatch to the 60 Training Battalion at Kinmel Camp on 26 August for a court-martial. It was agonisingly delayed until November 1916.

At that time Councillor Tal Mainwaring was vehemently protesting about the County's action in declaring that there was a vacancy at Abergwynfi boys' school because of Morgan's absence from his post. The issue of whether conscientious objectors should be permitted to remain at their teaching posts was a hot topic in south Wales. Morgan's case ranks alongside two other such celebrated cases, those of Jimmy Edmunds of Cardiff and Dan Griffiths of Llanelli. Difficulties could arise when a tribunal considered that an objector should remain in his normal employment, but where the post concerned had been filled during the tribunal process. In other words, regardless of any difficulties that the length of the process may have caused the employer, the latter should not have prejudged the tribunal's outcome.

Mainwaring's allegation was that decisions of policy towards the employment of objectors as teachers seemed to depend as much on the political composition of the local authority involved as the merits of the case.

When Morgan eventually received the Court's decision it transpired to be a sentence of 112 days' hard labour. However, the Central Tribunal were much quicker to summon him than the court-martial. |It resolved that he was a class C objector[100] and released him from Wormwood Scrubs on 2 December 1916.

Morgan did not take advantage of the opportunity to continue his teacher training so he was further transferred to 60 Training Battalion at Kinmel. He again refused to comply with orders and was returned to the Scrubs and then[101] to Walton Prison in Liverpool, where criminal prisoners were still being held. The primary punishment, in many cases the most severe, was psychological rather than physical. The most fortunate conscientious objectors were those who could devise ways to cope psychologically with loneliness, doubt, depression and loss of ability to concentrate. Some objectors coped by taking an active role in challenging the situation in which they found themselves, but Morgan does not appear to have done so. Fenner Brockway[102], who was also imprisoned at Walton, wrote from there claiming that 'one man in three at Walton was in hospital or under examination for weight loss.' Records held at Carlisle stated that 'On 1 December 1917 Morgan was experiencing mental illness' and 'losing his mind'. He was accordingly transferred to the County Asylum at Rainhill, Liverpool. At the start of the second war Morgan married Glenys Murphy. He lived until 1953.

Walton Prison, Liverpool

Thomas Henry Williams (1898–1951)

Most Cwmafan boys found work in the coal mines or tin-works: but Thomas, the fifth child in his family, worked on a farm. The Williams' lived at Finers and David's Rows.

Our first knowledge of his objection to military service was of his £2 fine at Port Talbot 'last Thursday, 5 October 1916, for failing to report, remanded and awaited a police escort.'[103] The succeeding months would see Williams being sent to an army barracks where his refusal to obey orders would result in a court-martial, a fine and imprisonment. It is likely that his time at Shrewsbury Prison followed his final appeal to the Central Tribunal, having been imprisoned at Wormwood Scrubs pending that appeal. Clearly the Tribunal's decision did not provide the outcome that Williams desired, hardening his attitude.

Many Cwmafan residents have travelled to Shrewsbury by train, but few have alighted on platform eight. The now disused platform is screened from passengers waiting on the adjacent departure platform for south Wales by a large concrete wall. Many have wondered why the wall was put there. The reason for erecting it was so that passengers on adjacent platforms could not see prisoners joining or alighting trains at platform eight. Williams was just one of the prisoners and conscientious objectors who alighted there during the First World War.

The prisoners' wall at Shrewsbury station. Platform eight is on the left of the wall.

The Dana: Shrewsbury Prison

His arrival at Shrewsbury is estimated as sometime in January 1917. It is intriguing to consider what happened to Williams, and why, in the course of the next six months or so. In July 1917 Philip Snowden MP asked a question in parliament[104] about Williams' condition: 'whether he was being force fed and whether his operation has led to physical injuries including the development of goitre in his neck, and whether steps will be taken to discontinue this treatment?' Less than six months later Snowden's concerns about Williams were shown to be justified. A fellow inmate at Shrewsbury, Arthur Horton of Manchester, became seriously ill. After fourteen months' incarceration he complained of under-feeding, and, unable to keep warm he developed pneumonia. Although he was granted a release he was too ill to be removed and died in prison on 16 January 1918[105].

The prison is mentioned in 'On Moonlit Heath and Lonesome Bank' which is part of the book, 'A Shropshire Lad', by A.E. Housman. The proximity of the prison to Shrewsbury railway station is highlighted in the verse:

They hang us now in Shrewsbury jail:
The whistles blow forlorn,
And trains all night groan on the rail
To men that die at morn

Shrewsbury Prison was the birthplace of the Howard League for Penal Reform. It should be noted, however, that this is not the same Howard as the Rev. Howard of Cwmafan, 'The Pugnacious Pacifist', who visited jails to check on the welfare of conscientious objector prisoners. Williams married Mary E. Mills in 1920.

Jack Woolcock (1880-1952)

Jack Woolcock and his brothers ran the family coal merchants' business from Brynheulog Terrace, in Cwmafan. Jack was both an ILP and NCF member who, in July 1916, was arrested with Dan Edwards, taken to Port Talbot Police Court, fined forty shillings and taken on the mid-day train, to Cardiff[106]. Lemuel Emanuel was also detained with them at Cardiff Barracks for twelve days before being sent to Buttrills Camp at Barry. The 'special treatment' Woolcock received at Barry and a general explanation of Field Punishment can be found in Dan Morgan's biography. It took a year for the War Office to respond to alleged cases of 'special', or coercive, treatment like these. Following mistreatment of objectors at the 3rd Cheshire Regiment at Birkenhead Barracks, a circular was sent to prisons on 19th September 1917.

> 'In cases of disobedience the correct procedure was for objectors to be immediately placed in arrest and remanded for trial by court-martial, unless a minor punishment is awarded or the soldier elects to accept the award of his commanding officer. If ignored, the Army Council will seriously consider whether the officer concerned, who has been guilty of a grave dereliction of duty and disregard of the law, can be permitted to retain his command.'[107] The circular was not adhered to in many cases.'

Nevertheless, on 10 August 1918, Philip Snowden had to ask a question in the House of Commons about Woolcock's treatment. After the war Woolcock's family business had to be abandoned. Woolcock tried to gain work in the mines but he suffered episodes of unemployment between the wars.

The Absolutists

'It is not the fear of physical death in the trenches that has led to our remaining in prison, but rather of spiritual death which we believe must follow our assent to any conscription scheme, military or civil.'
(Clifford Allen's letter to Lloyd George from Parkhurst Camp, 31 May 1917.)

When he was Secretary of State for War, Lloyd George, had sworn to make obstinate objectors' lives as 'hard as possible', because he doubted their true motivation. Daniel Watters' cartoon below depicts his attitude. The true absolutists would accept nothing but absolute exemption from conscription. Their belief was that it was inconsistent to refuse government work outside prison and then to accept it inside. Mailbag making in prison might simply free others from their normal work to make munitions.

The Port Talbot objectors to be described below may not have been as definite in their intentions as Clifford Allen of the NCF when he wrote at length to Prime Minister Lloyd George. The Port Talbot men's behaviour and their views may have progressed to the absolute position they took. The reason that some are recorded here as potential absolutists is simply because they were close to the 'limits of endurance.'[108]

Lloyd George *(Wikipedia) (L)* and as depicted by Watters of Cwmfan (R)

119

It is worth considering the prospects that Allen described he was about to face because that is what the Port Talbot 'absolutists' faced. Following his third successive sentence of imprisonment with hard labour for two years, Allen wrote:

> 'This will mean that...I shall have to spend the whole of my sentence in strict solitary confinement in a cell containing no article of any kind. . . I shall have to rest content with the floor, the ceiling and the bare walls. I shall have nothing to read and shall not be allowed to write or receive even the rare letters permitted hitherto, and shall live for long periods on bread and water.'

The Port Talbot men who may be considered as Absolutists were:

John Selwyn Jones   *Evan David Mort*
Dan Morris   *Christopher R. Scott*

Prisoner and George Maitland Llewelyn Davies-another Welsh absolutist in Winson Green Prison

John Selwyn Jones (1897-1958)

Jones, a Congregationalist from Castle Street, Port Talbot, was a tinplate worker from the age of 14 who applied for exemption on grounds of conscience. The tribunal's decision was that he be offered exemption from combatant service only but this was not acceptable to him.

It is not known whether Jones worked at the same tinplate works as Willie Rees, but they were near neighbours in Castle Street and their journey through the tribunal system was shared for most of the way. At the Margam Appeal tribunal on 25 March 1916, held at Aberafan Police Court, Jones, appeared with four others[109]. These, including Willie Rees, were dealt with in the usual way, namely a fine of forty shillings and then an escort to Cardiff Barracks. In April 1916 at Cardiff 4 Western, both Jones and Rees again refused to sign papers for conditional exemption to join the Non-combatant Corps.

Jones was automatically referred to Kinmel in June for a court-martial. This was duly forthcoming, but not until 18 July. Its decision was that he was to serve a stretch of two years' hard labour at Walton Prison, Liverpool. So, too, would Willie Rees[110], both sentences being subject to an appeal at Wormwood Scrubs. On 28 August, the Central Tribunal upheld the sentence imposed at Kinmel and sent Jones to Cardiff Prison with an option to serve the remainder of it by joining the Home Office Scheme. Jones accepted and, from 1 November 1916, he spent seven months on the scheme at Llanon reservoir before rejecting it and being returned to prison. By January 1919, Jones had served two sentences and almost two years in prison. A month later conscientious objectors went on hunger strike in ten prisons.

Jones married Violet Tucker in 1927 and thereafter lived at Bracken Road, Margam. He continued to work as a manager in the steel and tinplate industry.

Dan Morris (1892-1963)

Dan Morris was from a family of eight children of London Terrace, Cwmafan. Unlike his brothers, who were employed at the Copper Miners Tinplate Works and the Rhondda and Swansea Bay Railway, he was employed as a postman. Such employment became significant: it meant that he had an opportunity to communicate with people about ILP and NCF business during his post rounds. Morris had not only become a Cwmafan ILP member, he also, conveniently, became the organisation's Secretary. It was not his employment as a postman that got him into trouble, however; trouble occurred when he allegedly distributed NCF anti-conscription leaflets, but not during those post rounds.

On Sunday afternoon on 18 June 1916 an anti-conscription meeting was held by the National Council for Civil Liberties, at Gallipoli Square, Taibach. It was held there 'to avoid attention from the authorities because of their recent activity which unfortunately resulted in four of their comrades finding themselves in the police court'. It was chaired by Alderman Harry Davies of Margam, the speaker was Fred Bramley, and its purpose was to demand the repeal of the Military Service Act. Morris, brothers William and Jenkin Williams[111] and Tal Mainwaring had previously been charged with distributing literature in support of Bramley's demands. These were considered to be offences under the Defence of the Realm Act. Llewelyn Williams K. C. defended, but each defendant received a fine of ten pounds and a guinea costs, or imprisonment in default.[112]

Neither Morris nor Mainwaring paid their fine. As a result, Morris was sentenced to two month's imprisonment at Swansea Gaol, with Tal Mainwaring receiving a sentence of three months. Soon afterwards, in July 1916 Morris was notified by the Postmaster General that his services as a postman were no longer required' because of his imprisonment. W. C. Anderson raised his case in the House of Commons.[113]

> 'Another man, Dan Morris, a local postman has not only gone to prison, but he loses his situation as well. I think that if it is at all possible, the Home Secretary should cause some investigation to be made in this case, which I would suggest is harsh and vindictive, and see what can be done in regard to what, in my opinion, is a grave public scandal. I do suggest very strongly that this sort of thing is a travesty of justice'.

Not only was Morris to fall foul of the Defence of the Realm Act, as described, he was soon to suffer from the application of the Military Service Act. Three weeks after his release from Swansea Prison he was again arrested. On Monday 15 August 1916, PC Cole called at London Terrace to apprehend him for failing to report to the recruitment office when called up. At Aberafan Police Court[114] the bench, comprising William Jenkins in the Chair, Major Gray and Percy J. Jacobs, charged Morris with failing to join the army.

Morris had stated, when arrested, that he was a conscientious objector, and was given leave to make a statement to court. He said: 'Under the new army order of June 24 all conscientious objectors were to be released to take their appeals to the Central Military Tribunal. Therefore, I request my release until my case is heard at the Central Military Tribunal.'

When Gray said that Morris was called up before the army order was made, Morris replied: 'All men are going to be released irrespective of the decision of previous tribunals. They were all deserters, too. They did not give themselves up willingly.' Gray added that 'He has been evading the police for three weeks', to which Morris retorted 'Recuperating in Pembrokeshire in preparation for the anticipated trials'. Gray then suggested that 'we adjourn till next Monday when the Hon FC Bailey of Cardiff will be present'.

The fact that Morris was deemed to be a member of the 20th Welsh by the Army, but not by himself, meant that he was escorted on the 11.30 am train from Port Talbot to Cardiff Barracks, not arriving until 6pm. By the time this was reported in the newspapers, he was facing a court-martial at Kinmel Camp, on 26 August. Morris' court-martial's proceedings were reproduced in Chapter Two.

The court determined that both he and Aneurin Morgan should meet with two years' hard labour, commuted to 112 days. By the time he was required to attend the Central Tribunal at Wormwood Scrubs on 20 September, the harshest part of his sentence had been completed and he and Aneurin Morgan were reported by the Society of Friends to be in good spirits[115].

The Central Tribunal, surprisingly, assessed him to be a Class B objector. This meant he could propose to the tribunal where he should be placed. Presumably the Tribunal felt that his dismissal from the Post Office was unfair and that its best course of action was to persuade him to join the Home Office Scheme. He soon found himself at Newhaven Work Centre[116] and probably realised that this was not the generous choice it might have appeared. It was a convenient way to remove him and his activities from Port Talbot. Perhaps he felt that the authorities could not be trusted and that he would be no worse off by refusing to co-operate once more. The upshot of this was that, three months later, in December 1916, he was reassigned to Warwick Prison for a period of eight months. Thereafter, from August 1917, he was sent to Dartmoor before being returned, finally, to Wormwood Scrubs.

In 1923 he married Catherine Thomas and lived on Margam Road.

A letter by Daniel Oliver Harries[117a] of Gorseinon describes his welcome on return from Dartmoor and the solidarity shown by Dan Morris and colleagues.

'They gave me a hearty reception at the station (I utterly broke down). Dan Griffiths[117b] (Llanelli, his brother Ben and his wife (who have been here on holiday), Dan Morris,[117c] Bob,[117d] other comrades from Cwmafan, Briton Ferry, Albert Lewis[117e] (Neath), some from Neath, Merthyr, Aberdare, Ystalyfera, Pontardawe, Treharris and Rhondda Valley greeted me. Albert Lewis and the Cwmafan comrade have me to supper every night, they call for me and when I do go, there are new potatoes (sent from Cwmafan), kidney beans, Williams' coffee for me (Williams the phrenologist, Swansea Arcade), tea and cocoa, why, they are leaving no stone unturned to restore my health, sardines and plenty of bread and butter, Albert Lewis with a tin of salmon and jam to finish up.'

Evan David Mort (1890–1962)

Evan David Mort of Cotton Row in Taibach worked originally as a behinder in the copper rolling mills before securing later employment at the Crown Patent Fuel Works. Gradually, Mort took an interest in politics, becoming a Dockers' Union representative and a member of the ILP. It was from this background that Mort's extraordinary journey as an absolutist conscientious objector emanated.

Mort's application for exemption from service was on grounds of conscience only, because he declined to appeal on the grounds of caring for his dependent, widowed mother. When offered non-combatant duty his acerbic reply was that the work of the RAMC was 'like a man baling out a leaking boat instead of finding the leak'.[117f] 'The only way to save life,' he said, 'was to stop the war.'

His application was refused, and refused again at the Glamorgan Appeal Tribunal on 28 March 1916[118]. There he declared that his unyielding beliefs were so strong he would go to prison even though, with compliance, he still might be exempted to care for his dependent widowed mother. At his first court-martial by the 20 Welsh at Kinmel in August 1916, he received a penalty of two years' hard labour, to be commuted to four months, and subject to appeal.

The Central Tribunal heard the appeal quite promptly, on 24 August. Mort was classified as a genuine CO, class A, eligible for referral to the Brace Committee which might allow him to do work of national importance at a work centre. For many, this was preferable to imprisonment and getting caught up in the 'cat and mouse' Act. Mort accepted the scheme, but only for some six months, before he rejected it by absconding from Llanelli Waterworks' work centre at Llanon with a large group of others.[119]

On 14 May the following year he was attending his second court-martial at Kinmel's 57 Training Battalion, where his original sentence, which had been served, was repeated. It should be remembered that each court case was the result of a further refusal to acknowledge military authority. The sentence was again served, but five months later Mort was attending his third court-martial by LN Lancs at Felixstowe. On 20 October, the duration of his sentence was changed to eighteen months' hard labour, commuted to nine months. Another, fourth, court-martial was to follow at Felixstowe in June 1918 and yet another sentence of two years' hard labour was the result.

Cotton Row, Taibach, in the 1930s *(Port Talbot Historical Society)*

Mort was, therefore, one of the most intransigent of all the Welsh objectors, having been court-martialled four times. Only one Welsh objector, Emrys Hughes (Keir Hardie's son-in-law) exceeded Mort's tally, having been tried at five court-martials.

Christopher Richard Scott (1886–1976)

Christopher Scott was born on Christmas Day, 1886. When he was due for conscription he lived at Somerset Street, Taibach, and worked on the Great Western Railway as a signalman. He was to become a key figure in Port Talbot's early Labour Party history. In 1910, aged twenty-three, he had joined the Amalgamated Society of Railway servants at New Milford, now known as Neyland. He was soon elected for union activities. These undoubtedly led him into the ILP, first as a member, then as a Committee man. Soon Scott was to become Chair of the ILP and Labour Representation Committee in Aberafan as well as Secretary of Mid-Glamorgan ILP, along with Henry Davies as its President.

In January 1916, at the Dockers' Hall in Port Talbot, Scott chaired a meeting called 'to protest against any measure of military service being thrust upon any section of the workers'[120]. Previously the ILP Council had given its opinion of any conscription Act: that '…conscription would so outrage the liberty and conscience of the individual that the council… decided… to call on the men of the ILP to resist its operation[121]. At the same meeting in the Dockers' Hall, a resolution by Tom Llewelyn of the Steelmakers' Union was carried. Supported by Tal Mainwaring and both Henry and Harry Davies, it resolved 'that this meeting of Aberafan and Port Talbot trades unions declares its strongest opposition to compulsory military conscription, believing conscription to be a violation of the principles of civic freedom.[122]'

Copies of the resolution were sent to the Prime Minister, to the Secretary of State for War, Arthur Henderson, the local MPs and the press. But conscription soon came to Britain with the Military Service Act, on 2 March 1916. From that date all single men and childless widowers aged 18-41 years were required, when called, to report to a local recruitment office. Port Talbot seems to have been an early target to test the Act. By 28 March 1916, Scott had appeared both before Margam local Tribunal and the Glamorgan Appeal Tribunal[123], with his application for exemption being refused and the decision upheld.

Scott also chaired a meeting,[124] attended by W. C. Anderson in August 1916, in which it was resolved to call on the British Government 'to use every effort to prevent the Right of Asylum in Britain, which is contained in the proposal to deport all Russians of military age, unwilling to enlist in the British Army'. Anderson highlighted the better treatment in France of such 'political refugees'.

The great part of Scott's wartime narrative remains silent for now. Given his background and his activities in the ILP, it seems likely that he would have exhausted the exemption process and become an absolutist. Somewhere, no doubt, his curriculum vitae is recorded in a fellow objector's diary, but it is not to be found in the NCF records that still exist.

He married Margaretta James in Carmarthenshire late in 1918 and was still working as a GWR signalman in 1939, living at Felinfoel, near Llanelli. Margaretta ran a poultry small holding there until she died in 1963. Richard Scott died in the Autumn of 1976.

Outcomes unknown

'Such things matter not one jot when men's consciences are aroused' (Lord Roberts)

Where there is much uncertainty about individual objectors' experiences and history, they are included in this section. They are:

John Brown	*Philip Phillips*
Percy Warren Davies	*John Studt*
S. Jones	*David John Evans*
John George Mills	*Daniel Samuel*
Ebenezer Morris	*William Williams*

John Brown (1895–1973)

John Brown was from Pantdu, Cwmafan. His mother had been widowed twice and had brought up twenty children. John was a coal miner whose reasons for applying for exemption are unclear, but he does seem to have been associated with the ILP, so his motivation may have been primarily political. Apply he did, but he was denied by the Margam Tribunal on 3 March 1916.[125] The Appeal Tribunal referred him to a colliery tribunal, presumably to verify that his occupation was a coal miner and that this work was essential to the war effort. Nevertheless, he may still have refused to undertake this work on the conscientious grounds that he did not want to support the war effort, either for humanitarian or political reasons.

Had he refused, he would have been referred to the Central Military Tribunal at Wormwood Scrubs whose task was to determine how genuine his objections were. By the time the proceedings had taken place the Home Office Scheme would likely have come into force so that he could be given alternative work detached from the direct war effort. Thereafter little is known of him, except that, in 1919, he married Margaret Davies and died aged seventy-eight.

Percy Warren Davies (1893–1962)

Although Davies came from a Neath railway family, he lived in Caradoc Street, Taibach and attended Aberafan Boys' Board School where, in 1900, he was the sole scholarship pupil from the school. Davies was a congregant of the Church of England, a member of the NCF and, later, the Communist Club. At his local tribunal he declined an offer to join the Royal Army Medical Corps, or to do work of national importance. He made no appeal against tribunal decisions and consequently found himself in Wandsworth Prison, from January until March 1917. During Davies' time there, the prison Governor was dismissed for the maltreatment of an objector, but just prior to this, Davies was transferred to Winchester Prison by order of the General Officer Commanding and does not seem to have been maltreated:

> 'Mr P. W. Davies of the Port Talbot Branch of the NUR,[126] a member of the Head Office staff of that union, has now, at Winchester Jail served five months of his sentence of two years' imprisonment as a conscientious objector. A few days ago his colleagues at Unity house sent a visitor to see him and found him in good health.'[127]

Winchester held around a hundred COs at this time. Their communication with each other was quite enterprising: morse code was one medium used, created by tapping on the pipework to correspond with adjacent cells. The second method, which was never discovered by warders, was the production of a newspaper. It was written on toilet paper and contained essays, poems and humour and was bound using canvas from mailbags.

Normally, at this stage, an objector would appeal the sentence of a court-martial to the Central Tribunal. If Davies did so it would be his first such appeal. Possibly the Tribunal intervened in his case without an appeal in order to maintain good industrial relations on the south Wales rail networks. There were strained relationships between the railwaymen of Port Talbot and their employers' at this time. This arose from the railway companies' willingness to release their staff for military service in the 'comb-out' process.

It is possible that no appeal to the Central Tribunal was made and, if one was made, whether it resulted in anything other than a return to his normal work, for Davies to re-establish the deteriorating relationships between the rail men and their employers. Davies married Elizabeth M Griffiths in 1922.

S. Jones

Who was the S. Jones that was court-martialled at Kinmel on 18 July 1916 and sentenced to two years' hard labour at Walton Prison? What was the outcome of his appeal to the Central Tribunal on 18 July 1916? The objectors who attended the tribunals at this time were those who experienced some of the worst treatment in the hands of the authorities. Therefore, 'S. Jones' should be identified and remembered. To do so, a search in the 1911 census of Port Talbot area for any S. Jones born between 1875 and 1900 was made. The search revealed twelve possibilities for the identity of S. Jones.

All that is known of Jones' case comes from a newspaper article which contained the following information. 'S. Jones' was an NCF member and one of the group of Aberafan men arrested on 25 May 1916, as absentees. It appears that he was not a 'badged' man who could be permitted to stay in his normal job, rather than be conscripted. However, the possibility exists that, despite being badged, he made a stand against conscription on principle and underwent the whole of the tribunal process.

It may be assumed that Jones appealed against the local tribunal's decision and that the appeal was unsuccessful because he failed to report for service and was arrested as an absentee. He was court-martialled at Kinmel on 18 July and was sent to Walton Prison, Liverpool to commence his sentence of two years' hard labour. The sentence was probably subject to an appeal to the Central Tribunal.

Aneurin Morgan was also remitted to Walton Prison in August 1916. It is uncertain whether Morgan and Jones were there at exactly the same time because Jones was last recorded at Llanon Reservoir Work Centre on 2 November 1916.[128] By December Morgan was experiencing mental illness and one asks whether Jones' presence would have given him support. It remains unknown whether Jones was still at Walton at the time absolutist Arthur Emlyn Thomas of Briton Ferry arrived at the prison.

John George Mills (1895–1952)

John George Mills was a hairdresser who lived in Gwendoline Street, Aberafan and a near neighbour of James Price of the NCF. He was not the only Port Talbot hairdresser to object to conscription: Lemuel Emanuel was another.

Readers may be better informed about Mills than the writer. It is known that he was at Cardiff Barracks on 19 May 1916. After that the NCF's Conscientious Objectors' Information Bureau (COIB) lost track of him. It is uncharacteristic of the COIB to lose track of anyone because it normally ensured it was kept well-informed about objectors' movements and treatment, whether they were NCF members, or not. One can speculate that Mills decided to relent and accept military discipline. Some objectors did so at this juncture, but not very many. Otherwise, Mills would still have had difficult decisions to make during the time he remained in the army reserve. Nevertheless, throughout the process of court-martial, tribunals and serving his sentences, most of the decisions about how and where his life would be spent would be made by others.

Ebenezer Morris (1892–1968)

Morris was born into a farming family at Llandough in the Vale of Glamorgan. Both he and his father were also colliery ostlers when the family came to live at Ty Canol Farm, in Pontrhydyfen. He was content to remain in the household of fifteen until he was arrested by Sergeant Evans to appear at Port Talbot Police Court[129] on the same day as Lewis Emlyn Jones, of Cwmafan. Morris told the bench: 'I have been bad', meaning ill. Lieutenant W.

E. Rees gave evidence saying: 'he had refused to go before the medical board or to do anything'. Apart from his apparent liking for farm life, Morris' motivation for not reporting is unknown: he may not, in fact, have claimed grounds of conscience. On the other hand, he may have become known to the police, having previously been denied exemption on grounds of conscience. He married Ethel Burrows in 1922.

Philip Phillips (1885–1969)

Phillips was a gardener and former steel smelter who lived at Pont-yr-Arian, Baglan.[130] Nothing is definite about his motivation for applying for exemption on grounds of conscience. A religious, independent, rather than political, stance to be exempted seems most likely in his case. It was put before Aberafan Tribunal in March 1916. Phillips hesitation at the Tribunal suggests that he had not been as prepared to face the bench as local members of the NCF who were given guidance by their local branches on how to respond to the standardised, predictable questions and comments from some of the tribunal members. Objectors sometimes replied with standardised, predictable answers, too especially because, at this time, the Aberafan Tribunal was routinely offering non-combatant status to applicants.

The dialogue in a very short hearing went as follows:

> '*Chair:* You would rather be killed than kill a German? –Yes
> *Mr W. E. Rees (Military Representative):* and your brothers and sisters killed also?
> *Philip Phillips, the applicant:* (after hesitation) –Yes
> *Mr Rees:* Then you don't deserve to live
> *Chairman:* You are in a bad way I believe (laughter)
> *The clerk:* You would not dig trenches? –No
> *Mr Rees:* Carry the wounded? –No
> *The Chairman:* As a non-combatant you would have to dig trenches
> *Applicant:* What are more important – potatoes or shells?
> *The Chairman:* Shells I should say, and that you'll probably find out.'

Phillips was, indeed, offered non-combatant service[131]. It is not known whether he accepted this or whether he appealed against the decision. His trajectory during the rest of the war awaits discovery. He married Gladys M. Milton in 1922.

John Studt (1893–

A handwritten NCF and Conscientious Objectors' Information Bureau record of September 1918 details a person with the surname of Steed, or Stood from Port Talbot. Diligent and painstakingly efficient though these organisations' record keeping was, transcription errors, though few, were possible. That is why one must consider that John Studt's name was erroneously recorded.

If that is the case then it can be said that John was probably the son of Henry and Emma Studt, an amusement caterer whose address was Fairfield, Aberafan. Fairfield is the name of a street, which connects Lister Avenue and Julian Terrace. The Studts had lived there for at least fifteen years when young John, who had been assisting in his father's catering and amusement business, was called-up. He was arrested as an absentee on 5 June 1916. The Conscientious Objectors Information Bureau lost track of him after that date.

David John Evans (1880–1940)

David Evans was born in June 1880. He was a married miner from Graig y Tewgoed, Cwmafan when he was first remanded for being an absentee in February 1917. His reason for not reporting was that he had been ill and was still under the doctor's care,[132] but his summons to court had followed an application for exemption on conscientious grounds. Eventually Evans[133] did appear at the Magistrates' Court in August 1918, where he was fined £3 and then escorted to Cardiff Barracks. It can be assumed that Evans was offered the chance to join the Home Office Scheme, but it cannot be assumed that he accepted any such offer. Therefore, the details of how, when and where his time was spent during the remainder of the year are yet to be determined, hopefully from family records or fellow objectors' notebooks.

After the War Evans became a colliery repairer. He died at Graig y Tewgoed in 1940.

Daniel Samuel (1893–1949)

In 1918 the Daniel Samuel of Cwmafan, who was remanded for being an absentee, was unquestionably a conscientious objector.[134] However, two Daniel Samuels were born in Cwmafan in 1893. Daniel Samuel, the conscientious objector, was a collier born on 31 August who lived in Tymaen Street with his mother Mary, grandmother May, sister Beatrice and brothers Idris and Ivor Glyn.

His early tribunal history remains unknown, but to be arrested as late as August 1918 gives us some indication of both his earlier and later history as an objector. It seems he may have once been 'badged' as a miner and then 'combed out' from his job in 1917, propelling him through the tribunal system. After arrest he was fined £3 at the Magistrates' Court, along with David John Evans, and escorted to Cardiff Barracks where he was court-martialled on 29 August by the 3rd South Wales Borderers for not obeying orders. His sentence was six months' hard labour at Wormwood Scrubs, pending any appeal he wished to make to the Central Tribunal. Thereafter, it is likely that he was one of the last to be incarcerated, and one of the last to be released in 1919.

At some point after release, Daniel left the pit for a tin-works. Misfortune was to meet him. For some reason he became incapacitated whilst working there. He never married, but lived with his widowed mother at the Oakwood Inn, which, in 1939, was run by his elder sister, Elizabeth Morris.

William Williams (1890–1918)

Thomas William Williams was born in 4 Tewgoed Row, Cwmafan. The young coal miner had married in 1915 and had made his home at Carlos Street, Port Talbot. In the Autumn of 1918 he died of influenza at twenty-eight years of age, leaving Sarah widowed. He was regarded as 'a robust fighter for the cause of socialism, pacifism and trade unionism in the district, and was compelled to endure many hardships for his convictions'.[135] The hundreds who attended his funeral wore red-rosette buttonholes and the 'Red Flag' was sung over the grave. From the windows of the Hardie Institute hung a flag of black velvet with the words 'We mourn the loss of a comrade', sewn in red letters. 'The Cwmafan, Aberafan and Taibach branches of the ILP will record William Williams' name as one of the list of heroes in the battle for socialism.'

When William Williams appealed for exemption at Aberafan Tribunal in March 1916[136] he submitted a written statement of application. Henry Davies also appeared to speak for him. Davies referred to Lord Roberts, one of the most successful military commanders of the nineteenth century, and a keen advocate for conscription. Roberts had made known his views on conscience in dealing with 'another group of conscientious objectors who had refused military duty in Ireland in defence of the British Constitution'.

> 'I have some knowledge of military discipline and I should like to bring home to you something of its meaning and limitations. If you penetrate deep enough into the depths of human nature you will unfailingly reach in each one of us a stratum which is impervious to discipline or any other influence from without. The strongest manifestation of this truth lies in what men call conscience – an innate sense of right and wrong, which neither reason nor man-made laws can effect. It is no use to make an appeal to the constitution or to threaten pains and penalties. Such things matter not one jot when men's consciences are aroused. And if this demand be renewed the army will be brought to destruction.'

Despite Davies' brilliant argument for Williams the application was refused. It should be noted that, in May 1916, another William Williams, but this time of 18 Tewgoed Row, his brother Jenkin, Daniel Morris and Tal Mainwaring of Cwmafan ILP were charged with distributing circulars 'likely to prejudice recruiting' in Cwmafan.[137] Whether or not Thomas William Williams was in a prison or work centre, or on a furlough when he succumbed to influenza is not known.

Conclusion to this chapter

The conscientious objection that took place in Port Talbot occurred in four phases:

The first was prior to the introduction of conscription in March 1916 when some who objected to taking human life volunteered to take part in non-combatant activities. Only one person, David John Jones, who joined the Welsh Students' Company of the Royal Army Medical Corps, came into this group.

The second phase was by far the most important and turbulent. It took place immediately after the introduction of conscription until April 1917 when almost sixty men who were culled as conscripts refused. The tribunals sometimes heard a dozen or so of these cases at a time, whilst on the streets, and in Port Talbot's halls, mass anti-conscription meetings were held and the leaders imprisoned.

A third phase was evident after the lifting of various occupational exemptions in April 1917, when some of the Port Talbot objectors were 'combed out' from jobs which had previously been 'occupational exemptions'. The Military Service (Review of Exemptions) Act's aim was to provide a million more men for the army. This phase was not hugely significant for the district in terms of the number of men who had their exemption removed: only half a dozen or so were affected. However, they were taken from industries like the railways that were already under great strain. The effect was to sour labour relations by conflating industrial conscription and military conscription even further, at a time of great difficulty in the conduct of the war.

The fourth phase involved those who reached conscription age after 1916, or were part of a second 'comb out' of conscripts. In 1918 all exemptions, except those of conscience, could be cancelled. These young objectors mostly attended tribunals, and were arrested, individually. The recording of some of these cases, such as Thomas Henry Williams and David John Stephens, was assiduous, but later recording was sometimes less thorough than earlier cases and, consequently, several may remain undiscovered.

Port Talbot objectors saw the insides of at least twelve prisons, six other work centres, a further six army barracks' cells and one asylum during the course of the war. Families usually knew where the objectors were but public awareness of the events involving many of the objectors was low during the war. At the introduction of conscription, a collective culling of objectors and their tribunals was quite well reported. So, too, were the DoRA prosecutions later in 1916. The reaction of trade unions to the 'combing out' in 1917 also received some publicity. Very often, however, the experiences of many individuals simply escaped the attention of newspapers and, hence, the general public. It was left to the *Pioneer* and other newspapers to report on the fate of many individuals in south Wales and, even in supportive journals, what reports were made sometimes consisted of the briefest of details.

Conscription did not end with the Armistice on 11 November 1918, nor did the internment of objectors. Britain did not wish to end conscription until its allies did likewise and the peace treaty would forbid conscription in Germany. It was still necessary, therefore, for the NCCL to organise a 'No Conscription Sunday' in March 1919, with meetings held at Aberafan, Briton Ferry, Cwmafan, Kenfig Hill, Maesteg and elsewhere.

At the Armistice, around 1,500 objectors were still in confinement and deaths, diseases, work stoppages and hunger strikes had become common. In April 1919, a 'release plan' was formulated: the first to be released were those who had served two years or more. It took the authorities some time to decide that this would include those who had received remission. Releases were done slowly in small groups in order not to cause antagonism with demobilising soldiers who feared loss of employment to the objectors. In May 1919, the 650 still incarcerated comprised the oldest and youngest: those who had been inside for less than twenty months, having just reached eighteen, and those conscripted after raising the enlistment age from forty-one to fifty-one. It took until August 1919, for the last batch to be released.

It is possible that some young Port Talbot objectors, like Daniel Samuel, were detained until the end. However, press reporting of objectors was less assiduous in 1918 than in 1916, so it may be that some Port Talbot objectors who fell into this category went unreported. It is clear that several of Port Talbot's outright objectors were interned until very late: David Davies of Cwmafan was still detained in May 1919, and Evan Mort comes to mind as one who may have been detained even longer.

The next chapter will consider the local support that the objectors received from both individuals and various religious, political, and trade union organisations and how that support was demonstrated.

Notes for Chapter Four

The Port Talbot objectors

[35] T. E. Nicholas 'To a sparrow', translator Wil Ifan, accessed on line at www.terrynorm.ic.net, 13 August 2016.
[36] Alison Ronan 'Unpopular Resistance: The rebel networks of men and women in opposition to the First World War in Manchester and Salford'. (Manchester 2015).
[36a] Duncan, R. 2015 'Objectors and resisters' p114
[37] Llewelyn, as before.

The Non-combatants

[38] H. C. Deb 06 March 1918 vol 103 cc1958-9 1958 and 26 Mr King.
[39] *Glamorgan Gazette*, 31 March 1916.
[40] *Cambria Daily Leader*, 18 October 1916.
[41] *Glamorgan Gazette*, 31 March 1916.
[42] *Labour Leader*, 25 May 1916.

The Schemers

[43] *Glamorgan Gazette*, 31 March 1916, reported as 'Joseph N. Davies'; *Labour Leader*, 25 May 1916.
[44] *Glamorgan Gazette*, 31 March 1916, reported as 'Joseph N. Davies'; Labour Leader, 25 May 1916.
[45] Some of these events are based on entries found in the notebook of a fellow objector named Collins, whose notes are in Leicestershire Records Office.
[46] 'The Oxford Dictionary of Christian Thought', (Oxford, 2000).
[47] *Herald of Wales*, 28 October 1916.
[48] *Glamorgan Gazette*, 31 March 1916.
[49] *Cambria Daily Leader*, 9 July 1918; *Herald of Wales* 13 July 1918.
[50] *Glamorgan Gazette*, 31 March 1916.
[51] *Glamorgan Gazette*, 31 March 1916.
[52] A. Leslie Evans, 'A History of Taibach and District' (Port Talbot, 1982).
[53] *Glamorgan Gazette*, 31 March 1916.
[54] *Glamorgan Gazette*, 31 March 1916.
[55] J. Ivor Hansen, (1968), as before.
[56] *Glamorgan Gazette*, 3 March 1916.
[57] *Labour Leader*, 4 May 1916.
[58] *Cambria Daily Leader*, 17 April 1917.
[59] *Cambria Daily Leader*, 13 September 1917.
[60] David Cleaver, 'Conscientious objection in the Swansea area' in Morgannwg vol 28 pp48-53, Glamorgan History Society (Cardiff, 1984).
[61] *Y Dernas* (the Nation) was an anti-war newspaper in the Welsh language.
[62] *Pioneer*, 15 July 1916.
[63] *Pioneer*, 15 July 1916.
[64] *Glamorgan Gazette*, 3 March 1916.
[65] *Herald of Wales*, 3 June 1916.
[66] *Herald of Wales*, 3 June 1916.
[67] *Herald of Wales*, 20 May 1916; *Labour Leader* 25 May 1916.
[68] Daniel Rees Michael also lived in this row.
[69] *South Wales Weekly Post*, 18 March 1916.
[70] *Cambria Daily Leader*, 22 June 1918.
[71] *Glamorgan Gazette*, 31 March 1916.
[72] *Labour Leader* 25 May 1916.
[73] *Cambria Daily Leader*, 22 May 1916.
[74] *Herald of Wales*, May 20 1916.
[75] *Herald of Wales*, 3 June 1916.
[76] *Glamorgan Gazette*, 31 March 1916.
[77] *Labour Leader*, 2 May 1916; *Herald of Wales*, 20 May 1916.

[78] *Cambria Daily Leader*, 22 November 1916.
[79] 29 April and 4 May 1918.
[80] Hartshorn was then Chief Miners' agent for Maesteg District and an ILP member.
[81] *Herald of Wales*, 27 May 1916.
[82] *Glamorgan Gazette*, 31 March 1916.
[83] *Cambria Daily Leader*, 22 May 1916.

Workers of national importance

[84] John Morris in 'A Time for Peace' accessed at http://www.thechristadelphians.org.uk (13 August 2016).
[85] *Herald of Wales*, 3 June 1916.
[86] *Pioneer*, 23 September 1916.
[87] *Glamorgan Gazette*, 31 March 1916.
[88] *Glamorgan Gazette*, 10 March 1916.
[89] *Glamorgan Gazette*, 31 March 1916.
[90] *Glamorgan Gazette*, 31 March 1916.
[91] *Glamorgan Gazette*, 31 March 1916.
[92] *Glamorgan Gazette*, 31 March 1916.
[93] *Cambria Daily Leader*, 16 April 1916.

Tortured and tormented

[94] *Herald of Wales*, 3 June 1916.
[95] *Merthyr Pioneer*, Saturday 22 July 1916.
[96] There was a voluntary aid detachment (VAD) Hospital at Howbury Hall, which provided field nursing services.
[97] Allen was NCF Chair and a conscientious objector.
[98] *Merthyr Pioneer*, Saturday 19 August 1916; 31 March 1916; *Glamorgan Gazette and Pioneer*, 15 July 16 and 19 August 1916.
[99] *Pioneer*, 22 July 1916.
[100] Class C objectors could receive temporary exemption whilst undergoing training.
[101] *Pioneer* 26 August; 2, 9 and 23 September 1916.
[102] David Boulton, 'Objection overruled' (Dent, 2014) p 258.
[103] *Cambria Daily Leader*, 14 October 1916.
[104] *Cambria Daily Leader*, 25 July 1917; *Herald of Wales*, 28 July 1917.
[105] Boulton, as before, p 254.
[106] *Pioneer*, 15 July 1916.
[107] Boulton, as before, p 254.

The Absolutists

[108] David Boulton's description of the effects of maintaining an absolutist stance.
[109] *Herald of Wales*, May 20 1916.
[110] *Pioneer*, 19 August, 1916.
[111] William of 76 Gower Street, Aberafan and Jenkin of Cunard Road.
[112] *Herald of Wales*, 17 June 1916.
[113] *Pioneer* 5 and 19 August 1916.
[114] *Glamorgan Gazette*, 18 August 1916.

[115] *Pioneer*, 23 September 1916.
[116] *Pioneer*, 19 August 1916, and 2 and 9 Sept 1916
[117a] 35 year-old Harries (Chum) was the founder of Gorseinon ILP and a CO. He was sent to Dartmoor with WI Thomas after both were absent without leave from Talgarth work camp
[117b] A teacher, author and CO, sarcastically called 'The New Dock Diogenes'.
[117c] Morris was Cwmafan's ILP Secretary. He had been imprisoned at Swansea under DoRA. As a CO he was also at the Scrubs, Warwick and Dartmoor.
[117d] Probably William John Roberts of Gorseinon, Glamorgan NCF's branch secretary & CO
[117e] Lewis was a Neath Borough auditor and CO.
[117f] *Cambria Daily Leader*, 7 March 1916
[118] *Glamorgan Gazette*, 31 March 1916.
[119] Dr Roscoe Howell; 'Llanelli's water, past and present'; Created 21 March 2013 www.llanellich.org.uk/files/232-llanelli-water-past-and-present accessed 12 April 2016.
[120] *Glamorgan Gazette*, 14 January 1916.
[121] *Pioneer*, 30 October 1915.
[122] *Glamorgan Gazette*, 14 January 1916.
[123] *Glamorgan Gazette*, 31 March 1916.
[124] *Pioneer*, 19 August 1916.

Outcomes unknown

[125] *Herald of Wales*: 'Socialist in Court', 3 June 1916.
[126] The NUR was an industrial union founded in 1913 by the merger of three unions.
[127] *South Wales Weekly Post*, 6 October 1917.
[128] *Labour Leader*, 25 May 1916; *Tribunal*, 10 August 1916.
[129] *Cambria Daily Leader*, 2 January 1917.
[130] In 1916, Baglan lay within Briton Ferry Urban District Council's boundaries, whereas today it is in Port Talbot following changes to local government. For this reason, it is appropriate to include his case with the Port Talbot objectors along with another Baglan objector, Robert J. Davies.
[131] *South Wales Weekly Post*, 18 March 1916.
[132] *The Herald*, 24 February, 1917: 'Local Police Courts'.
[133] The Pearce Register contained three unidentified 'D. Evans' who were court-martialled at Cardiff. They were E. D. Evans, D. J. Evans and D. L. Evans.
[134] *Herald of Wales*, 17 August 1918.
[135] *Pioneer*, 23 November 1918.
[136] *Glamorgan Gazette*, 10 March 1916
[137] *Pioneer*, 17 June 1916.

Chapter Five:
Local support

'They spread their political gospel at every opportunity, and often in the open air ... on railway station square, at the side of the Grand Hotel, outside the Central Schools, on the Park and on Gallipoli field.'

(J. Ivor Hansen)

Introduction

THE PREVIOUS CHAPTER RECORDED the individuals from Port Talbot who had resisted conscription through the tribunal system. They were not alone, however, in opposing conscription and war. Other individuals, who were not eligible for service, or had been exempted, were also against conscription and played important roles locally to support the objectors. This chapter will identify some of the support, explaining the roles of both the individuals and the organisations involved.

Support for the seventy-four Port Talbot objectors whose experiences were detailed in Chapter Four is represented in the diagram on the next page.

1. The objectors themselves are represented by the innermost circle, number one.
2. Their local support, which is the subject of this chapter, is represented as ring number two.
3. Ring 3 represents Welsh support from outside the immediate area of Port Talbot is represented as ring three.
4. Support from elsewhere in Britain is the outermost ring, number four.

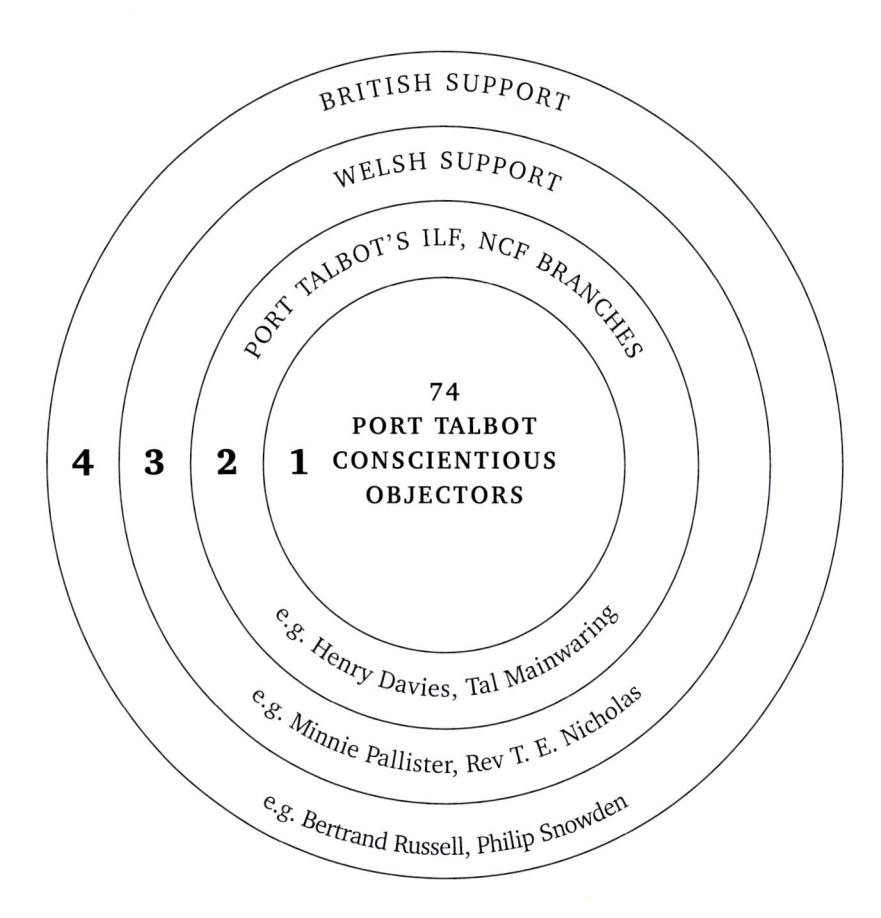

```
         BRITISH SUPPORT
           WELSH SUPPORT
        PORT TALBOT'S ILF, NCF BRANCHES
              74
          PORT TALBOT
  4   3   2   1  CONSCIENTIOUS
              OBJECTORS

       e.g. Henry Davies, Tal Mainwaring
       e.g. Minnie Pallister, Rev T. E. Nicholas
       e.g. Bertrand Russell, Philip Snowden
```

The pattern of local support and opposition

Much of the local support came from the three ILP branches at Aberafan, Cwmafan and Taibach, from the local NCF, and from groups within the miners, the steel and tin-workers and the railwaymen's unions. In general, the Labour Representation committee and the TUC nationally supported the war, but the ILP did not. To this hard core of support can be added some additional support from the chapels. Overall, the pattern of support, both for and against the war, was complex.

ILP badge

141

The chapels and churches

Some chapels supported the war and some did not. Some refused their facilities for peace meetings and others had to step in. For example, the refusal by Cwmafan's Methodist chapel to permit a 'Peace by Negotiation' meeting in March 1917, resulted in its diversion to Zion Baptist Chapel. 'Local jingos and conservatives attempted unsuccessfully to disrupt the meeting on the spurious grounds that it should be held in English, rather than Welsh!' Similarly, because of the previous incident, the Rev. T. E. Nicholas' meeting scheduled for Bethania, Cwmafan was transferred to the ILP centre a few days later. Although the Church in Wales in Port Talbot, showed support as an organisation for the war, a number of its individual congregants did not. Percy Warren Davies and Willie Rees were among these.

The relationship between some of the religious denominations and the ILP became strained. This was reflected in an ILP-originated newspaper article[138] which castigated some of the churches and chapels:

> 'The Sunday meetings arranged by the ILP at Cwmafan have become very popular. Although timed not to clash with religious services, and although the object of the meetings is in accord with the essentials of Christianity, the churches are doing their best to prevent the attendance of the youths by prolonging the religious services to an unusual extent. This narrow mindedness, vindictiveness and intolerance of the elders of the church is alienating the thoughtful young men from the chapel.'

On 9 January 1916 an anti-conscription meeting,[139] under the Chairmanship of Christopher Scott of the rail union, was held by Aberafan and Port Talbot trade unions to 'declare its strongest opposition to military service, believing conscription in any form to be a violation of the principle of civic freedom, hitherto prized as one of the chief heritages of British liberty'. Tom Llewelyn of the Steelsmelters moved the resolution and William Wyatt of the Dockers seconded it. Councillor Harry Davies of Taibach supported it for the Miners, with Tal Mainwaring, D. J. Jenkins and Alderman David Rees also speaking in support of the resolution.

The concern of the meeting was that 'men in civil employment should not be brought under military law'. If they were, then industrial action could be curtailed or prevented altogether. To emphasise the depth of the meeting's concern, copies of the resolution were sent to the Prime Minister, the Chair of the Parliamentary Labour Party, the Secretary of the ILP and the local MP. Later, in January, the Military Service Act brought conscription into effect.

Port Talbot had three ILP branches at Margam, Cwmafan and Taibach. Together they formed the Aberafan Labour Representation Committee, which was ably chaired by Lance Waters (1915), C. R. Scott and Tom Llewelyn of the Steelsmelters (1917). Of the three branches, Cwmafan was the strongest, having Dan Morris as Secretary and Harry Davies as Chairman. Its strength can be gauged from the fact that when extra funds were needed for its activities in 1918 the branch quickly raised £12, its 2016 value being £1113.

Some key figures who supported objectors from the ILP and the NCF, will be examined here, principally through the activities of Tal Mainwaring, the Secretary of Taibach ILP, and Harry Davies of Cwmafan. Mainwaring was an anti-conscriptionist who was exempted from military service but whose NCF activity saw him jailed for a Defence of the Realm offence. In contrast, Christopher Scott and Lance Waters, both ILP Chairmen, were also jailed during the war, but as conscientious objectors. In their absence Mainwaring was able to offer them support, and carry out many of their activities, during their absence. Daniel Watters of Cwmafan's reflections on the events at this time as a lay ILP member will enhance the picture.

The ILP/Labour Representation Committee was well-organised, with a lecture Secretary in Morgan Jones and a Marxist economics class run by Comrade Dick Bennetta. Its Executive committee included postal worker J. J. Franklin (Secretary), David Rees, Mayor in 1917, fitter Harry Batey, George T. Owen and Jenkin Williams. Not surprisingly, trade union support for the ILP was strong, involving Rees Llewelyn of Margam, the south Wales organiser for the Municipal Workers' Union, William Jackson, President of the Tin and Sheet Millmen's Association and also the rail unions.

The railway unions and their members in the district experienced serious problems as a result of the Military Service and the Defence of the Realm Acts, which brought results to a head in 1917. The effect of a second Military Service Act was to put extreme pressure on the rail workers of the district. As previously-badged members were 'combed out'[140] for military service, the hard pressed rail workers struggled to keep essential wartime services operating, using excessive overtime and labour substitution, but with precious little reward. To add insult to this injury, the heavy-handedness of Port Talbot police in interpreting the Defence of the Realm Act was winning few friends amongst the railmen. This came to a crisis point when a local branch Secretary of the NUR was taken to Port Talbot police station. The books and papers he was carrying, which were the Union's property, were examined. This action sufficiently inflamed the membership of Port Talbot, Maesteg and Cardiff No 5 branches for a mass meeting to be immediately called on Sunday 1 October[141] by A. J. Williams, the south Wales organiser of the NUR. Mr J. H. Thomas, the anti-conscription MP for Derby, addressed the meeting and clarified the limits of the state's rights to protect its citizens, calling for 'no repetition of the incident' and pointing out that the incident had taken things 'too far when the liberty of the subject was interfered with in this way'.

That opposition to conscription and war had gained some strength by 1918[142] after the 'comb-out' of its members in 1917. One result of this included a threat of labour withdrawal by the Port Talbot and Maesteg branches of the Locomotive Enginemen and Firemen's union. A joint resolution stated their position unequivocally, saying they were engaged in a 'persistent fight against the substitution of men employed on the footplate'. This was typical trade union business: the replacement of skilled men by unskilled. Aberafan and Margam tribunals joined forces to each send a deputation of three members to interview Sir Auckland Geddes, the Minister for National Service, about the recruitment matter[143].

There was an aspect, too, of international politics contained in a resolution which called the government to engage in 'immediate negotiations (to allow belligerent nations) to achieve self-determination with no annexations or indemnities.' The union stated that it would continue to support war aims as long as these objects were being pursued but, if the government failed to open negotiations it would act in resisting the government's manpower proposals. In other words, they would strike.

If that was not enough, the Maesteg branch endorsed an appended resolution:

'that this meeting strongly protests against the repeated imprisonment and penalisation of conscientious objectors as a violation of the clauses of the Military Service Acts intending to safeguard the historic right of individual freedom of conscience and opinion and demands their immediate release from prison and penal settlements.'

It was unsurprising, therefore, that the rail union, which had representatives who were ILP and NCF members, could find common cause with the objectors who were fighting against both conscription and the civil rights they claimed they were being denied by the Defence of the Realm Act.

By 1918, under the auspices of the National Union of Railway Workers, the unions were turning their attention to an ending of the war and a post-war settlement. TC Morris of the NUR presided over a meeting at the Grand Theatre, Aberafan to discuss these matters. Bob Williams spoke for the National Transport Union, Ernest Bevin for the dockers and Henry Davies for the miners.

The South Wales Miners Federation

The 'miners' will be considered through the organisation called the South Wales Miners' Federation. It ('The Fed') was formed in 1898 following a six-month strike and defeat. Henry Davies of Cwmafan had urged the Welsh colliers to join the Miners' Federation of Great Britain and, after the 1898 strike, it did. The Fed was so called because it was organised on a federal basis with twenty districts and a miners' agent for each. It did not have an anti-conscription or anti-war policy but it became linked with those matters through the likes of James Winstone. He was the miners' agent for eastern valleys in 1901 who became vice-president in 1912 and then President in 1915, the year he was defeated at Merthyr General election by C. Butt Stanton, the pro-war advocate. A Baptist lay preacher and an ILP member, Winstone was not a pacifist, having a son in the army, but he supported anti-conscription activities.

In July 1917, at the Dockers' Hall, Port Talbot, William Davies presided over thirty-six delegates representing 7,540 miners. They heard a resolution from Argoed Lodge 'protesting against the tendency to infuse the system of elementary education with the spirit of militarism by the instruction of military drills and methods in elementary schools and the formation of cadet corps in secondary schools'.[144] The motion was carried and copies were forwarded to the Board of Education and to Glamorgan Education Committee.

The miners and steelworkers were not always in complete harmony. Vernon Hartson, the chief miners' agent for Maesteg District and an ILP member, had indicated prior to a Conference at the Grand Hotel, Port Talbot that the new Aberafan constituency was 'earmarked as a miners' constituency.' This attracted a strong editorial reply;[145] 'seeing that the most populous parts of the constituency consist of iron, steel and tinplate industries and that the ILP has a tremendous following, it is a bit surprising to find the miners, or rather the miners' leaders claiming the seat without deigning to consult the other workers.' It continued to say that 'the choice of candidate should fall on the best man, whatever his vocation.'

Hartson was brought up amongst primitive Methodists in Monmouthshire and built up a reputation as a level-headed chief miners' agent for Maesteg District who had 'steered the miners' minds away from dangerous agitation' and spurred coal production'. In 1918 he was elected MP for Ogmore and became Post Master General in MacDonald's 1924 government.

In November 1918, Frank Hodges of the Miners' Federation of Great Britain came to the new Theatre in Taibach to remind everyone that 'Social Reconstruction' was a necessary part of the post war settlement and that it was necessary for all the unions to work together to achieve it.

In the event the Aberafan nomination went to Robert Williams, an anti-war advocate who previously had represented neither miner, nor steelworker but transport workers. Williams lost the 1918 election to Major John Edwards; leaving one to speculate on the effect of the minor schism amongst the trade unions may have affected the result.

The steelsmelters

Under Tom Llewelyn, the position of the steelsmelters on conscientious objection was clear; they were deemed to be soldiers under the Military Service Acts and the union would treat them as such; the fact that they did not bear arms was irrelevant.

The **NCF** will be examined through several individuals: John Morris, the branch secretary of Cwmafan NCF, Henry Davies, Tal Mainwaring and Daniel Watters.

Joe Branch (1869–1954)

The 'dockers' and their union's position on war and conscription are presented in this chapter through the person of Joe Branch and Robert Williams, who is discussed in the following chapter.

Branch was a founder member of the Aberafan ILP and its President from 1904 until 1934. In 1905 he was a founder member of mid-Glamorgan Labour Party and its Chair until it became Aberafan Parliamentary Division in 1918. Len Williams was a Briton Ferry delegate to Aberafan Labour Party. He claimed that 'The man responsible, more than anyone else for getting him (Ramsay Macdonald) into the constituency was Joe Branch.'[146]

Joe Branch

Branch was the son of a Cwmafan-born tinman. He was born and lived at 22 Lowther Street in Briton Ferry before his family moved to Railway Terrace in 1891.[147] At an early age Joe became a washman/tin finisher in Vernon Tinplate Works alongside his two elder brothers and soon became involved in trade unionism. By 1903, he was a Briton Ferry Urban District councillor and father of Irene Olive Branch. His growing political experience enabled him to go on and chair the council for five years, and, as a result of this, he became an ex-officio magistrate on Neath Magistrates' bench.

Branch's family often received visiting ILP speakers at their home even before Branch became Chair of Briton Ferry ILP: John Bruce Glasier is recorded as a guest on census night, 1911. Branch was then Chair of Briton Ferry Urban District Council, an Associate of the NCF (being outside military age), and a founding committee member of Briton Ferry Public Hall. Branch had also been one of the founder members of the Mid-Glamorgan Divisional Labour Party in 1905, until it became part of the Aberafan division. The year 1912 saw him become chair of Briton Ferry ILP and, in 1914, local Secretary of the Dockers' union, being Llanelli based for some ten years.

During World War One Branch was a staunch pacifist and, in 1916, he was prosecuted for handing out anti-war leaflets outside Briton Ferry's

Bethel Chapel. It is necessary to record here that the pastor of the chapel, the Rev. James Llewelyn, and its deacons, gave evidence in court. As a result, after the court case, Branch never again attended Bethel. At Joe Branch's funeral, significantly and appropriately, the Rev Trevor Evans of the pacifist Jerusalem Church officiated.

After his appointment as South Wales District Secretary of the tinplate section of the Transport and General Workers' Union (TGWU), Branch was in close touch with its then General Secretary, Ernest Bevin. Similarly, in his position as Chair, over many years, of Aberafan & District Labour Party, he had regular contact with Ramsay MacDonald, MP for Aberafan and first Labour Prime Minister in 1924. Not surprisingly perhaps, with contacts such as these, Branch became a Member of the Court of Governors of the University College of Swansea and attended its first meeting at the Guildhall in May 1920. No wonder that Len Williams, a fellow ILP member, considered him 'a very well-educated man'.

After 1922, when Briton Ferry Urban District Council was merged with Neath, he continued to represent Briton Ferry on the larger body. In 1932–33 he was Mayor and father of the council for several more years. A serious deterioration to his eyesight in 1934 caused him to retire from his TGWU post and his thirty-year long Presidency of Aberafan ILP.

At the age of 65, Alderman J. O. Branch retired from fully from his temporary post of Tinplate District Secretary but lived for twenty more years. His contribution to the Aberafan Labour Party, as an elected representative of the working man and the working man's family, was enormous; as was his wider contribution to a just society through his trade union and political activities. In this respect, perhaps all his beliefs, and his abilities to apply them, came into clear focus during his pursuit of peace and justice at the 1916 trial of the ten ILP/NCF members. Then, as President of the local branch of the ILP he said:

> 'I thought if the Christian Church would not speak out ... to call public attention to the barbarities imposed on men ... then it was the duty of someone else to do it.'

Joe Branch spoke out – for all of us.

Henry Davies – Cwmafan (1870–1953)

Davies was baptised in Cwmafan on 23 January 1870. At the age of twenty-three he married Mary Ann, and lived at 8 London Terrace, Cwmafan. Originally a miner, he was appointed the rate collector for the Parish of Michaelstone Lower of the Neath Poor Law Union and a member of Glamorgan County Council. Henry Davies was the leading ILP figure in Cwmafan, an NCF associate, and a frequent official at political and anti-conscription events throughout west and mid-Glamorgan, being President of Mid-Glamorgan ILP. Perhaps, above all else, he was an auto-didact of the highest order.

Henry Davies
(West Glamorgan Archives)

In July 1914, Davies was reported as 'delivering a stirring address' in support of Women's Suffrage, along with David Rees, Mayor of Aberafan, at the recently formed branch of the Women's Suffrage Society.[148]

We first hear of Davies in connection with conscription when an early attempt to hold an anti-conscription meeting took place, in December 1915, at the Grand Hotel, Port Talbot. It was thwarted when members arrived to find the doors locked. The event was transferred outdoors to a much colder Bethany Square, and that was not the last time it was necessary to hold meetings outdoors, or at secret venues. During one such meeting Davies made allegations that Councillor Percy Jacobs, the Mayor of Aberafan, had gone through the district advising the adoption of conscription. Jacobs denied the allegations and Davies' feelings on the war were expressed in a verse that he wrote in February 1916:

> *Blessed are the peacemakers, so Christ said,*
> *But men have lost the message;*
> *The world is strewn with sick and dead*
> *For nothing-but a mess of potage.*

Davies also became something of an expert on the conscription aspects of the Military Service Act. In March 1916, at the Glamorgan Appeal Tribunal at Port Talbot, Davies told the tribunal that he believed the instructions from the Home Office made it very clear that the tribunal had the power to grant absolute exemption from conscription. The chair, Mr F. W. Gibbins, retorted: 'If you understand all the instructions that are being issued, Mr Davies, you must be very clever. I don't.' Davies was right, however, because the official circular from the Home Office had said: 'Absolute exemption can be granted in these cases if the tribunals are fully satisfied of the facts'[149] and that 'The man who honestly and as a matter of conscience objects to combatant service is entitled to exemption'.

Davies also contributed to the *Pioneer* newspaper under the pen-name of *Democritus*, reporting on the progress and whereabouts of the conscientious objectors and ensuring that events such as the trials and imprisonment of the Defence of the Realm offenders were well-reported.

Davies was to Cwmafan what Joe Branch was to Briton Ferry: a leader with charisma. Their charisma was apparent when both represented their members at important legal proceedings. In Davies' case, the Glamorgan Gazette, of 31 March 1916, reported on a tribunal at which he represented no fewer than thirteen Port Talbot conscientious objectors who had refused non-combatant status. No wonder he was once also referred to as the *Welsh Keir Hardie!* The biographies of those he represented were presented in Chapter Four.[150]

Davies worked closely with Tal Mainwaring. Hansen wrote that 'They read every book they could lay their hands on, on the subject of socialism. Henry Davies had such a thirst for political knowledge that he was seen to dip his hands in a basin of cold water in order to read a book after returning home after a night shift.'

Later, in May 1916, he was charged by Superintendent Ben Evans with obstruction at an NCF rally in Bethany Square, Aberafan. Charges were also laid against three other local councillors who had spoken at the meeting: ILP Councillor Harry Davies of Taibach, ILP Councillor Tal Mainwaring of Margam and James Price, a miner and member of Aberafan Town Council, the Chair of the meeting.

A week previously the police had raided the ILP centre in Cwmafan and confiscated all the branch's literature, including the *Everett* and *Repeal the Act* leaflets. A subsequent court case resulted in charges against Tal Mainwaring, Dan Morris (Cwmafan ILP's Secretary) and ILP members Jenkin and William Williams for distributing circulars likely to prejudice recruiting. A parallel tribunal was held at Neath early in June 1916 in which Joe Branch was the principal defendant in a class action against him and nine others from Briton Ferry.

At the West Glamorgan Appeal Tribunal on 17 April 1916,[151] the similarity of an objector's written claim with several others was pointed out, alleging that Davies had written them all. In turn, Davies protested that a member of the tribunal, Alderman Davies, was 'thrusting his political views upon the appellant' when an objector claimed himself to be an international socialist. Davies was called to order, but another supporter then 'became demonstrative.'

A further meeting, chaired by Davies, was the cause of much trouble. It was held under the auspices of the NCCL at Gallipoli Square in Taibach on 18 June. At the meeting Fred Bramley, the TUC General Secretary, called for the repeal of the Military Service Act. This resulted in four members being charged, with imprisonment for Morris and Mainwaring, because they refused to pay their fines. A fuller description of their committal can be read later under the heading of *Tal Mainwaring*.

None of this deterred Davies. In July he chaired more public anti-war meetings in Cwmafan and Taibach. One involved Richard Wallhead and yet another Bertrand Russell in which he spoke 'to a large and appreciative audience near Cwmafan police station'.

On 10 July, the ILP's Rees Llewelyn, the south Wales Organiser of the Municipal Workers, presented a motion, seconded by Davies, 'that Margam Council strongly protest against the action of the police in persecuting British citizens for exercising acknowledged public rights by addressing a meeting at Bethany Square ... (and) ... to put on record a strong protest against the suppression of meetings at Taibach and other parts of the district ... (and) ... that the council decide to convene a public meeting to petition the proper authorities to restore to the people the right to free speech, and to demand of the government to pass a bill for the conscription of wealth.'[152]

Was it not also Davies who wrote under the nom de plume of 'Democritus'[153] to chastise the authorities for discrimination against the ILP and NCF in denying them their civil rights of assembly?

> 'Bethany Square, Aberafan, has been from time immemorial the vantage ground for all types of meetings, political, secular and religious. The Free Churches, Plymouth Brethren, Anti-Socialist Union, Naval League men, the ILP and various other organisations have used the spot for the exposition of their creeds and opinions, but since the war one organisation has been prohibited from holding meetings there. It will require no

strain on the imagination to guess what organisation that is.

The excuse of the police for this arbitrary preclusion of the ILP from Bethany Square is obstruction. True the place is verging on the highway, but other bodies can hold meetings there on any day of the week when vehicular traffic is at its height and the police like good Levites pass without a word of objection, but when the ILP starts a meeting, even on a Sunday when traffic is nil, the majesty of the law is evoked to curb the right of free speech-of course ILP free speech.'

Davies' energy was relentless: later that year he was at Briton Ferry Public Hall supporting Ethel Snowden in her call for peace negotiations.

In January 1918 a special conference of the ILP branch for the new Parliamentary division of Aberafan was held and Henry Davies was chosen as candidate.[154] That would have made a fitting epitaph for Davies, but events in his life had taken a sharp turn. In the course of doing work for the local Poor Law Board, he was personally arrested by none other than Superintendent Ben Evans, prosecuted for fraud and received a jail sentence. In March 1918, Llais Llafur, for whom Davies was a leader writer[155] under the pen name of 'Carrusk' reported the case in detail. Its report can be found in Appendix Six.

He was also later defeated in the County Council elections by none other than Percy Jacobs. At the end of the war, efforts were still being made to nominate Davies in opposition to William Jenkins JP, the well-known miners' leader, as the Labour candidate for the newly-created Aberafan constituency.[156] In the event Robert Williams, of the National Transport Federation and ILP, got the nomination. He lost it to the coalition Liberal, Major John Edwards, who in the 1924 General Election surrendered it to one James Ramsay MacDonald.

This might have ended all Davies' hopes of furthering his political ambitions, but it did not do so altogether. Although he lost his place, from being the front runner, for selection as a Parliamentary candidate, he became the Mayor of Swansea, in 1946.

> 'Harry Davies' work on behalf of the bottom dog has been purely disinterested. His labours have sprung from a desire to benefit his fellow man, and his steadfast adherence to principles in face of the vilest abuse, and sacrifice of his own personal interests

place him in the forefront of trustworthy men to whom the workers can relegate their cause'.

There can be little doubt that Davies was guilty of the alleged offences. One must, however, question how those offences were detected. Were the defalcations discovered in the normal course of auditing, or was there a speculative attempt by the authorities to incriminate him? More ominously, were there similar attempts against other ILP members? A second case, which aroused this suspicion followed: under the heading 'Engine driver charged with coal theft'[157]. David Jones, an ILP member engine driver at Baldwins and an overseer for Cwmafan was charged with stealing seven pounds of coal, value two pence[158]. In this case it was the Manager of Baldwins who spoke in defence of Jones as an 'exemplary employee'. Surely, this was a vindictive prosecution.

The last word on Henry Davies must come from Len Williams[159] of Briton Ferry: 'When Bertrand Russell became a conscientious objector, he came to Cwmafan, and he said, meeting Henry Davies, that he was the most well-read working man that he had ever met.'

Tal Mainwaring (1890-1968)

Seventeen of the cottages in Cwm Brombil were once occupied by the Mainwarings. Tal was the son of colliery blacksmith/farrier Samuel Mainwaring, who worked at Morfa pit. Ten days after Tal's baptism at Beulah Chapel, Groes, in March 1890, disaster was to befall the family. Five minutes after Sam descended the pit, a huge explosion occurred beneath him. Tal's two uncles, Noah and Thomas, were on duty in the bowels of the pit. Both died, along with eighty-five others, including thirty-three-year-old next-door neighbour, William Barras, the pit manager. The village became the scene of utter confusion and the school, which Tal's brother William attended, closed for a week.

Tal and his brothers, William, David and John, nevertheless became underground workers. The family, no doubt, fully understood Keir Hardie's castigation of the House of Commons in 1895 for not adding condolences to the families of the 257 victims of the Pontypridd pit disaster to their congratulations on the birth of Edward as royal heir to the throne.

After leaving school Tal joined his father at Morfa pit, at first as a surface worker, and later as a tram driver. By the age of eighteen he was a committee-man at his pit lodge and by the time he was twenty-three he was chairman.

'About this time there were emerging two men, both working in the coal industry, who dedicated their lives to socialism and to the affairs of the town. They were Alderman Harry Davies and Tal Mainwaring. They spread their political gospel at every opportunity and often in the open air.'[160]

Tal Mainwaring became interested in politics in his early twenties and by his late twenties was active in local politics. He became a Margam District Councillor, and an ILP and NCF member, working alongside ILP Secretary, Daniel Morris of Cwmafan. During 1914 the militants in the South Wales Miners' Federation were winning victories in their demands for higher pay and the following year, at a coalfield conference, a strike for a new wage agreement was called for. There existed an 'unconscious anti-war feeling' in the coalfield.[161]

In April 1915, Mainwaring was Taibach's delegate to the ILP National Conference at Norwich. At a Margam District Council Meeting 'on 14 December 1915,'[162] when a resolution was passed to set up a committee to

Morfa Colliery

consider what steps could be taken to stimulate recruiting, the motion was opposed by Mainwaring, a noted pacifist.'[163] When conscription came in 1916, Mainwaring was an early supporter for exemption from military service on political grounds, becoming Port Talbot District NCF Secretary, but he was not a conscientious objector, as many imagined. Tal Mainwaring was 'badged', meaning he was exempted from military service because his employer saw his employment in the pit as work of national importance. This was very convenient for the ILP and the NCF. It meant that Mainwaring could continue without too much interruption to his political activities from military service tribunals and the sentences they imposed. Yet it was whilst carrying out these activities that he was imprisoned for offences under the Defence of the Realm Act in June 1916.

Tal's activities in the NCF continued. One reason why he was anti-war was very clear: as a trade unionist he was concerned about military law in the pits, meaning that there could be no effective trade union action under a regime of militarism.[164] After a No Conscription Fellowship rally at Bethany Square, Port Talbot, in May 1916, Mainwaring was charged with obstruction, along with fellow Margam District Councillor Harry Davies, James Price of Aberafan Town Council and Henry Davies, of Cwmafan, the former member of Glamorgan County Council.

> 'Tal Mainwaring spoke with a pleasanter tenor voice (than Harry Davies), with his head thrown back defiantly, and with his hands grasping the lapels of his coat. Although I heard both men speak many times in public, I never heard them employ much humour, but Tal could lampoon opponents occasionally with dry humour. During one of Ramsay MacDonald's first general election campaigns locally, Tal devoted much of one speech to the columns of hostile press, and he caused many grins by referring to two newspapers as "The Daily Wail" and the "Western Mule".'[165]

On Sunday 18 June, an anti-conscription meeting was held in the afternoon, under the auspices of the National Council for Civil Liberties at Gallipoli Square, Taibach. It was chaired by Alderman Harry Davies. The speaker was Fred Bramley and its purpose was to demand the repeal of the Military Service Act. The reason given for holding it in that particular spot was reported: 'to avoid attention from the authorities because of their recent activity which unfortunately resulted in four of their comrades finding themselves in the police court.'[166] Following the fines imposed on Mainwaring and others, which they had refused to pay, Mainwaring was imprisoned for three months; Morris for two months.

If this was not enough, the authorities had also requested a private court hearing to destroy documents held at the ILP centre. It was reported on the day Mainwaring was taken to prison[167] that the titles of some of the documents seized were 'Baby clinics' and 'Help the babies.' The documents had been held there since 1910.

'Great waves of enthusiasm witnessed the departure of Councillor Tal Mainwaring and Dan Morris en route to Swansea Gaol from Aberafan station last Saturday evening (24 June)'.

> 'The police endeavoured to persuade them to pay, and showed their willingness to serve distress warrants on them but the two comrades refused their offer. ... Eventually the authorities sent for them at 5.30 pm and this time they were followed to the railway station by hundreds of enthusiastic people to see them off. Some of the crowds climbed the platform palings; women wept; and the men sang themselves hoarse and waved their headgear. Their attention was now diverted by the arrival of the train packed up with its Saturday night load of visitors to town. These people never left the platform, but were caught up in the well of enthusiasm and again the Red Flag was sung – this time with renewed vigour and joined in by the Aberafan Male Voice Party, who were leaving by the same train. It was an impressive scene. The singing having ceased a voice shouted out 'Are we downhearted'? "No" responded a thousand voices. Again and again this cry went up. And now silence reigned. Councillor Harry Davies had suddenly risen to speak and the few remarks he was able to make were generously punctuated with applause and "hear, hear". Movements on the platform indicated the departure of the train. Porters bawled out warnings and the guard hurried along the platform as best he could to close the doors. A green flag was waved, a shrill whistle sounded from the engine, and thus departed, the Comrades were gone – but the spirit remained.'[168]

After the first fortnight in Swansea jail Tal Mainwaring was already able to speak of his prison experiences and repeat Madame de Stael's pronouncement: 'I never knew what freedom was until I went to jail'. When he was released from jail on Saturday, 9 September, a demonstrative crowd of 2,000 awaited him in Port Talbot. Shortly afterwards a social was held in his honour at the Co-operative Hall in Taibach.[169]

On 10 July, 'arising from the suppression of public meetings at Bethany Square and elsewhere by the police under the Defence of the Realm Act, Rees Llewelyn and others had endeavoured to persuade the (Margam) Council to convene a public meeting to petition the proper authorities to restore the right of free speech. The suggestion provoked bitter feelings and the chairman was forced to close the meeting.'[170]

By October 1916 Mainwaring was already able to speak of his prison experiences at an NCF fund-raising social event in Briton Ferry. In his speech he spoke of 'political prisoners', the result of which was his prosecution. However, the ILP members of the British Steelsmelters' Union had ensured that it was Union policy to welcome back COs (and those serving sentences for sedition it seems) on the same basis as soldiers from the front.

The ILP branch at Taibach had no meeting rooms, so it was the private homes of members or officers such as Tal Mainwaring and Councillor Davies, which were raided. This was the equivalent of raiding the offices of a major political party today. On 13 January 1918 the Pioneer reported that the Magistrates Bench gave permission for Inspector Ben Evans to seize 25,000 leaflets from Mainwaring's home under S.51 of the Defence of the Realm Act. This, it should be noted was *before* there had been any evidence of public distribution and was given in his absence whilst he was in prison.

On another occasion: 'At Tal Mainwaring's house they were less successful, finding only the current number of the *Tribune* together with a number of pamphlets entitled "British Prussianism". And here again it reflects no great honour on the methods adopted by the civil authorities in raiding a man's house in his enforced absence.'

Mainwaring experienced a bout of pneumonia in 1917, which attracted much public sympathy in the area. His prison experiences were the motivation to set up a fund for the welfare of the dependents of south Wales conscientious objectors. Minnie Pallister, the President of Monmouthshire ILP and 'Wales' great woman orator', wrote to the *Pioneer* newspaper[171] in December under the heading 'You and Tal Mainwaring'. She said:

'I should have no anxiety for the welfare of the dependants of our south Wales conscientious objectors for a month or two. The very last thing comrade Mainwaring did, before he was seized with pneumonia, was to hand me donations received at my Port Talbot meeting, and it is largely his devotion to the ILP and the NCF, and consequent neglect of his own health, which brought on his illness. We all rejoice at his recovery.'

She continued by suggesting that further donations to the fund he created would be the best way for people to show their appreciation of his good works.

His attitude to the war was admirable: 'If we desire 'a durable peace ... all the peoples have to admit some guilt and share some blame for permitting their respective governments to pursue a foreign policy which was conducted behind the backs of people and which represented the material interests of capitalism and which ultimately brought about this war without the knowledge and consent of the peoples.'[172]

In 1917 the South Wales Miners' Federation 'decided to ascertain the views of the British labour movement on a Peace Settlement so that such views could be made to the labour movements of the belligerent powers and, on 8 October, a coalfield conference refused to assist in the recruitment of colliery workers into the army.'[173] That was at a time when Mainwaring and Harry Thomas of Cwmafan were shortlisted for a check-weighman's role at Oakwood colliery. They 'have received a very high testimonial regarding their qualifications for the job. The management, it is said, is extremely anxious that neither of them shall have the position.'[174]

Tal Mainwaring went on instead to become a check-weigher at Bryn colliery, and then a miners' agent. The latter position was one of 'considerable responsibility and had commensurate power and influence ... leadership by the agents could affect the whole industrial and political tenor of their districts. The quality required by these men were ... those of moderation, of financial acumen, pragmatism and administrative skill: not a recipe for a zealot'.

In 1933 he was elected to the executive of the South Wales Miners' Federation. He went on, too, to become Mayor of Port Talbot, not just once, in 1924–25, but again in 1952–53, also becoming a Freeman of Port Talbot Borough. It was his and Harry Davies' motion of May 1919, requesting the amalgamation of Aberafan and Margam Councils which had been instrumental in the creation in 1922 of the borough. Heol Taliesin in Cwmafan was named after him.

Tal married Dora Evans in 1919 and had five children. One, Frederick Samuel was Dai Mainwaring's father. Tal's grandson, Dai, was not very close to his grandfather because Dai's parents had moved to Birmingham. However, as a boy he did sometimes meet his grandfather … Dai remembers one occasion, at Villa Park football ground, when they attended an England v Wales soccer match in 1958. Tal not only related the tale of his imprisonment in Swansea, but he also told of a visit to the USSR in the 1920s (with TUC General Secretary, Fred Bramley, and Bob Williams, Secretary of the National Transport Workers' Federation). The purpose of the visit, which coincided with the Labour Day celebrations, was to discuss the formation of a new, international, group of trade unions. Bernard Mainwaring, a nephew of Tal, claimed that Tal spoke over the radio to Britain to describe the march-past. The schedule also involved visiting the Kremlin and each member of the delegation was presented to the General Secretary of the Central Committee of the Communist Party of the Soviet Union: Tal had whispered to Dai that he could not forget Josef Stalin's eyes, as they seemed to be so full of cruelty. Fred Bramley died in office the following year.

Fred Bramley
(TUC collection)

John Morris (1875–1945)

Morris was born at Church Square in Cwmafan, but as the family grew in size, a move was made to London Terrace. John was the much elder brother of Dan Morris, and worked as a tinplate bundler. The move to London Terrace was the likely point at which John became involved with labour politics. Eventually he became a very active NCF Branch Secretary at Cwmafan, at the time of Dan's troubles with the law.

His daughter, Kate Morris, was a member of the local Women's Labour League, a pressure organisation to promote the political representation of women in parliament. Both Cwmafan NCF and the league had connections with the Amalgamated Society of Railway Servants. It is unsurprising that later visits to Port Talbot were made by several notable socialist women such as Margaret Bondfield.

Daniel Watters (1865-1947)

Dan Watters was born and bred in Cwmafan, but was not related to Lancelot Waters' family. On leaving school he first worked in a tinplate works and lived at Ebbw Vale Row. After marriage, now a coalminer, he moved to Hazlewood Row. Most of his neighbours were copper workers and it was not long before Dan also moved into copper smelting work. By his mid-thirties, he had spent over a decade in all three of the industries that characterised Cwmafan, coal, copper and tinplate. These years undoubtedly provided him with much political insight.

When war approached Watters, now living at Ynysygwas Terrace, had gained even more industrial experience and political awareness through his ILP membership. He did not support the war and, being over the age to be conscripted, joined the NCF as a proud Associate Member. It was this experience that motivated Watters to express his views on topical issues in the form of political illustrations. Often these were drawn in family autograph albums where several cartoons of Lloyd George appeared, showing the Prime Minister's harsh attitude towards conscientious objectors. He was also graphically eloquent on the role that women were playing politically during

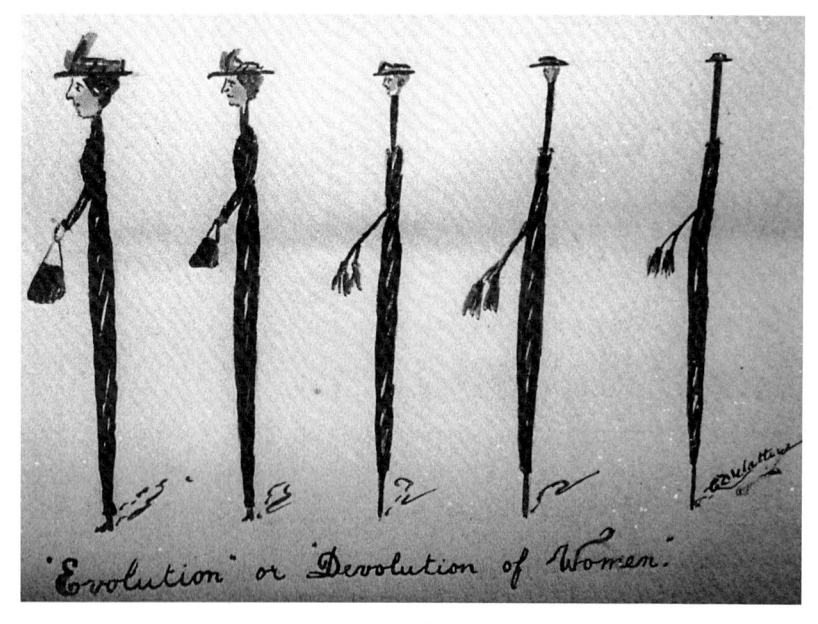

Evolution or devolution of women? *(Philip Mort)*

the war, particularly the schism that was emerging amongst them as to whether they should or should not support the war. His cartoon 'Evolution or devolution of women'[175] is interesting for a number of reasons: the image shows a progression of female figures towards a headless torso. This could be likened to a weapon of war; a bayonet on a rifle.

The topic of evolution, following the themes of Darwin and others, was still a divisive issue whilst devolution had not yet gained its modern meaning and was defined as *degeneration*.[176] Was Watters saying that support for the war by some of the suffragette movement would damage their cause? Given his membership of the ILP and NCF in Cwmafan, it seems likely that Watters would have supported women's suffrage and been bitterly disappointed by those who supported the war, which had led to a *devolution* of women. There may be other explanations linked to press comments at the time, but this hypothesis seems to be the most likely.

Watters' biography demonstrates how the political culture of Cwmafan enabled an elementary educated, working class, boy to comprehend contemporary domestic and international affairs. He then used this understanding to engender an awareness amongst the population that they were exposed to much tendentious militaristic propaganda. That was not all: it is clear that Watters and his contemporaries in the ILP were not merely against war and conscription; they also positively advocated progressive social change.

Conclusion

This chapter considered the local support that the objectors received, from both individuals and various religious, political, and trade union organisations, and how that support was demonstrated.

The next chapter will consider the national support that the Port Talbot conscientious objectors, their supporters and supporting organisations, which were described in this chapter, in turn received from nationally-known individuals and organisations.

Notes for Chapter Five

[138] *Pioneer*, 8 September 1917.
[139] *Glamorgan Gazette*, 14 January 1916.
[140] Shortly after becoming Prime Minister, Lloyd George reneged on pledges given to Trades Unions in 1916 that 'badged' members would not be affected.

[141] *Pioneer*, 29 September 1917 and 6 October 1917.
[142] *Pioneer*, 23 February 1918.
[143] *Cambria Daily Leader*, 27 November 1917.
[144] *Cambria Daily Leader*, 31 July 1917.
[145] *Pioneer*, 12 January 1918.
[146] David Egan and Richard Lewis South Wales Miner's Library: Transcription of audio tape AUD/282 (Swansea 1974).
[147] Lowther Street and Railway Terrace were demolished in 1973.
[148] *Glamorgan Herald*, 11 July 1914.
[149] *Glamorgan Gazette*, 11 February 1916.
[150] Joseph N Davies, Albert Rankin Evans, William Grane, Edward Haycock, John Haycock, Joseph Llewelyn, Arthur Millington, David Mort, William Mainwaring, Daniel H. Phillips, Christopher R Scott, William Arthur Thomas and Lancelot Thomas Waters
[151] *Herald of Wales*, 22 April 1916.
[152] J. Ivor Hansen, 1968, as before.
[153] *Pioneer*, 8 September 1917.
[154] *Pioneer*, 19 January 1918.
[155] Martin Wright, 'Wales and Socialism: Political Culture and National Identity c 1880–1914' (University of Cardiff, PhD Thesis, 2011).
[156] *South Wales Weekly Post*, 26 January 1918; Pioneer 26 January 1918.
[157] *Herald of Wales*, 25 February 1918; *Cambria Daily Leader*, 2 March 1918.
[158] Its equivalent value in 2016 is £0.63.
[159] David Egan and Richard Lewis, as before.
[160] Hansen J. Ivor, 1968, as before.
[161] Hywel Francis and Dai Smith, 1980, as before.
[162] A. Leslie Evans, 'Minutes of Margam UDC', in: Transactions of Port Talbot Historical Society no 3 Vol III, (1984).
[163] Mainwaring was only a 'pacifist' in common usage of the term. He was not a conscientious objector, but he stood up for their rights, especially not to be conscripted.
[164] *Glamorgan Gazette*, 14 January 1916.
[165] J. Ivor Hansen, 1968 as before.
[166] *Pioneer*, 24 June 1916.
[167] *Pioneer*, 24 June 1916.
[168] *Pioneer*, 1 July 1916.
[169] *Pioneer*,23 September 1916.
[170] A. Leslie Evans, as above.
[171] *Pioneer*, 8 December 1917.
[172] Letter to the *Pioneer*, 11 August 1917.
[173] Francis and Smith – as before.
[174] *Pioneer*, 13 October 1917.
[175] The cartoon may be a reversal of an idea of Sarah M. Severance, the American women's suffrage advocate. She wrote on the Devolution and Evolution of Women in order to express her views on the inequality experienced by women in historic European and Asian cultures, women's employment and responsibilities to family and church
[176] *Oxford English Dictionary*.

Chapter Six:
National support

*'To preach war is fine
but to preach peace is politics'*
                                            Rev Rees Powell, Briton Ferry[177]

Introduction

THE GROWTH OF THE ILP and the NCF in south Wales was encouraged by many nationally-known speakers who spent considerable time visiting the coal-mining valleys and the steel and tin-plate manufacturing centres along the industrial coastal strip. They advocated many of Keir Hardie's policies and, through their messages, sought to apply them. The phenomenon of speakers visiting such areas as Port Talbot had started at the beginning of the twentieth century, when industrialisation was already well-established, and continued after the war. The speakers, whether economist, philosopher, politician or religious in background, were aware of the imminent dangers to peace and to the labour market posed by the toxic mix of industrialism, colonialism and capitalism.

When their efforts to promote peace failed to prevent the outbreak of war, their visits increased in number to explain how secret treaties had led to war, the dangers of conscription during the war and the perils for peace of post-war reparations and annexations. To some of the populace the visitors were most welcome, but to the state, all too frequently, they were seen as a threat to its increasing militarism and, therefore dangerous and subversive.

These visitors, like the Port Talbot conscientious objectors and the men at the front, were prepared to pay for their beliefs. And pay they did. Many of them suffered imprisonment, torture, deprivation and mental illness.

They fought against many of the injustices of the tribunal system and the cruel sentencing under the Defence of the Realm Act. They became political prisoners who fought for the rights of women and children and, particularly, the fight for freedom of expression and conscience. In daring to defy the establishment, they, alongside the suffragettes, the Port Talbot objectors and their supporters, fought for causes that gained some of the human rights that we enjoy today.

They were not alone. Many members of the public, as well as the organisations to which they belonged, gave them direction, support and legitimacy. This chapter will examine the national organisations and some key nationally known visiting speakers, including women visitors.

The Independent Labour Party

The prefix 'independent' indicated independence from the Liberal party, and not the Labour Party. After the 1892 general election the Trade Union Congress (TUC) proposed the foundation of a new party and a year later the ILP was founded in Bradford, with Keir Hardie as its first Chair. It, along with the TUC, the Social Democratic Federation and the Fabian Society, played a central role in the formation of the Labour Representation Committee. This committee was the forerunner of the Labour Party, which was formed in 1906. The ILP was affiliated from 1906 until 1932.

The Cwmafan ILP Branch was one of Wales' strongest, a fact attributed to its recruitment levels and strong leadership in the mines, steel and tinplate works and railways, where membership was mainly drawn from manual trade unions. Several of its leaders were Town Councillors. In Cwmafan ILP it was customary for members to refer to each other as 'comrade'. 'The ILP's Sunday meetings were timed not to clash with religious services, but the 'churches (were) doing their best to prevent the attendance of youths by prolonging the religious services to an unusual extent.'[178] This alienated many young men from the churches.

The Union of Democratic Control (UDC)

The Union of Democratic Control's purposes were: to campaign to ensure that foreign policy would be under parliamentary and not militarist control; to promote negotiations to take place after 1918 in order to prevent future conflict and to campaign for a peace settlement that would not humiliate defeated nations or result in artificial boundaries which could cause further future friction. Of importance for Port Talbot, in terms of Aberafan Parliamentary Constituency, was that Ramsay MacDonald, was amongst its founders alongside Charles Trevelyan, Arthur Ponsonby and E. D. Morel. The UDC was effectively a coalition of the ILP and Liberal critics of the war. Its policy was adopted entirely by the ILP in 1915 and President Wilson's 14-point post-war Peace Program was based on the UDC's policy. I have seen no evidence of the UDC having any members in Port Talbot area but much sympathy with its aspirations was, nevertheless indicated by events.

The No Conscription Fellowship (NCF)

The NCF had many members in the Port Talbot area, doubtless because it encompassed religious and secular objectors alike. The Fellowship believed that arms should not be borne to take human life, which was sacred. The national organisation advised members eligible for conscription how to present their cases for absolute exemption on grounds of conscience and offered some support to families. The movement was well-known for its efficient administration of the Conscientious Objectors' Information Bureau under Catherine Marshall which enabled it to trace and record the whereabouts of its incarcerated members. It is from NCF records that the identities of many of its members in Port Talbot have been discovered. The Pearce Register has drawn on Marshall's records to create a national database of conscientious objectors.

The NCF's founders were Bertrand Russell, Clifford Allen, from Newport, and Fenner Brockway. Morgan Jones of Bargoed was a very influential early member. He anticipated the introduction of conscription and its scope. Before it was introduced, the NCF asked men between eighteen and thirty-eight whether they were opposed to engaging in combatant activities and those who said 'yes' were its first members. The Fellowship was a confluence of religious and political dissent. It existed from November 1914 until November 1919, before it eventually merged with the Peace Pledge Union and became the *No More War* movement. It was originally only open to men liable for conscription and had 100,000 members in 1916. The organisation exhibited aspects of both pacifism and civil liberties and was organised as a semi-covert organisation, modelled on Sinn Fein and the Suffragette models.

The south Wales branch was formed at Briton Ferry on 19 June 1916, when Morgan Jones was elected as its branch chair. Bertrand Russell visited Port Talbot in July 1916 in his capacity as the NCF's national Chair.

The Fellowship of Reconciliation (FoR)

The Fellowship was founded in 1914 by Henry Hodgkin, a British Quaker, and a German Lutheran, who was once Chaplin to the Kaiser. The Rev. Richard Roberts of Blaenau Ffestiniog was its first Secretary and Wales' George M. Ll. Davies, a conscientious objector with Jenkin William James at Knutsford, was also a founder member. The Fellowship was not a passive peace movement: it was anti-war and for reconciliation and placed a strong emphasis on the individual's conscience to achieve these. It eschewed biblical references stressing that love is the only basis for human society but, as Christians, members were forbidden to wage war and urged co-operation with non-Christian faiths. It played a prominent role in acting as a support network for Christian pacifists during World War One, especially concerning the difficult choice of whether or not to become a conscientious objector. It is possible that Port Talbot's David John Jones, the theology student, was a member.

Despite the FoR's membership being small in number, the emphasis on individual responsibility by the Quakers and the FoR may have helped to give rise to the notion that conscientious objectors acted individually and alone. For Port Talbot's objectors, whether socialist or religious, nothing could be further from the truth.

Women's organisations and visits to Port Talbot

Women visitors played an important part in supporting peace and anti-conscription activities in Port Talbot during the war. Their support was largely facilitated through the ILP, many of whose members also belonged to organisations, which fought for women's rights. The ILP supported both peace and women's rights.

The Women's Freedom League's (WFL) is an important example. Its formation had taken place in 1907, when seventy members broke off from the WPSU. The autocratic behaviour and preference for violent protest advocated by Emmeline and Christabel Pankhurst of the WPSU, in order to win the vote for women, was unwelcome to others, like Charlotte Despard, who joined the League to secure the vote through democratic means and peaceful protest.

When Messrs Beith, Parkes and Fagan of the League visited Port Talbot in 1910, their call was for the 'return of an MP in favour of votes for women'. Little pacifism was yet spoken of. However, in 1914, the ILP hosted a meeting of the Women's Suffrage Society (NUWSS) under the chairmanship of Henry Davies. This would turn out to be a significant event for the ILP in Port Talbot because of the reciprocity that was generated by members of the NUWSS such as Charlotte Despard and Maude Royden. They were also members of the WFL and, as the WFL's peaceful protest to secure the vote gradually became aligned with a more general pacifism, the WFL supported the Women's Peace Council to achieve a negotiated peace settlement. This was especially the case after the introduction of conscription.

Organised through Cwmafan's Kate Morris of the National Federation of Women Workers (NFWW), and chaired by James Price of the ILP, Margaret Bondfield's visit in November 1915 was aimed at emphasising the difference between women and men's earnings for similar work. She also revealed in her speech, 'Let my country awake', her interest in the Union of Democratic Control and a peace settlement.

The 1916 cartoon by Cwmafan ILP member Dan Watters demonstrated that the political role of women was already a matter of considerable interest in Port Talbot – at least for the ILP. Indeed, when Ethel Snowden spoke of the need for a 'lasting and honourable peace' in December at Briton Ferry it was Henry Davies of Cwmafan who chaired the proceedings. In October 1917, Mrs Anderson-Fenn[179] spoke at Cwmafan and the New Dockers' Hall of the 'Women's Peace Movement'. The visits of these women not merely provided serial reminders of the issues of peace, anti-conscription and women's rights, they cemented them together. Minnie Pallister, Wales's ILP organiser ensured that these reminders continued during her visits. In November 1918 she explicitly called for workers' wives to join the ILP.

Meanwhile, in December 1917, Ethel Snowden had visited. She was Philip Snowden's wife and a founder member of the Women's Peace Crusade, the first popular campaign to link feminism with anti-militarism. The crusade's main demand for a people's peace was made through non-violent protest. Her aim was to encourage Port Talbot to form a branch. She succeeded, following a rousing call for 'a speedy and democratic end to the war'. Shortly afterwards, in February 1918, Charlotte Despard spoke at Cwmafan of the 'Qualification of Women Act and its implications'.

One very important woman who did not visit was Catherine Marshall, the NCF's Parliamentary Secretary, and Acting Secretary after Clifford Allen's imprisonment. She, instead, ensured that, as Port Talbot's male members were being imprisoned, their whereabouts and experiences were continually tracked and recorded.

The spectrum of interests of the women visitors therefore included military and industrial conscription, peace, pacifism, socialism, mothers' and children's rights and universal suffrage.

Mrs Anderson Fenn

Mrs Anderson Fenn visited Cwmafan and the New Dockers' Hall Port Talbot in October,1917 . She was a delegate to the 1919 Zurich Congress of the Women's international League for Peace and Freedom. The Congress urged the Peace conference then meeting in Paris to include a Women's Charter in the final peace treaty. The twelve-point charter included equal suffrage, equal pay and opportunities in employment and education and economic support for mothers.

Zurich Congress of the Women's international League for Peace and Freedom 1919
Included are Margaret Ashton, Harriet Briggs, K. D. Courtney, Mrs Crawford, Charlotte Despard, Gertrude Eaton, Mrs Anderson Fenn, Miss I. O. Ford, Mrs Giles, Miss Hardcastle, Huth Jackson, Mrs Pethick Lawrence, E. M Leaf, Chrystal Macmillan, E. Macnaghten, Catherine Marshall, Annot Robinson, Miss Royds, Mrs Rollo Russell, A. Salter, M. Sheepshanks, Mrs Philip Snowden, Mrs Swanwick, Ellen Wilkinson, Dr Ethel Williams and T. Wilson. *(TUC Collection)*

William Crawford Anderson (1877-1919)

Billy Anderson spoke up in Parliament about matters of conscription and civil rights in Port Talbot and was already a key national ILP figure when he raised the subject of the raid on Cwmafan ILP centre.[180] He was exhaustively educated at the instigation of his mother, an ardent radical. In Aberdeen he attended meetings of the Social Democratic Federation before he became Chair of the shop assistants' union in Glasgow. At Glasgow branch of the ILP, he gained a strong reputation as a public speaker, addressing audiences on subjects ranging from Tariff Reform to National Service.

Billy Anderson

By 1908 he was elected to the ILP's National Administration Council. Fenner Brockway believed that his position, together with his warm manner, helped maintain party unity and succeeded F. W. Jowett as ILP Chair in 1910. He wrote *What means this labour unrest?* and then launched the *Daily Citizen* with Ramsay MacDonald in 1912. Anderson aimed to reassure Labour that their suspicions of the ILP were ill-founded. He advocated the nationalising of land, writing *Socialism, the Dukes and the Land*.

He was a national figure when he spoke with reference to the recent charges brought against Tal Mainwaring, Dan Morris and Jenkin and William Williams under the Defence of the Realm Act. In the first part of his speech he dealt with the raid and then proceeded to deal with Tal Mainwaring's case. He said:

'The next case I want to draw your attention to is a prosecution under the Defence of the Realm Act at Port Talbot Police Court on June 8 when a man named Mainwaring, who was a socialist and a local Councillor, was charged with an offence under Section 27 of under the Defence of the Realm Act at a meeting about conscription on May 7, and three other men were charged with distributing leaflets. The men were defended very brilliantly by my honourable and learned friend, the Member for Carmarthen Boroughs (Mr Llewelyn Williams). The Mainwaring speech, in my opinion, ought never to have been made the subject of a prosecution. There is reason to believe, if the Home Secretary wants information on this point, that this matter was instigated not by the military authorities, not by any responsible military officer, but by Mr Percy Jacob, the Mayor of Aberafan, who is chair of the Aberafan Military Tribunal, and who that morning left his own police court to sit in judgment upon this case.

If the Home Secretary will care to look into this matter, he will see that Councillor Mainwaring's speech had absolutely nothing to do with recruiting. It was never in his mind to influence recruiting, and if you are going to stretch that Act so that you are going to bring a charge that a man in such a case is prejudicing recruiting, there is not one critical word spoken, either in this house or outside that could not, by stretching of this sort, be brought under the measure. Or, Mainwaring made no reference to recruiting and it showed very clearly what the police attitude was. Just listen to this slight dialogue between the defending counsel and Inspector Rees, who warned the speakers before they started that if they did speak trouble would be likely to follow.

Mr Williams: 'Were you prepared to prevent him speaking?'
Witness: 'I know his general views; I had that in my mind at the time.'
Mr Williams: 'You were prepared, before he opened his mouth, to prevent him making a public speech?'
Witness: 'I had an idea what he would say'.

In Germany, where everything is wrong, the police very often go to the meeting, and when something is said of which they do not approve, they hold up a hand and the meeting is stopped. We have very often laughed at that and condemned it; and said how much better off we were in this country, but here are the police, before a man opens his mouth, take it upon themselves to warn him that every word he is going to say is going to be taken down, and that the man is likely to get into trouble. The whole purpose of this penalty was to put down the meeting. There was no question of the defence of the realm being involved in the matter. Councillor Mainwaring is a man of high character, respected locally, a man who has held meetings without a word of interruption and he has gone down for three months under the sentence.

Another man, Dan Morris, a local postman, has not only gone to prison, but he loses his situation as well. I think that if it is at all possible, the Home Secretary should cause some investigation to be made in this case, which I suggest is harsh and vindictive and see what can be done in regard to what, in my opinion, is a grave public scandal. I do suggest very strongly that this sort of thing is a travesty of justice.'

His opposition to the war and support for the Clyde Workers' Committee cost him his parliamentary seat in 1918. He died of influenza in 1919, having just completed a further book: *The Menace of Monopoly. An argument for Public Ownership.*

The significance of Anderson for Port Talbot's war resistance was that he gave an early and reasoned lead to the ILP to denounce support for the war. 'Each country in turn, largely through the influence of its jingo press has been stampeded by fear and panic ... powerful armaments' interests have played their sinister part, for it is they who reap rich harvest out of havoc and death'. Apart from the crucial issue of free speech, Anderson also highlighted, during the war, how civil-military relations were threatened through loss of civilian control to the military and how justice was threatened when there were clear conflicts of interest in the case of people like Percy Jacobs, who appeared to act as both prosecution and judiciary because of his roles in the tribunal and police court.

Rev. T. E. Nicholas (1879–1971)

Thomas Evan Nicholas' life was motivated by the radical aspects of the gospels. The resulting convictions he espoused were to fight for the disadvantaged, fight against injustices and war and comment on the battle between capitalism and the working class. He first worked at Treherbert as a stonemason before deciding to enter the ministry. In order to do so he enrolled at Gwynfryn School in Ammanford where he absorbed Christian Socialism and married. He expressed himself through the pulpit; he was ordained in 1901 and accepted the invitation in 1904 to join Capel Seion in Glais.

Rev. T. E. Nicholas
(Wikipedia)

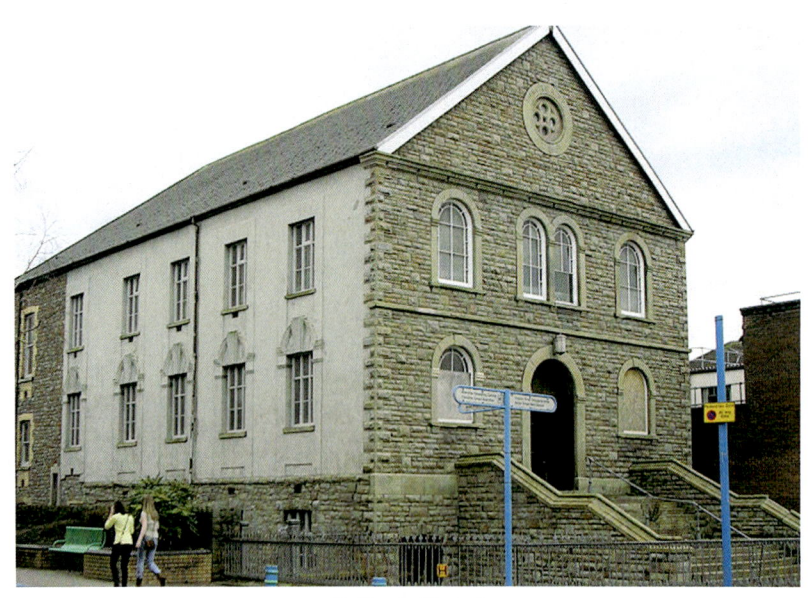

Bethania Chapel

The Pembrokeshire-born poet, preacher and advocate for the weak joined the ILP in 1905 in his efforts to help in unionising the agricultural and industrial workers of Wales. Over the next decade he developed into a passionate Welsh advocate for socialism and, at the same time, became a favourite of the Glais miners because he stood by them in their disputes.

After he left Glais in 1914 he wrote a series of articles on the 'Unjust War' for the *Pioneer*, which Keir Hardie had asked him to edit in Wales. The newspaper featured local news but Nicholas also ensured it covered matters such as socialism, peace, justice, equality, nationalisation, politics and education. This brought him under the suspicion of the authorities for the first time.

His stature can be measured by the fact that he delivered Keir Hardie's funeral address in 1915. Just like the Rev. Rees Powell of Briton Ferry, he was unafraid of delivering political messages from his own pulpit at Glais or anywhere else. That is exactly what he did at Bethania Chapel on 18 June 1916.[181] In 1918 he even stood, unsuccessfully, for Parliament at Merthyr against the war supporter, C. B. Stanton. During the 1920s and 1930s he supported the Soviet system, but in 1940 was arrested for supporting fascism and was interned in Swansea and Brixton prisons until public pressure resulted in his release.

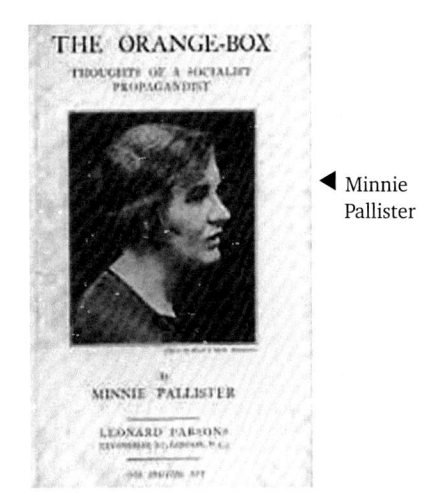

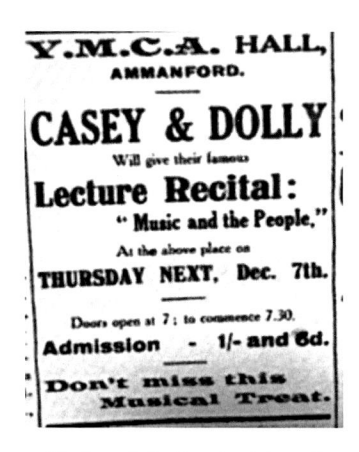

Music and the People: Advert for a Lecture Recital

Minnie Pallister (1885–1960)

Minnie Pallister's early life in was spent in Brynmawr where her father, a Methodist minister received preferment. She was an excellent piano player and elocutionist and was a teacher by profession. At the University College of South Wales and Monmouthshire she gained a double first, studying social and economic questions and doing much fieldwork with local families.

In June 1914, Pallister was elected President of Monmouthshire ILP, the first woman to hold such a position in Wales. In this role she spoke at events throughout south Wales. After speaking in Llanelli, the *Llanelli Star* described her as 'Wales' Great Woman Orator'. Keir Hardie described her as 'A new meteor on the horizon'.

Pallister was concerned about the welfare of children and not only encouraged women to use their vote, but to vote ILP, so that the party's policies for child welfare could be put in place. When she visited the Dockers' Hall and Taibach, in November 1918, on a two-day visit organised by the ILP and Co-op Guild, she encouraged workers and their wives to enrol in the ILP. She linked child welfare to her anti-conscription stance: in a speech at the Olympic Rink, Merthyr, she said: 'the government is irresponsible for children to the age of eighteen and then steps in and claims them as their own'.

In her travels around Wales Pallister spoke at peace meetings which were often attended by police officers and a police reporter. As the organiser of the NCF in Wales she had spoken in Briton Ferry of Butler, the Stockport conscientious objector who had died after he contracted tuberculosis on his third confinement in Preston prison. His mother's request for relief on health grounds had been refused by the Home Office.

Pallister was speaking in the open air on Cimla Common, Neath in August, but the rain, or was it the police presence, that resulted in a small crowd? At Briton Ferry in December 1918, at a meeting to support Reverend Herbert Morgan as ILP candidate for Neath, she was supported by a very large crowd. When she returned there in March 1924, she could take advantage of the occasion to promote her recently written book: 'The Orangebox: thoughts of a Socialist Propagandist'.

Pallister was sufficiently accomplished as a pianist to accompany the celebrated violinist, Casey, on his ILP-supporting 'lecture recitals' around south Wales, when Dolly, his regular pianist, was not available. Casey even suggested a national tour together 'to present a new common foundation for an international brotherhood'. The Amman Valley Chronicle reported that 'a serious truth lies in his remarks'. Pallister inscribed her adherent's notebooks with such quotes as this, from William Morris:

> 'Then that which the worker winneth
> Shall then be big indeed
> Nor shall half he reaped for nothing
> By him that sowed the seed'.

She also composed an election battle song for Ramsay MacDonald's campaign in the Aberafan constituency. It was to the tune of *Men of Harlech*:

> 'Ramsay, Ramsay. Shout it.
> Don't be shy about it.
> Labour's day is bound to come,
> We cannot do without it.
> On then Labour, on to glory
> 'Twill be told in song and story,
> How we fought at Aberafan
> On Election day'.

Bertrand Russell (1872–1970)

Russell was one of the foremost philosophers of the twentieth century, but to the general public he was best known as a campaigner for peace and as a popular writer on social, political and moral subjects. 'During a long, productive and often turbulent life, he published more than seventy books and about 2,000 articles, married four times, became involved in innumerable public controversies, and was honoured and reviled in almost equal measure throughout the world.'[182]

Bertrand Russell

He was Welsh, born near Cwmbran, in Monmouthshire. His early life was tragic because, before he was six, his parents, sister and grandfather all died and he and his brother were brought up by his grandmother, with Bertrand being educated at home and studying mathematics joyfully. His isolation came to an end when he entered Trinity College in Cambridge. Russell was a Lecturer there, having written the *Principles of Mathematics* in 1903 with A. N. Whitehead, and having become a Fellow of the Royal Society.

During the War he took an active part in the NCF. He was dismissed by Trinity College after being fined a hundred pounds for writing a leaflet criticising a sentence of two years' imprisonment for a conscientious objector. The war had a profound effect on his political views, in which he abandoned his inherited liberalism in favour of a thorough-going socialism.

Russell was the author of the *Everett* leaflet. It had described the dismissal from his post of a Lancashire teacher who was a socialist conscientious objector and received terrible treatment in prison. The ILP's possession and distribution of the *Everett* and *Maximilian* leaflets in Port Talbot led to the police raid on Cwmafan ILP Headquarters, on Tal Mainwaring's home, and the charges against Mainwaring, and others under the Defence of the Realm Act.

In July 1916 Russell delivered public speeches on his Welsh tour, organised by the NCAC and NCF and with ILP endorsement. His theme was that the war was a war between governments and not between peoples. On the afternoon of 2 July a meeting in Gallipoli Square, Taibach[183] was reported:

Russell at the BBC microphone

'Here one perceived a man that suggested the carelessly dressed student. Dressed in a suit of rough brown cloth, ravelled neck-tie, slouched hat and low boots, one could easily have mistaken this Professor of Mathematics for a typical working class orator. His speech was tinged here and there with a little humour, and one really expected it from the habitual smile that characterised his face. It was not an eloquent, but rather a simple and direct address for an age of reason and rational thought; for a 'just, lasting and honourable peace'. 'Newspapers in this country have kept from us things that we ought to know. It is not well-known in this country that Germany, for some time past, has had no intention whatsoever of retaining Belgium at the end of the war, and that they are willing to evacuate Belgium as a condition of Peace. We were told when this war began that it was a war on behalf of Belgium, and a very large number of men have lost their lives in that belief. The Germans are willing to evacuate Belgium on the day that peace is made. You cannot say that we are fighting on behalf of France. You know that the French nation has suffered terrible and appalling losses of men. Those of us who are aware of the feeling in France know that the French people are very desirous of peace. The Germans and Austrians are very desirous of peace, and you will find the same opinion in the United States. 'the prolongation of war . . . is due to our unwillingness to enter into peace negotiations, is due to our jealousy of German trade, and our accumulation of hatred'.

'It would be far better to spend these enormous amounts of money on the education of the country, rather than in using it to waste human life.'

Present were seven police officers and a shorthand reporter, apparently working on behalf of the police. A police official was heard to say of the

The Grand Hotel, Port Talbot

ILP after the meeting to a fellow officer: 'We have just about finished them now'. Chairman (Mr Henry Davies) was in his usual form, later suggesting that the officer should 'develop a better sense of observation' because the ILP branches were anything but finished.[184]

Afterwards Russell expressed his surprise at the amount of anti-war feeling in the Port Talbot area when he wrote to Ottoline Morell from the Grand Hotel, Port Talbot, on 4 July:

> 'The state of feeling here is quite astonishing. The town subsists on one enormous steelworks, the largest in south Wales; the men are starred, and are earning very good wages; they are not suffering from the war in any way. But they all seem to be against it. On Sunday afternoon I had an open air meeting on a green; there were two chapels on the green and their congregations came out just before I began. They stayed to listen. A crowd of about 400 came, not like open-air meetings in the south when people stay a few minutes out of curiosity, and then go away; they all stayed the whole time, listened with the closest attention and seemed unanimously sympathetic. The man who has been organising for me here works twelve hours every day except Sunday in the steelworks. Their energy is wonderful.'[185]

The Banning of Bertie *(Emily Johns/Peace News)*

Following Russell's speeches at Port Talbot and Briton Ferry, he made a further speech in Cardiff which is depicted in the poster above. The text reads: 'Britain's greatest leading philosopher Bertrand Russell was banned under the Defence of the Realm Act from a third of the country for an anti-war speech he expressed in Cardiff on 6 July 1916'.

Russell's own description[186] of this event was:

> 'My speeches to munitions workers in south Wales, all of which were accurately reported by detectives, caused the War Office to issue an order that I should not be allowed in any prohibited area.... At the War Office General Cockerill had beside him a report of my speeches in south Wales and drew special attention to a speech I made in Cardiff saying there was no good reason this war should continue for another day ... such a sentiment made to miners or munition workers was calculated to diminish their ardour ... I was encouraging men to refuse to fight for their country.'

Russell spent much time in south Wales that year. He later visited Merthyr and attended the *Peace Conference*, and an anti-conscription meeting organised by the National Council for Civil Liberties in Cardiff on 10 November. When offered a post at Harvard, his Majesty's Government, in August 1916, did 'not consider it to be in the public interest to issue a passport to enable Mr Russell to leave the United Kingdom at the present time'.

In 1918 Russell spent six months in Brixton prison for writing a pacifist article in the NCF journal *Tribunal*, suggesting that the American Army might be used as strike breakers. This was a continuation of Newbold's theme and indicated how widely the Defence of the Realm Act was being interpreted. Russell was initially sympathetic to the Russian Revolution in 1917, but a visit to the Soviet Union in 1920 left him with a deep distaste for Soviet communism. He ceased to be a pacifist in the 1930s with the rise of Hitler. In 1950 he received the Nobel Prize in literature for 'championing humanitarian ideals and freedom of thought'; he became a founder member of the CND in 1958 and was imprisoned again in 1961 for his part in a CND (Campaign for Nuclear Disarmament) demonstration. He also became Chair of the World Disarmament Campaign.

Philip Snowden (1864-1937)

Philip Snowden was one of the most prominent people to campaign against the war and to argue for an early peace. In Parliament he defended the principles of conscientious objection and took up matters concerning objectors from Port Talbot. He first visited the town in October 1907 to attend an eight-day event held by the Aberafan and Port Talbot Temperance Mission.[187]

He was a Methodist weaver's son from west Yorkshire. It was his father's tenacity that enabled him to continue his education to become an insurance and civil service clerk, until he became crippled by a spinal disease. He became convinced of the ILP's ideology after researching a speech for his local Liberal Party on *The Dangers of Socialism*. He attended political meetings and wrote and lectured for the ILP, losing his first election in Burnley in 1900 but winning Blackburn for the Labour Party in 1905 for the Parliamentary Labour Party to be born. Soon he turned to the ILP, becoming Chair for the

Philip Snowden

first time, from 1903 to 1906, and prominent in national politics.

Up to 1914 the ILP gave much publicity to the growth of the private arms industry and the growth of overlapping directorships, with Snowden contributing books, including one entitled *Dreadnoughts* and *Dividends: Disarmament and the Arms Race*. He correctly predicted that general conscription would follow once the conscription of single men was conceded. Snowden also moved an additional clause in the Military Service Bill to safeguard the persistent objector from the death penalty.

He visited Briton Ferry in September 1916, having been denied the use of Neath Town Hall to speak on *Current Politics*. Councillor John Morris of Neath said 'Why, the name of Philip Snowden stinks in the nostrils of every patriot'. George Lansbury, however, was permitted the use of the Hall to speak on *High Food Prices*.[187a]

Snowden was not a pacifist but he was against conscription and was regarded as the ILP's shrewdest foreign affairs spokesperson. He discerningly exposed in Parliament the inconsistencies, unfairness and irregularities of many Military Service Tribunals and the treatment of conscientious objectors. Snowden ensured that a clause was inserted into the Military Service Act to safeguard persistent objectors from receiving the death penalty under its provisions.

The reason Snowden was effective in Port Talbot was because of the strong NCF organisation in the area. It was able to feed him information about local injustices, through the NCF's nationwide intelligence organisation, on which he could question the authorities. Snowden knew the answers before he asked the questions. The whole point of his questioning was to put the answer on public record. On 25 July 1917, he asked whether Thomas Henry Williams of Cwmafan was being force fed at Shrewsbury Prison, and whether this had led to the goitre in his neck. Similarly, on 10 August 1918 he raised the matter of the mistreatment of Jack Woolcock, Dan Edwards and Lemuel Emanuel when held at Barry Army Camp.

Snowden's stance during the war was unpopular with his constituents and he lost his seat in 1918, but in 1922 he was back in the Commons. After MacDonald's appointment as Prime Minister, in January 1924, Snowden was appointed Labour's first Chancellor of the Exchequer. In his budget he reduced duties on some foodstuffs; reduced spending on armaments and provided money for council housing. He did not realise how serious unemployment had become, however, and criticised the Liberals' Keynesian ideas expressed in its 1929 election manifesto *We can conquer unemployment*.

In 1927 he repudiated the ILP, in favour of the Labour Party proper, for its increasing militancy in drifting 'from evolutionary socialism to revolutionary socialism' but Labour emerged as the largest party in the 1929 general election and Snowden became Chancellor. His policy was considered by many to be an obstacle to tackling unemployment and the Great Depression. When he and MacDonald broke with Labour policy in 1931 by joining the National Government, they were expelled from the Labour Party.

Disappointing though Snowden's economic policies were for most people, he represented the interests of Port Talbot objectors in the House of Commons. His stance against conscription and his parliamentary techniques were brilliantly conducted, thus making him an especially significant person in the eyes of many in the town. He continued his contact with Port Talbot after the war: in 1919, for example, he attended the Labour Day celebrations at the Grand Theatre.[188]

Richard C. Wallhead (1870-1934)

Dick Wallhead was a lecturer, socialist and journalist who visited Port Talbot several times and was well-liked by many in the town. Before World War One he was organising secretary for the ILP and Labour candidate for Coventry. He was opposed to the war. Wallhead came to Port Talbot in his national ILP capacity on 16 January 1916 when he spoke on the 'Nemesis of Nations' at Aberafan Public Hall. He retained his connection with Port Talbot and south Wales between the wars.

Wallhead (L) with Keir Hardie

In July 1916 he spoke at two open air meetings; one was in Bethany Square where his topic was on 'Britain after the war'. A third meeting, held indoors at the Public Hall was packed with an enthusiastic audience to hear him give 'a great address on *Peace Negotiation*'. He spoke yet again in December 1917, at another outdoor event Briton Ferry for which he was subsequently fined £50 at Neath, and in default four months' imprisonment under the Defence of the Realm Act.

'For false statements likely to prejudice the recruitment, training, discipline and administration of His Majesty's forces in speeches at Briton Ferry and at Cwmdu (Maesteg) on 12 September. Amongst other utterances it was alleged he said that boys of eighteen did not join for the duration of the war, but that they would be the Regular Army of the future.'[189]

His exact words were:

'There are a lot of women in the field. You mothers take warning: you who have sons of eighteen years are under the impression that your sons are joining for the duration of the war. But that is not so. Every lad of eighteen years joins, but for the regular army of the future. I know there is posted up in every barrack room notices to the effect that boys of eighteen years will be kept for the regular army in the future. Commanding Officers have also told them on parade and therefore we have also got conscription in the worst form.'

'Considerable interest was evinced at Neath one Friday in connection with the presentation of the case against him. There were four summonses. The defendant was legally advised by Mr Edward Roberts (Dowlais) and the prosecution for the Home Office was taken by Mr Edward Powell, Neath. The cases had been adjourned two weeks to allow Mr Wallhead to prepare his defence.'

Sergeant Williams was cross-examined by the defendant and admitted not having taken a verbatim report of the speech, but the passages in question so impressed him, he said, that he went straight to the police station and reported them. PC Lisk said he distinctly heard the defendant say that boys of eighteen would be the army of the future. Captain Hamilton Kerby Shore, of the Adjutant-General's Department at the War Office, said the Defendant's statements were absolutely untrue: no such notices were posted up in barrack rooms.

Mr Wallhead argued on legal grounds that the proceedings were irregular and that there was no written record of what he had said. He only spoke about permanent militarism. He pleaded guilty to the second charge regarding the notices and was fined £25 in each of the two Briton Ferry cases, or in default four months' imprisonment. He was ordered to pay costs in the Maesteg cases. Advocate's fee of five guineas was allowed.

He was sent to Swansea Prison for four months, but was released after two. In March 1918, he related some of his recent prison experiences to a big meeting of the Briton Ferry ILP. Two years later he became Chair of the ILP nationally for two years. He again came to Briton Ferry on 20 February 1922, before winning Merthyr from the Liberals and holding the seat until his death in 1934. Indeed, Richard Collingham Wallhead was one of only five ILP MPs to retain their seats after the 1931 election – a fine tribute to his Merthyr predecessor, Keir Hardie.

Robert (Bob) Williams (1881–1936)

Williams was born in Swansea and worked as a coal trimmer at the docks, becoming a Labour Councillor from 1910, the first Secretary of the National Transport Workers Federation and a leading member of the Union of Democratic Control. In July 1914 he assured the Parliamentary Labour Party of full support in the country for any anti-war activity in the House of Commons. When he spoke, under the auspices of the No Conscription Fellowship, at Briton Ferry Public Hall in 1916, it was to explain how he believed that democratic control of foreign policies could be achieved through international trade unionism. He repeated these ideas with H. J. Harford of the *Herald* in August 1917 at a full-to-overflowing Ebby's Olympic Cinema in Cwmafan.

Robert (Bob) Williams

Securing the candidature for Aberafan constituency, in the election of 1918, was not a straightforward matter for him. At a Labour Conference in the Dockers' Hall, Aberafan in May, William Jenkins, the Afan Valley Miners' agent implied that Williams was an ILP nominee. George T. Owen and Henry S. Batey, Executive members of the Aberafan Divisional Labour Party, wrote to the press[190] in reply to a scurrilous letter from Jenkins to say that he was properly selected by the Division. Such rifts in the party could not have helped Williams: standing on behalf of the October Revolution (Labour) Party, he failed. Major John Edwards[191] won the seat for the Liberals with 62.8% of the vote, with Williams realising 35.7% on a 71.4% turnout.

Nevertheless, he had other important things to attend to which he dealt with most successfully. The first was to re-establish links with German transport unions after the war. Johann Doring, of the German dockers recalled an encounter in Amsterdam in 1919: 'We saw the British comrades, Robert Williams, Harry Gosling and Ernest Bevin ... when comrade Williams saw us, he took three or four great strides and stretched out his hand. Bevin was also affected, saying it was 'A very happy meeting which will ever live in one's memory.' Williams went on to consolidate this rapprochement at the ITWF Congresses at Vienna and Hamburg in 1922 and 1924. At the latter he castigated both German financiers and Allied militarists for coercing the Germans into impossible reparations. Perhaps this was his finest hour and perhaps, accounts for his five years' presidency of the International Transport Workers' Federation (from 1920 to 1925).

Williams joined the Communist Party in 1920 and visited Moscow with a deputation of British trade union officials to discuss the formation of a new, international group of Trade Unions – the Red International of Trade Unions. Williams was a potential Labour party leader, but he was not everyone's preference. 'I had heard (Bob Williams) recently in the Grand theatre address a mass meeting with an inflammatory speech which ended with the scorching peroration; "I believe in revolution; peaceful if possible, but revolution".'[192]

Although the transport workers were a signatory to the Triple Alliance with the National Union of Railwaymen and the Miners Federation of Great Britain, Williams' union failed to support the miners when their wages were cut as a result of de-control of the mines in 1921. That was *Black Friday* but, in 1925, the government agreed to grant a temporary subsidy to the mining industry to avoid wage reductions. That was *Red Friday*.

In the meantime, Ramsay MacDonald won the Aberafan seat for Labour in 1924 with a 28.2% swing and, from 1925–6, Bob Williams became chair of the Labour Party. After criticising the miners during the 1926 strike, Williams (having become General Manager of the Daily Herald, a job he held from 1922-30) was deselected as a Labour candidate. After supporting Ramsay MacDonald's apostasy to the National Government, Williams could find no work, a factor that was a likely contribution to his suicide in 1936.

Llewelyn Williams KC [193] (1867-1922)

Llewelyn Williams represented Port Talbot anti-conscriptionists in a civil rights case whose charges arose from alleged breaches of the Defence of the Realm Act. He was from a Carmarthenshire[194] Congregationalist family and received his education at Llandovery College and Oxford University. From 1891 he edited the *South Wales Star* at Barry, before being elected as MP for Carmarthen Boroughs in 1906. He had opposed the Boer War, but at the start of the war in 1914, when enlistment was voluntary, Williams 'committed himself to the view that this was a holy war on behalf of Christian virtue'.[195] The introduction of the Military Service Acts in 1916 'deeply alienated many liberals who had accepted the necessity, even the righteousness of the war, but now saw universal male conscription as deeply injurious to the rights of free citizenship.' Williams virulently opposed conscription by word and deed and his opposition would be played out in places such as Briton Ferry and Port Talbot.

Llewelyn Williams

In 1910 Williams had helped to disestablish the Welsh church to become the Church in Wales. By 1912 he had taken silk, becoming the recorder of Swansea and leader of the south Wales judicial circuit. By the summer of 1916 he was to appear in defence of the anti-conscriptionists of Port Talbot and Briton Ferry. His involvement at Port Talbot arose from two cases involving breaches of the Defence of the Realm Act. The first was on Sunday 8 May in which Messrs Mainwaring and both Henry and Harry Davies spoke under the chairmanship of James Price. This case was particularly significant because the accused were elected representatives. They were found guilty of obstruction and fined forty shillings.

The next case, which was linked to the second, attracted the involvement of Llewelyn Williams to appear for the defence of Tal Mainwaring, Dan Morris and brothers Jenkin and William Williams. The charge, in which Mainwaring was the principal defendant, was that early in June his speech in front of a crowd of some 400-500 at Bethany Square, Port Talbot, was alleged to be a breach of S27 of the Defence of the Realm Act because 'it was calculated to prejudice the recruiting and discipline of the troops'. The defendants in the case contended that the Military Service

185

Act was 'not for the defence of the country but for the conscription of the labour of the country'.

Captain Martin, the Military Representative, had taken 'grave exception' to Williams representing the defendants. Martin later denied saying this, so the bench allowed Williams to continue. The bench found the defendants guilty, but took a 'lenient view', fined Mainwaring £25[196] and awarded costs against them.

The case in Briton Ferry saw Joe Branch of Briton Ferry, President of Aberafan ILP, as principal defendant, with nine other co-defendants accused of distributing anti-conscription pamphlets following a police raid on Briton Ferry's ILP premises in May. The Neath bench was less tolerant this time, fining Branch fifty pounds[197] and the others twenty-five. Nevertheless, the *Pioneer*[198] reported 'Counsel's brilliant defence in the Briton Ferry case'. This was based on three principal arguments:

Firstly, as put forward in a previous Merthyr case, that the leaflets were factual and, rather than discouraging people from becoming conscripts, the leaflets merely pointed out the penalties that would be incurred by those who resisted conscription. The second argument was that the 'Maximilian' leaflet portrayed Christ as a conscientious objector and that to ban its distribution would, effectively, be banning the Bible. Thirdly, if the purpose of imprisonment was a deterrence and not punishment, then imprisonment was not appropriate since no leaflets had been distributed since the 30 April.

These events did nothing to improve Williams' relationship with Lloyd George, who would become Prime Minister in December 1916. Williams' liberal opposition to conscription set him against his one-time friend for the remainder of the war, but before he died Williams attempted to affect a reconciliation with the Prime Minister.

James Price (1875–1964)

Lewis James Price was born at Llanfrechfa, near Cwmbran and came to Aberafan to work as a coal miner. After meeting his future wife, Florence, the family lived in Gwendoline Street and raised five sons and two daughters. Price was a Labour Councillor on Aberafan Town Council and also an NCF and Aberafan Military Service Tribunal Member.

In May 1916, trouble arose over his membership of the tribunal. A meeting was suspended[199] on the grounds that Price was not a suitable member because of his NCF interests. The suspended meeting had followed an earlier meeting against conscription, held elsewhere, that Price had chaired. At a Council Meeting, the Mayor, Percy Jacobs, who was also the chair of the tribunal, moved for a suspension of Council standing orders to ask for Councillor Price's appointment to the tribunal to be revoked. It was alleged that comments Price had made at the meeting were unpatriotic and a breach of the Defence of the Realm Act.

Mr Miles Thomas, the town clerk, was asked to read the qualifications for appointment to a tribunal for the Council. Price stated that the Council had no right to discuss the matter because his membership of the NCF had no bearing upon his work as a councillor. In any case, the council should have listened to what Price had to say before making such allegations.

Whether there was any need to determine if Price had, indeed, 'broken the law' by presiding over an NCF meeting is doubtful. The upshot of all this was that, a few days later, W. C. Anderson, the Labour MP, asked a question in Parliament[200] of Runciman, the President of the Local Government Board, 'whether he was aware that Councillor James Price, a miner and Labour representative on the Aberafan Town Council, has been a member of the Aberafan Tribunal and has performed his work with fairness and impartiality; whether he is aware that because Councillor Price presided over a meeting against conscription, the Recruiting Officer for the area, backed up by the Military Representative to the Aberafan Tribunal has demanded that Councillor should resign his seat on that tribunal and that the Recruiting Officer insisted that Councillor Price had broken the law by presiding over a meeting against conscription and whether there is anything in the rules and regulations to justify this action and, if not, what action he proposed to take?'

Mr Hayes Fisher replied by saying that 'It is, of course, desirable that members of tribunals, whatever their personal opinions, should refrain from any action which might appear to throw doubt on their impartiality'. Mr Anderson then asked 'Does that apply to both sides or only to one side?'. Fisher clarified by saying: 'It certainly applies to both sides' and confirmed that Price remained a member of the tribunal.

At 64 years of age Price, now living with his wife at Norman Street was still working as a blast furnace labourer when war again came. Price lived until 1964, having reached his 89th birthday.

Notes for Chapter Six:

National support

[177] *Cambria Daily Leader*, 24 April 1918.
[178] *Pioneer*, 8 September 1917.
[179] She was a delegate to the 1919 Zurich Congress of the Women's International League for Peace and Freedom. The Congress urged the Peace conference then meeting in Paris to include a Women's Charter in the final peace Treaty. The twelve-point charter included equal suffrage, equal pay and opportunities in employment and education and economic support for mothers.
[180] *Pioneer*, 5 August, 1916.
[181] *Pioneer*, 9 November 1918.
[182] *Encyclopaedia Britannica*.
[183] *Merthyr Pioneer*, 8 July 1915.
[184] *Merthyr Pioneer*, 15 July 1916.
[185] Nicholas Griffin, 'Selected letters of Bertrand Russell – the Public Years 1914–1970' (2001).
[186] Bertrand Russell, Autobiography 2nd Edition (2000).
[187] *Glamorgan Gazette*, 18 October 1907.
[187a] Cambria Daily Leader, 4 August 1916
[188] *Cambria Daily Leader*, 6 May 1919.
[189] *Pioneer*, 8 December 1917.
[190] *Pioneer*, 25 May 1918.
[191] Major Edwards DSO MP, the newly adopted candidate for Aberafan Liberal Labour Association.
[192] J. Ivor Hanson, as before.
[193] *Carmarthen Weekly Reporter*, 14 January 1916.
[194] *Herald of Wales and Monmouthshire*.
[195] Kenneth O. Morgan, 'Peace Movements in Wales 1899–1945', *Welsh History Review* Vol 10, no 3 p 410 (1981).
[196] £2,320 at 2016 values, accessed at http://www.thisismoney.co.uk. (13 June 2016).
[197] £4,623 at 2016 values, as above.
[198] 17 June 1916.
[199] *Herald of Wales*, 20 May 1916.
[200] *Llais Llafur* 27 May 1916; HC Deb 23 May 1916 vol 82 c197.

Chapter Seven:
Conclusion

A NUMBER OF QUESTIONS which were posed in earlier chapters can now be considered. Some were factual questions such as age, religious affiliation and marital status of the objectors. These will be answered below and tabulated in Appendix Eleven. Beyond these, more fundamental questions need to be answered. Foremost amongst these is the question 'what was the legacy of these men?'

The objectors' ages

Of the objectors from the Port Talbot area whose ages are known, the mean age was 25.5 years. The youngest, David Jones, was called up at age 18 and the oldest, Jack Woolcock, was thirty-six. Over sixty per cent were in their twenties when called up. There were no Absolutists called up over the age of thirty.

Where exactly did the objectors come from?

An analysis based on the 70 percent or so of the objectors with a known address tells us that the most frequently reported home of objectors was Cwmafan. The village was distinct topographically from other 'town' areas because it was a large village, which lay in a well-defined valley setting. Almost half of Port Talbot's objectors came from here, with other large, but smaller, clusters elsewhere.

However, distinguishing precisely whether a man's home address was Aberafan, Port Talbot, Taibach or Margam is a little difficult because the boundaries are ill-defined.

What work did the objectors normally do?

The objectors in the Port Talbot area were drawn from three main occupational groups: the metalworkers, the coal miners and the rail workers. Although Port Talbot is regarded as a 'steel' town, with almost half of its objectors being classified as steelworkers, most, so classified, were actually tinplate or sheet workers who produced flat steel products. One in five was a miner and approximately one in five was a railway worker. The remaining objectors included eight who were teachers or from other trades and services. A comparison with nearby Briton Ferry is interesting. In Port Talbot the occupations of objectors were more varied, whereas the concentration of metal-workers and those in manual industrial occupations was much greater in Briton Ferry. What differentiates Port Talbot, in terms of the employment of anti-conscription objectors, is that a substantial cohort of rail workers was involved, including several influential figures such as Christopher R. Scott, the ILP Chair and Percy Warren Davies, the NUR official.

Were there any important political affiliations?

Twenty-five objectors were known to be ILP and twenty-four NCF members. The link between the ILP and the NCF was very strong; indeed, in nineteen of these cases they were members of both ILP and NCF. Some ILP members also had religious motivation to resist. Usually these were nonconformists for whom the description 'Christian socialist' may be apt. A number are also likely to have held philosophical objections close to the ILP's political stance, whilst others were likely to be more humanist in nature.

Were there any significant religious influences?

Approximately twenty-five per cent of the religious affiliations of the objectors are known, so comment must be made with a caveat. The predominant religious motivation was nonconformist, but one or two Church of England objectors were recorded, as well as a minister of religion and a trainee minister. Port Talbot did not seem to have a local nonconformist minister like the Rev. Rees Powell of Briton Ferry who advocated socialism from the pulpit. Nevertheless, even without a Powell, Keir Hardie's adage that 'there will never be true Christianity without socialism' still depicts the blend of politics and religion that drove Port Talbot's resisters.

Did the objectors act alone?

The NCF and ILP generally had a coherent anti-conscription and war policy for its members to follow, but no similar policy existed for the religious organisations in Port Talbot. Few objectors were acting alone, with the possible exception of some religious objectors. No clear examples from Port Talbot were found of religious groups of objector belonging to a single congregation or even denomination. Such examples may have existed, but they have not been picked up because of the low number of objectors declaring a specific religious affiliation.

ILP and NCF members were not acting alone and this can be clearly seen to be so at tribunals where, both individually and collectively, they were supported by fellow members such as Henry Davies. It is not entirely clear why batches of objectors were sometimes dealt with collectively by the tribunals. It was unlikely to have been for the convenience of the applicants and is more likely to have been arranged for the bench concerned to deal with the large volume of cases in its hands.

What effect did the resistance have on family life?

Sixteen of Port Talbot's objectors were married when called-up;[201] a further twenty-four were single, but the marital status of the remainder, over forty-percent of objectors, is unknown. The direct impact on family life of the tribunal process and its consequences is hard to assess from empirical evidence because there is little in the public domain from Port Talbot objectors' families. Some idea of the impact on the objectors themselves can be gained from newspaper reports and diaries, such as the Penderyn Work Centre reports from Albert Rankin. Evidence of the impact of the objectors' treatment on families is also lacking.

Whether married or single, objectors' families lost income during the men's incarceration at the time of rising prices. Efforts were made by organisations, such as the NCF, and local supporters, such as Tal Mainwaring, to support objectors and their needy families with 'comfort funds'. There was sometimes mutual support between the objectors' families in neighbouring towns. Aberafan objectors and their families, for example, collaborated with those in Gorseinon and Neath to provide help, comfort and nourishment. In the public's eyes the objectors' families were regarded in the same light as the objectors. If an objector was loathed, all too often would his family be loathed. If an objector was admired, his family would also be admired.

The letter of Herbert Rees of Gorseinon written from Northallerton Prison, which is reproduced as Appendix Twelve, is most revealing: W. I. Thomas is said in Rees' letter to be 'having the hard time' in Dartmoor, but is Rees telling the truth about himself? Or is he concealing it and putting a brave face on things to ease his family's worries? 112 days' hard labour was the most severe level of prison sentence at that time. Similar letters between Port Talbot's objectors and their families may still exist and it is hoped that this book will encourage their disclosure.

Did visiting speakers influence objectors?

The influx of celebrated speakers to Port Talbot during the war was not as strong as in Briton Ferry, but visits increased after the formation of the Aberafan constituency in 1918 and the election of Ramsay MacDonald as Prime Minister in 1924. The phenomenon of visiting speakers must not be taken to suggest that Port Talbot was unable to manage its own proselytising: far from it. In the political arena, as far as opposition to war was concerned, the likes of Tal Mainwaring, Henry Davies and their colleagues were coping very well on their own during the years of war. In the absence of radio and TV, which did not arrive till the 1920s and 1930s respectively, it was only newspapers and public speaking that would inform the populace on political affairs. The *Pioneer* was founded by Keir Hardie to support the ILP's policies and it was mainly the *Pioneer* that publicised both the visiting speakers and the fortunes of the Port Talbot resisters.

During the 1920s many of the issues raised by the war such as the peace settlement, reparations, housing, women's and children's rights and welfare continued to be hotly debated in Aberafan constituency. In many ways these discussions were simply a continuation of the issues raised by the fight against conscription and war, and the desire for an equitable peacetime settlement for all. With the constituency's MP as Prime Minister, the matters raised in Port Talbot received acute attention. Most were concerned with socialist and trade union affairs, but other important issues were debated, too. Among the visitors debating them were George Lansbury, Frank Hodges, Jack Jones, James Maxton, Emanuel Shinwell, Bob Smillie, Maude Royden, Herbert Samuel, Harold Laski, C. T. Cramp and Herbert Samuel.

Were Port Talbot's objectors stereotypical?

One of the stereotypes described in Chapter Three was that objectors were generally despised and rejected in their communities. This was not the case in Port Talbot. The Bamford brothers, for example, were presented with gifts on their return home from Princetown Work Centre. The local Steel Smelters Union's policy was to treat objector-members returning from prison or work centre as they would treat soldier-members returning from the front. Anti-conscription activists, too, such as Tal Mainwaring and Dan Morris, were supported by large crowds on their way to and from prison.

Could the objectors have been regarded as selfish, indolent and cowardly? Certainly some tribunal members said so. Whether they thought so is another thing, remembering that some of the tribunal members were deliberately using such terminology to induce objectors to fight, or at least agree to non-combatant service. No Port Talbot tribunal chairman had the empathy of George M. Ll. Davies' court-martial Chairman who sentenced him to prison with the words 'I am condemning a far better man than myself.'

To say that the objectors were deviant might be acceptable as a mathematical description because they formed less than 0.25% of the entire population and around 1.4% of those eligible to be conscripted. In terms of the social norms propagated by the military authorities to encourage enrolment, they were depicted as morally deviant. The fact that they simply dared to differ from the norms advocated by such propaganda, however, cannot lead one to the conclusion that they were deviant.

The only way in which they constituted a national danger was because of the resources taken from the military effort to prosecute and incarcerate them. The deliberate isolation of the resisters' was to prevent them from influencing the general population with ideas that did not suit the state's often undemocratic policies. But, as has often been said, the number of objectors involved in terms of the numbers enrolled was a very small percentage.

The objectors may not have been seen as upstanding and honourable citizens at the time because their raison d'être was to demonstrate the evils of militarism, and to offer a better alternative. As events were to show, as the war progressed and afterwards, many were later to receive support from disillusioned soldiers as well as local recognition by the electorate.

The resisters may never have become heroes in the military sense but their arguments that voluntarism and co-operation was a better answer than conscription and war did gain some acceptance eventually.

Was Port Talbot aberrant?

This question was first asked about Huddersfield by Cyril Pearce[202] for two reasons: firstly, due to the higher-than-expected incidence of conscientious objection in the population compared with other places; secondly, because of the general tolerance which was afforded to the war resisters. When the question was again raised about Briton Ferry, similar answers were again forthcoming: the strength of opposition in Briton Ferry repeated Pearce's findings about Huddersfield.

The Port Talbot research demonstrates that another group of communities existed which showed a higher-than-expected prevalence of conscientious objection and tolerance towards its anti-war dissidents. It is therefore becoming increasingly misleading to continue to suggest that such places are unrepresentative of the country as a whole.

On the other hand, it can be argued, the cases of Huddersfield, Briton Ferry and Port Talbot, taken together, account for the work of no more than a dozen Military Service Tribunals from a national total of 1805. Nevertheless, the fact remains that where detailed, empirical research has been undertaken, the findings point to a common conclusion: that the strength of opposition to conscription and war has been much understated. As a result of these three studies, and a small number of others, the Pearce Register is now approaching 20,000 entries of objectors to conscription.

What was the legacy of the men and women who dared to differ?

The main legacy of Port Talbot's defiance of authority in the First World War was in the field of civil liberties. The activists and their supporters in the area did not wish to limit government: in some areas of public life: they actually wished to see more government intervention. Their wish to limit it was in areas where such intervention was not legitimate. The government actions so bitterly resented were its refusal to accept freedom of conscience, speech and movement. The right to be free from unreasonable searches of one's home by the authorities was another hotly contested matter. The result was that Port Talbot produced many prisoners of conscience, whose experiences would, later, assist in prison reform.

Mainly through the ILP, the denial of women's right to vote brought civil rights and civil liberties matters together in Port Talbot. The awareness in the town of the need for an early and equitable peace settlement, and the town's association with organisations such as the Union of Democratic Control, gave the town a more internationalist outlook.

Political prisoners and prisoners of conscience

It is debatable whether objectors should be classified as political prisoners or prisoners of conscience. Here we will simply say they were prisoners of conscience. With the exception of certain religious groups, freedom of conscience for moral and political objection to conscription and war was never fully accepted by the state during the First World War. The resisters and their supporters in Parliament and elsewhere, nevertheless, succeeded in achieving recognition for the civil rights of conscientious objectors by getting Army Order X passed so that court-martialled objectors would be sent to civil establishments, and not military, prisons.

Freedom of association and expression

Albeit less violently, the principles underlying freedom of association and expression were curtailed no less in Bethany Square, Port Talbot in 1916 than in Tiananmen Square in 1989. These two freedoms were so severely restricted during the objectors' prison sentences, that it can confidently be asserted that the conditions of detention were disproportionate to the objectors' 'offences'.

Prison and sentencing reform

It can also be said with some confidence that the decisions of the tribunals were often inconsistent and rushed, and that applicants often did not receive fair hearings. The detentions resulting from courts-martial were even more controversial. Prison sentences with solitary confinement, rules of silence, or task-conversation only, whether with or without hard labour, should never have been in the gift of the military; they were too closely connected with the political and operational motives of the civil and military authorities. The treatment meted out in Barry barracks to Port Talbot's objectors demonstrated the unacceptable face of war in the line of command, where the army had lost control over some of its officers.

The subsequent publicity about objectors' treatment in custody, whether exaggerated or not, has certainly helped in the argument for improvements in penal conditions and sentencing. The success in demanding vegetarian food at Winchester Prison, where Percy Warren Davies spent much time, was a modest, but symbolic and lasting improvement.

Internationalism

The socialist resisters had a strong internationalist outlook. Partly this derived from their belief that the war was unnecessary in the first place and was brought about by an undemocratic, secret foreign policy. Alongside this was their view that the war was waged for the benefit of the capitalist munitions manufacturers and imperialists on both the Allied and the Central Powers sides. The British workers bore no grudges against the enemy's workers, who were in exactly the same situation as the British workers. They envisaged that Britain's military conscription of 1916 threatened to become permanent industrial conscription later.

Universal suffrage

Gender discrimination in relation to the ballot box was most eloquently articulated through the ILP by Minnie Pallister. She connected the denial of the right of women to vote with mothers', children's and family rights. For good measure she threw in the right to object to conscription.

A record of failure?

The state's attempt to marginalise objectors was because conscientious objection, as is becoming increasingly apparent, was a wider social phenomenon than it has been comfortable hitherto to recognise. This marginalisation was achieved not just through incarceration, nor just through blatant censorship, nor by means of a dubious judicial system, but also through a subtle manipulation of public thought through moral propaganda and culture.

It is a tribute to Port Talbot's constituent communities that the men we have described in this book, whilst never treated as the heroes who fought, were rarely seriously marginalised or derided by the population as a whole.

It is because of their steadfastness, and the support that they received, that the pro-war propaganda did not entirely succeed in the Port Talbot area. Yes, Henry Davies of Cwmafan was indeed the Welsh Keir Hardie, and Evan David Mort and his comrades *should* be recognised alongside the likes of Eugene Debs, Bertrand Russell and John MacLean. Professor Kenneth O. Morgan should now have the last words. Was he, too, not thinking of the likes of Tal Mainwaring, Christopher Scott, Minnie Pallister, Bryn Roblin,[202a] their supporters and families when he commented on peace movements in places such as Port Talbot?

> 'Yet the ... movements recorded here offer more than a record of negativism or failure. On the contrary, their victories, often posthumous, played a crucial part in the political and cultural evolution of modern Wales.'

Notes for Chapter Seven:

[201] The Military Service Act of January 1916, which called up single men, was amended in May, 1916, to include married men.
[202] Cyril Pearce, 'Comrades in Conscience'. (London, 2014).
[202a] A World War Two objector who still lives in Cwmafan.

Appendix One:
Timeline of key dates affecting conscription

Date	Event
1914	
4 August	Outbreak of World War One
September	Friends Ambulance Unit (FAU) set up in France
November	The No-Conscription Fellowship established
1915	
August	Compulsory registration of men and women up to age 65 (Derby reviewed the census)
September	Results of census showed that almost five million men of military age were not in the forces
11 October	Introduction of the Derby Scheme – men were given the chance to enlist voluntarily or to 'attest' with an obligation to come if called up later on
November	First National Convention of the No-Conscription Fellowship
1916	
2 March	Compulsory conscription in Britain for all single men and childless widowers aged 18-41 years (Military Service Act 1916)
March	Creation of Non-Combatant Corps (NCC)
June	Compulsory conscription extended to all married men aged 18-41 years
August	Introduction of Home Office Scheme – work camps set up by the Home Office
1918	
November	Armistice signed; recruiting under the Military Service Act suspended
1919	
August	The last conscientious objector (CO) released from prison
November	Final Convention of the No-Conscription Fellowship held; NCF disbanded
1920	
January	Last of the men demobilised from the NCC
1921	
	Majority of tribunal records destroyed

Appendix Two:
COs motivations in Briton Ferry, Port Talbot and Huddersfield: a comparison

Huddersfield Population 107,821 18,864 eligible Places of worship 70	Motivation	Briton Ferry Population 8,456 1,836 eligible Places of worship 20	Port Talbot Population 28,500 4987 eligible Places of worship 50
	Socialist		
15	BSP		
1	Fabian		
7	ILP	6	25
7	SSS		
15	Socialist	3	
45		9	25
	Religious		
1	Anglican		4
18	Christadelphian		2
1	Congregationalist	2	4
1	Methodist	3	6
1	Primitive Methodist		
13	Quaker		
3	Wesleyan		
2	Roman Catholic		
	Baptist	6	3
2	Religious		5
	Plymouth Brethren		2
42		11	26
	Other		
1	FoR		
7	NCF	8	24
1	UDC		

199

	1	Moral and ethical		
	10		8	24
		Not Known		
	18		5	24
	115	Total COs	33	74

Rate of conscientious objectors per thousand of population objecting to conscription
Briton Ferry 19.06   Port Talbot 14.43   Huddersfield 6.1   National 1.4

Note: in the above table a person may be listed for more than one motivation.

Non-combatant Corps members at work on a military road

Appendix Three:

The Tribunals' and Police Courts' Membership

Margam Tribunal[203]

(Normally met at Port Talbot Police Station)

Edward Lowther	D. E. Jones	John David	Edward Edwards	Richard Evans	Rupert Hallowes[204]
Chair Railway & Dock Manager. Chair Margam District Council	Clerk	Councillor Rail Company Manager Bryntirion, Port Talbot nominee	'Elected' in preference to Labour Representation Committee	Councillor Bryn Mayor 1915	Councillor Assistant Manager, Blackplate Works, Cousin of Sidney Byass

William Lewis	Charles Routledge	Rees Llewelyn	F. B. Smith	John Walters	Lewis Jones
Councillor Margam	Chamber of Trade & Port Talbot Steelworks	Councillor Margam & chair	National Service Representative	Councillor Margam	Military

Aberafan Tribunal

The Town Council appointed seven of its members to administer the act in the Borough.[205] They met in the Municipal Buildings

Percy Jacob	David J. Williams	D. T. Owen	Aeron James	James Price	William Jenkins JP	David Rees
Mayor of Aberafan; Cynon Colliery Cynonville	Councillor Aberafan	Councillor	Councillor Aberafan	Labour Councillor, Aberafan Town	Miners' Agent, Cymmer	Councillor Mayor 1914

Mr **W. E. Rees** was the Military Representative

West Glamorgan Appeal Tribunal[206]
(Normally met at Swansea Guildhall, Neath or Port Talbot)

Alderman Hopkin Morgan	Mrs W. H. Miles	David Davies	F. W. Gibbins	J. Powlesland
Chair of Glamorgan County Council Neath	Alderman Swansea	Alderman	Director of Eaglesbush Tinplate Neath	ILP Member & Trade Union Official Swansea

David James	T. W. James	William Jenkins JP	Daniel Daniels	Joseph Edward Moore-Gwyn JP
		Miners' Agent, Cymmer	Crynant	Duffryn Clydach, Neath

Port Talbot Police Court
(Normally sat at Port Talbot Police Station)
In August 1916, the bench that heard Dan Morris' case was:[207]

S. H. Byass JP (Chair)	Herbert Evans	Alderman J. M. Smith JP	Harry A. Burgess
Owner of Mansel Tinplate; Director Port Talbot Steel Company & Port Talbot Railway & Docks Co. Mayor 1919		Mayor of Aberafan 1918	Carpenter Albion Road Baglan

T. Jones	Lewis Lewis	Robert Gibb	William Jenkins JP
	Gentleman 64 Baglan Road	Colliery Proprietor Danygraig Baglan	Miners' Agent, Cymmer

Charles Jones	Edward Lowther	Thomas Studley Goslin	George Lipscomb
	Railway and Dock Manager	Mayor 1917 Aberafan Councillor Baker & confectioner	Seamans' Missionary Margam Councillor

Appendix Four:

Prisons and work centres

The places listed were amongst those used to hold those guilty of certain Military Service and Defence of the Realm Act offences. Port Talbot men were held in those in **bold**.

Aberdeen, Dyce; Aldershot; Ayr
Ballachulish; **Bedford-Howbury**; Birmingham-Winson Green;
Blackdown; Brandon, Suffolk; Brockenhurst;
Caernarvon; **Cardiff**; Carlisle; **Carmarthen**, Caeo; Canterbury; Chelsea:
Clipstone, Crai; Cruachan
Dartford; **Dartmoor, Princetown; Denbigh (Asylum)**; Denton; Derby;
Ditton Priors; Dorchester Dublin, Mountjoy; Durham;
East Harling, Norfolk; Edinburgh, Calton; Ely; Exeter; **Felixstowe;**
Glasgow, Barlinnie; Glasgow, Duke Street; Garboldisham, Norfolk;
Gloucester; Grimsby;
Haverhill, Keddington; Hereford; Hornchurch; Hull;
Inverness; Ipswich;
Kew; **Knutsford;**
Leeds; Leicester; Lincoln; **Liverpool, Walton: Llanddeusant**; Llandebie;
Llangadoc; Loch Awe; Lyme Regis; Lyndhurst;
Maidstone; Maxton; Mold
Newcastle; **Newhaven**; Northallerton
Parkhurst Camp-Salisbury Plain; **Pembroke Dock; Penderyn**; Pendine:
Pentonville; Perth; Plymouth, Mutley; Preston;
Rathdrum, Co Wicklow; Redcar; Rhinefields; **Rhyl, Kinmel**; Richmond;
Rugeley;
Salisbury; Santon-Downham, Suffolk; Parkhurst; Seaford; Shepton Mallet
Shrewsbury; Sunk Island; Strangeways; Sutton; **Swansea;**
Talgarth; Tumble; Usk;
Wakefield; Walton; Warwick; Wandsworth; Weston-super-Mare;
Whitland, Red Roses; Wigtown: **Winchester; Wormwood Scrub**s;
Wrexham-Park Hall.

203

Appendix Five:

Significant events in Port Talbot opposing the war

Date	Event	Speaker	Location
1906			
		Robert Smillie	Taibach
1907			
October	Aberafan and Port Talbot Temperance Mission	Philip Snowden[208]	
1910			
January	To return an MP in favour of votes for women	Women's Freedom League: Beith, Parkes and Fagan[209]	Public Hall Aberafan
1914			
July	Women's Suffrage Society	Henry Davies	
1915			
7 November	Aberafan Mayor's Soldiers and sailors fund	Ben Tillett [210]	
29 November	Let my country awake	Margaret Bonfield[211]	James Price (President)
1916			
17 January	Nemesis	R. C. Wallhead[212]	Public Hall Aberafan
7 May	Making prejudicial statements	Tal Mainwaring[213]	Bethany Square, Port Talbot
10 May	Making prejudicial statements and distributing circulars	Tal Mainwaring, Dan Morris Jenkin Williams William Williams[214]	Cwmafan
13 May	Police raid on Cwmafan ILP centre		
14 May	Arrest on a charge of obstruction at an NCF meeting	Harry Davies, Tal Mainwaring, James Price and Henry Davies[215]	Bethany Square, Port Talbot

Date	Event	Speaker	Location
18 June		Rev. T. E. Nicholas[216]	Bethania Chapel Cwmafan
18 June	The effect of the military being posted to Wrexham	Dr Peter Price[217] (Wrexham)	Gideon Chapel Taibach
24 June	Modern Warfare: The Munitions and Military service Acts	Fred Bramley[218]	Gallipoli Square,
2 July	The war is between governments, not its peoples	Bertrand Russell[219]	Gallipoli Square, Taibach
11 July		Bertrand Russell[220]	Near Cwmafan Police station
18 July	Labour after the war	R. C. Wallhead[221]	Bethany Square, but 'moved towards the Forge Road Cinema.'
1917			
6 March	Attempt to break up 'Peace by Negotiation Meeting' failed	Rev. John Morgan Jones[222] (Merthyr)	Zion Baptist Chapel, Cwmafan
20 March	Peace Resolution	Rev. T. E. Nicholas[223]	Moved from Bethania Vestry, Cwmafan to ILP Centre
5 May		T. C. Morris (NUR) Bob Williams (NTU) Ernest Bevin (Dockers) Henry Davies (Miners)	Grand Theatre (Herald of Wales)
26 August	Stockholm Peace Conference	Bob Williams H. J. Harford[224] (London) H. Davies Chair	Ebby's Olympic Cinema, Cwmafan
15-16 September		Casey	Cwmafan
29 September		Noah Tromans[225] Mountain Ash with Tal Mainwaring (Chair)	Behind the Grand Hotel
30 September	Port Talbot Police and the NUR's civil liberties	J. H. Thomas MP[226] A. J. Williams (Chair)	

205

Date	Event	Speaker	Location
14 October	Women's Peace Movement	Mrs Anderson Fenn[227]	Cwmafan & New Dockers' Hall
20 October	War Aims	J. Hugh Edwards MP[228]	'Interrupted by Cwmafan & Taibach pacifists'
1 December		Tom Richardson MP[229]	New Dockers' Hall
2 December	Call for a 'speedy & democratic end to the war'	Ethel Snowden[230]	Cwmafan ILP
1918			
7 February	Qualification of Women Act & its implications	Charlotte Despard[231]	Cwmafan
9 March	The food problem	Bob Williams	Behind the Grand Hotel
1 November	Social Reconstruction	Frank Hodges JP[232] (President, Miners Federation of GB)	New Theatre Taibach
6-7 November	Call on workers and wives to join the ILP	Minnie Pallister[233]	Dockers' Hall Co-operative Guild
1919			
1May	Labour Day	Philip Snowden	Grand Theatre[234]

Appendix Six:

Henry Davies' trial

'Sentence of fifteen months'

At Cardiff Assizes on Tuesday, before Mr Justice Atkin, Henry Davies (48) assistant Overseer, who was charged on four counts with embezzlement, was sent to prison for fifteen months in the Second Division. The charges were:

1) Embezzling diverse sums of money amounting to £1023/12/9, the property of the Overseer of the parish of Michaelstone Lower
2) Making false entries in the collecting book with intent to defraud.
3) Making false entries in the monthly statements of the inspector of the poor and special ... rate,
4) Destroying two bank pass books relating to the poor rate account and the special expenses account.

Mr Villiers Meager (instructed by Mr Edward Powell, Neath) appeared for the prosecution and Mr W. Llewelyn Williams KC (instructed by Mr Gibson Davies) defended.

Mr Meager, in briefly outlining the facts of the case said that Davies was appointed Assistant Overseer for Cwmafan in January 1901. His duties were to collect the poor rate and special expenses rate, whilst he also had charge of the bank passbooks. At the audit for 1917 the prisoner did not put in an appearance, and the auditor wrote him a letter stating that there were grave irregularities discovered in the accounts. The audit was therefore adjourned for Davies' attendance. (The) total amount of the defalcations was £1023, although since these figures had been made it had been ascertained other small sums appeared to have been embezzled. From 1901 to 1915 prisoner had not been guilty of any defalcations.

In 1911 prisoner's salary was £217 per annum but in April 1917 it was reduced to £160, subsequently being increased to £200.

Lordship: how much did he collect per annum, I mean, how much was the turnover?
Mr Meager: about £6000. Mr Meager described the embezzlement as a deliberate one.

Police allegations

Superintendent Ben Evans said the prisoner was a man of good moral character, and he wielded a considerable influence in Cwmafan and district. 'I think from personal inquiries and what I gather', he added, 'I am inclined to believe this money has been to some extent supporting the propaganda of the socialist party in the district. Prisoner is a most prominent member, and has been actively interested in propaganda work for the last four years. He is a man who has given a considerable (amount) of trouble and has done a considerable amount of havoc to the young growing men of my town.'

Prejudicial effects

Mr Llewelyn Williams: Is that the only thing you have against the prisoner, that he holds these opinions which are prejudicial to the times?
Mr Williams: Have you ever prosecuted him for this propaganda? Witness replied that prisoner had been prosecuted for lecturing on the public highway and causing obstruction.
His Lordship: I do not think that will influence me in my decision.
Mr Llewelyn Williams asked permission to call the Vicar of Cwmafan and other people to testify as to character.
His Lordship said it would be of no use whatever as they knew the character of the man from the depositions.
Mr Richard Thomas, Cwmafan, said that eighteen years ago he attended the prisoner for a tubercular throat.

Prisoner's antecedents

Mr Llewelyn Williams said he would endeavour to explain what was almost inexplicable-the reason why a man of the prisoner's character should have descended to this sad and tragic position. He was a man of very poor parents and since the age of fifteen he had worked in a local tinplate works to earn his livelihood. He was a man of more than ordinary mental capacity and during the seventeen years he was working there he earned the respect and confidence of his fellow workmen. He was interested in the trade union to which he belonged and in the course of time was appointed secretary of the local branch of the union. He became district secretary and was appointed to. . .

Then he suffered from tuberculosis of the throat, and as a result he had to leave the works, and, unfortunately for him, took on his present position.

Mr Llewelyn Williams asked his Lordship to say that the prisoner had not taken the money for self-aggrandisement but had spent it on paying debts he had incurred to give his children a good education. For fourteen years he had kept a position without being guilty of any irregularity. During the period he had borrowed money from friends and when, in 1915, his friends came to him to repay the money he began a series of defalcations. Had he faced the position in 1915 he would have been a man of clean character. He had done this in order to repay his friends.

> *His Lordship:* it is very distressing to see a man of your position standing where you are. I do not want to add by word of mouth to the pain of your position. It is a sad thing to see a man who has yielded considerable influence on the members of the community in which he lives charged with an offence like this. It was a serious offence. It was a case where he had considered whether he would not send the prisoner to penal servitude. But he thought justice would be met by a sentence of fifteen calendar months' imprisonment in the second Division.

Appendix Seven:
Rankin's prison notebook

The men's entries in Bransby Griffiths'[235] album give a strong indication of their individual motivation and feelings. Rankin's entry was more subdued.

M. Jones of West Bromwich seemed to be referring to some of the local opinions of COs when he quoted Oscar Wilde. Wilde was, of course referring to the Devil's brigade as homosexuals, whereas Jones was referring to fellow conscientious objectors.

> *With slouch and swing around the ring*
> *We trod the fools parade*
> *We did not care, we knew we were*
> *The devil's own brigade.*

David Lewis of Merthyr made a philosophical entry, quoting Bacon:

> *Certainly, in taking revenge, a man is but even with his enemy*
> *But, in passing it over, he is superior*

Unsurprisingly, perhaps, J. C. Swanton, the Secretary of Pontypool NCF, was more political, perhaps alluding to the previous prosecutions in South Wales under the Defence of the Realm Act for distributing anti-conscription literature:

> *The people are in silence; Revolution is tearing from their mouth the bleeding gag.*

Peckham's Stanley F. Thomson returned to a strong political theme, offering words of caution about the post war settlement:

> *The working class and the employer class have nothing in common.*

There can be no peace as long as hunger and want are found among millions of working people and the few who make up the employing class have all the good things of life. Between these two classes a struggle must go on until all the toilers come together on the political as well as the industrial field and take hold of that which they produce by their labours through an economic organisation of the working class without any affiliation to any political party.

Ashworth of Mytholmroyd was more succinct, and was, perhaps, making a direct reference to actual events at Penderyn:

The contented wage slave is a clog in the wheels of progress

Alderson of Southport saw war and the state's involvement as a curtailment of Liberty, and said so firmly, but quite humorously:

War is a game that, were the people's wise,
Kings could not play at.

Adding: Author forgotten. Anyway, if he were still alive, his address would probably be one of HM prisons.

Walter Jones of St. Athan was well qualified to speak of Liberty since his arrest in August 1917, and subsequent incarcerations at Cardiff Barracks, Wormwood Scrubs, Knutsford and Dartmoor. Perhaps he was better qualified than Milton, whom he quoted and who, as Jones humorously pointed out, had never visited any of these places.

This is true Liberty, when freeborn men
Having to advise the public, may speak free.

On release from Penderyn, one objector, Bransby Griffiths of Briton Ferry[236], walked the twenty-two-mile journey home. Perhaps Albert Rankin walked with him and continued for three further miles to his Port Talbot home.

Appendix Eight:
Bibliography

Author	Year	Title	Publisher
Adams, Philip	2015	Not in Our Name; War dissent in a Welsh Town	Ludlow: Briton Ferry Books
Barlow, Robin	2014	Wales and World War One	Llandyssul, Gomer Press
Bibbings, Louise	2011	Telling tales about Men: Conceptions of conscientious objection to military service during the First World War	University of Manchester Press
Boulton, David	2014	Objection overruled	Friends Historical Society
Cleaver, D.	1984	Conscientious objection in the Swansea area	
Eurig, Aled	1987	Aspects of the opposition to the First World War in Wales	Llafur, Vol 4 no 4, 58-68
Evans, A. Leslie	1982	A history of Taibach and District	Port Talbot: Alun Books
Evans, A. Leslie	1992	Cwmavon Then and Now	Port Talbot Historical Society
Francis, H. and Smith, D.	1980	A history of the South Wales Miners Federation in the twentieth century	London: Lawrence and Wishart
Griffin, Nicholas	2001	Selected letters of Bertrand Russell – the Public Years 1914-1970	Routledge
Griffiths, Robert H.	2014	The Story of Kinmel Park Military Training Camp, 1914-1918	Pwllheli: Llygad Gwalch
Hansen, J. Ivor	1968	Portrait of a Welsh Town	MacDonald, Edinburgh
Hansen, J. Ivor	1971	Outline of a Welsh Town	Port Talbot: Daffodil Publications
Lewis, Bernard	2014	Swansea in the Great War	Barnsley, Pen and Sword

Llewelyn, Jen	2016	Pilgrim of Peace: A life of George M. Ll. Davies		Y Lolfa, Ceredigion
Lowe, Jeremy	1985	Welsh Industrial Workers' Housing 1775-1875		National Museum of Wales
Morgan, Kenneth O.	1981	Peace Movements in Wales 1899-1945		Welsh History Review Vol 10, no 3
O' Brien, Anthony Mor	1987	Conchie: Emrys Hughes and the First World War		National Library of Wales, Aberystwyth
Paige, James	1989	Rails in the Valleys		David and Charles
Parry, Stephen	2011	History of the Steel Industry in the Port Talbot Area 1900-1988		University of Leeds, School of History (Ph.D thesis)
Pearce, Cyril	2014	Comrades in Conscience		Francis Boutle, London
Port Talbot Historical Society	1984	Transactions No 3 Vol III		Port Talbot Historical Society
Rees, Arthur	2004	Some street and place names of the Port Talbot district		Port Talbot Historical Society
Rees, Dylan	1987	Morgan Jones, Educationalist and Labour Politician		National Library of Wales, Aberystwyth
Rees, Lynne	2013	Real Port Talbot		Bridgend, Seren Books
Ronan, Alison	2015	Unpopular Resistance		North West Labour History Society
Taylor, Warwick	2003	The forgotten conscript: a history of the Bevin Boys		Portland Press
Wright, Martin	2011	Wales and Socialism: Political Culture and National Identity c 1880-1914		Cardiff University, School of History, Archaeology and Religion (Ph.D thesis)

213

Appendix Nine:
Definitions and tribunal language

From the Concise Oxford English Dictionary etc.

Pacifism   The doctrine that the abolition of war or violence is desirable and possible; the support of arbitration in international disputes.

Militarism   The prevalence of military spirit or ideals as a valid policy for foreign affairs; undue influence of the generals on government.

Conscientious objector   One who for reasons of conscience objects to military service, etc.

Absolutist   The Military Service Act allowed for absolute exemption but tribunals were reluctant to grant absolute exemption from military service for reasons of conscience. It is not absolute exemption that made one an absolutist but one's absolute refusal to support the war effort directly or indirectly. Usually this was on religious grounds (such as Christadelphians or Quakers) or political grounds (such as Marxists). In fact, most objectors to conscription received absolute exemption for reasons other than conscience, such as ill-health. Some conscientious objectors who suffered ill health were exempted for health reasons rather than conscience.

Alternativists   Alternativists were those who were prepared to accept work of national importance which was clearly non-military to them. For example, the FAU or FSC. The ILP and the NCF did not discourage acceptance of this.

Army Order X	Army order X of 25 May 1917 enabled COs to be sent to the nearest public civil prison had and have their case reviewed by the Brace Committee, and if genuine, would be released from military prison to do work of national importance in a civil prison or work camp under the Home Office Scheme. The order was not retroactive, leaving hundreds of objectors in military prisons or guardrooms.
Brace Committee and Home Office Scheme (H.O.S.)	Brace was an Under-secretary at the Home Office whose Committee on the Employment of Conscientious Objectors ran the Scheme. It created Work Centres throughout the country in under-used prisons or as countryside work camps. It was aimed at avoiding the brutality that COs had experienced from the army or prison. Those who took part are sometimes known as *schemers*, but were paid by the police and many regarded themselves as political prisoners. The *Schemers* and the *Absolutists* bore the brunt of the persecution.
'Certified', 'badged', 'carded' or 'essential' occupation	These are the terms used to describe of a man exempted from conscription in order to continue his normal employment in a national important occupation. The tribunals classified this as a class 'G' objector. However, in 1917 more stringent criteria were applied to 'comb out' less essential workers for conscription. Many conscientious objectors were already in such work prior to conscription.
FAU	The Friends Ambulance Unit (FAU) was set up in France in September 1914 by a group of young Quakers; most of its 1200 members were pacifists.
Non-combatant corps	The corps was formed in March 1916, and existed until January 1920. It was an army unit for COs and subject to military discipline. Its members would not be required to fight or take life. The NCF and the Quakers repudiated this compromise arrangement, considering it to be part of the military machine.this compromise arrangement, considering it to be part of the military machine.

215

Pelham Committee and Work of National Importance	A Board of Trade appointed committee whose purpose was to advise Military Service Tribunals on the types of work that were alternative to military service but were of *national importance*. Such work included agriculture, forestry, food supply, shipping, transport, mining, education and public utility services. As a result, in Huddersfield, for example, two thirds of COs stayed where they were to do this work and did not go to prison or work camps. This situation also applied at Port Talbot, in the case of the Bamfords, for example.
Reserve	The *Schemers* moved from the army to the HOS by being transferred to Army Reserve Class W. The Home Office Scheme was civilian controlled and the men were paid by the police The NCF said that this meant COs so classified were still part of the military machine and liable to recall. COs were based in used prisons, asylums and workhouses and worked outdoors or indoors depending on the location. Typical outdoor work was timber cutting, road making; drain-laying; rail maintenance and agriculture. Indoor work was often mailbag fabrication; brush and basket making and rope-making.
The Cat and Mouse Act	The proper name for this 1913 Act of Parliament was the Prisoners (Temporary Discharge for Ill-Health) Act. When a suffragette (or, later, a conscientious objector) was sent to prison, it was assumed that she or he might go on hunger strike to cause problems for the authorities. The Act let prisoners get weaker until they had to be released from prison. On release they were unlikely to protest until they regained their strength. At that point they would be re-arrested and the cycle might start all over again.

Appendix Ten:

Letter from Northallerton Prison

Number 250 *Name H. Rees*

NORTHALLERTON PRISON *May 10th 191*

Dear Wife and Children,

Glad to inform you that I am still well and fairly happy and glad to note that you and the children are likewise. It was very sad to hear of the arrival of so many wounded soldiers and that they have had to convert the schools into hospitals to accommodate them. It does seem that the people are getting used to this kind of thing, that they are becoming indifferent to it. We must settle ourselves down to things as they are and hope that the end is not far off.

I am sorry that Ewart Williams and Edgar Griffiths have had to go; their mothers must be worrying after them. W. I. Thomas must be having a rough time on the scheme; he appears to be very unfortunate.

Regarding the book Mr Jones mentions, do not send it on, as it is forbidden, being political. Thank him for his kind offer. I may say that I wrote to David John last week and I asked him to send me a book entitled the Bible of Nature. I have not heard from him yet. I want to hear from you that Vi reads books that will benefit her.

I see from Mr Jones' remark that the war is still being waged furiously and that there appears to be no indication of an early peace. I am inclined sometimes to think that peace will come upon us without warning, as it were. We were plunged into it suddenly and it is quite possible that it will terminate suddenly. As he remarks, the losses on both sides must be stupendous and I am not surprised that there is great unrest in Germany as a result. If I am not mistaken there is going to be great unrest in our country too. What is Mr Jones' position under the new Act? Is there a possibility of him having to go? I hope he will not be called upon as it would leave Mrs. Jones in a very sorry position, on account of the rationing.

I have been studying shorthand now for some weeks and I am making very good progress at it. If I continue to study, I have every reason to believe that I will become proficient in due course. How are you getting on with the garden? Have you just finished it?

Just a few lines to Vi. Well Vi, although I am absent from home I am always thinking of you and Kenny, but last Saturday I was thinking of you all the day. I knew it was your tenth birthday and I was wishing that I were at home to see your smiling face. Never mind I will come home some day and then we will have good times together, won't we? Now Vi I want you to always to remember that we have a duty to perform while we live; that is, we must live good lives and useful lives. We must be kind to everyone and if we can do anything that will make others happy, it is our duty to do it. By doing this we will make ourselves happy. I would very much like to see you Ken and Mammy, but you know that because I refuse to be a soldier and kill GERMANS I am locked up here. You know that too the Germans have little children like you and Kenny and then they are killed the children cry because they will never see their fathers again. Isn't it a pity (just) the same if an English or Welsh father is killed; the children cry and are made miserable. It would be much nicer if the German and English fathers would agree not to fight but to stay at home with their children and try to make others happy. There is no reason why they should fight and kill each other; neither of them have seen the others before nor have they quarrelled with each other. But there are certain people in each country who quarrel then they put their innocent men to fight for them.

Mammy tells me that you are very fond of reading. I am glad to hear that because, by reading, we get knowledge, so I would want you to read the good books that I gave you Xmas 1916. Read them and tell Kenny what you read about. Also the thousand best poems –learn as many as you can. I did intend telling you about the nice flowers that are in the prison garden but I must leave (XXX) till the next letter. Remember your music too, as I intend giving you lessons as soon as I come home. I cannot conclude without expressing my thanks to Johnny for his contribution, brief as it was it set me thinking.

I do not agree with him when he refers to himself as an Embryonic Being. The fact that he could express himself in the manner proves that he has passed the Embryonic stage and that he is conscious of the misdirection of human energy and realises fully the possibilities of a better condition of society as he remarks that there is a better way of settling disputes and it has been proved times without number industrially the people have learnt that strikes are a savage method of settling disputes and that it hurts all concerned, the innocent as well, so they have practically the strike in favour of conciliation there are aspects of his remarks I would like to deal with ideas etc but space forbids so I conclude with fondest love.

HERB

Women's Peace Crusade (Emily Johns/Peace News)

Each branch of the Peace Crusade is represented by a banner-carrying protester, including Port Talbot and Briton Ferry representatives

Appendix Eleven:
Statistics for Port Talbot objectors

Area	Objectors with known address	Percentage of total
Aberafan	11	22
Bryn	1	2
Cwmafan	21	40
Margam	3	6
Pontrhydyfen	2	4
Port Talbot	7	14
Taibach	6	12
Total	51	100

11.1 Percentage of objectors from areas of Port Talbot

Occupation	Port Talbot %	Briton Ferry %
Coal	21	nil
Rail	16	3
Iron, steel		29
Tinplate	29	50
Teaching	11	3
Farming	6	nil
Others	13	15
Not known	4	nil
Total	100	100

11.2 Employment

Religion	Numbers	Percentage of total
Baptist	3	4.3
Calvinistic Methodist	2	2.9
Christadelphian	2	2.9
Congregationalist	4	5.7
Methodist	4	5.7
Plymouth Brethren	2	2.9
Church of England	3	4.3
Other	4	5.7
Not stated	46	65.6
TOTAL	70	100

11.3 Religious affiliation

Notes for Appendices

[203] *Glamorgan Gazette* 31 March 1916 and *South Wales Weekly Post* 26 February 1916.
[204] Brother of William Brabazon Hallowes, VC, of Graigavon House.
[205] *Glamorgan Gazette* 11 February 1917.
[206] *Herald of Wales* 25 March 1916 and 3 June 1916.
[207] *Pioneer* 26 August 1916.
[208] *Glamorgan Gazette* 18 October 1907.
[209] *Cambrian* 28 January 1910.
[210] *Cambria Daily Leader* 3 February 1916.
[211] *Cambria Daily Leader* 17 January 1915.
[212] *Herald of Wales* 22 January 1916.
[213] *Pioneer* 17 June 1916.
[214] *Pioneer* 17 June 1916.
[215] *Pioneer* 20 May 1916.
[216] *Pioneer* 24 June 1916.
[216] *Pioneer* 24 June 1916.
[216] *Pioneer* 24 June 1916.
[219] *Pioneer* 8 July 1916.
[220] *Pioneer* 15 July 1916.
[221] *Pioneer* 22 July 1916.
[221] *Pioneer* 22 July 1916.
[223] *Pioneer* 24 March 1916.
[224] *Pioneer* 1 September 1917.
[225] *Pioneer* 19 September 1917.
[226] *Pioneer* 6 October 1917.
[227] *Pioneer* 20 October 1917.
[228] *Pioneer* 27 October 1917.
[229] *Pioneer* 8 December 1917.
[230] *Pioneer* 8 December 1917.
[231] *Pioneer* 23 February 1918.
[232] *Pioneer* 9 November 1918.
[233] *Pioneer* 9 November 1918.
[234] *Cambria Daily Leader* 6 May 1919.
[235] Bransby Griffiths was a Briton Ferry conscientious objector who was also at Penderyn Work Centre.

Acknowledgements

In alphabetical order:

Hugh Adams. His original insistence that there was a story to be told has, once again, proved correct about Port Talbot, too.

Tony Allen, of World War One Postcards, for allowing me to reproduce the rare images from his collection.

Allen Blethyn of Taibach, when forensic differentiation was required between synonymous local names.

David Carpanini's for permission to reproduce his most admired work as the book's cover.

Martin Davies, Alltwen, deserves thanks for his continued work behind the scenes.

Maria Day for new information from about the Waters family.

Aled Eurig for his contribution regarding the religious aspects of conscientious objection in Wales.

John Fleming and *Jo Mundy*, for their intelligent appreciation of the subject when producing the design and layout.

Gethin Evans of Gorseinon for his permission to reproduce Herbert Rees' letter from Northallerton Prison.

Pauline Griffiths for giving me access to Bransby Griffiths' notebook.

Malcolm Hill for information about his uncle, Joe Branch, regarding Aberafan Constituency Labour Party.

Catherine James of Dolgellau for information on her father, Jenkin William James.

Damian Owen of Port Talbot Historical Society for providing electronic images from the Society's archives.

Cyril Pearce of Huddersfield, creator of the eponymous Register.

Mike and *Anita Phillips* of Mike's Newsagents in Briton Ferry for encouraging readership.

Jon Skidmore of Neath and Vienna, for the identification of military uniforms and badges.

Martin Wright of Cardiff University History Department, and Chair of Llafur, the Welsh People's History Society.

Port Talbot Library, for the provision of research facilities, the enthusiasm of the staff and for the launch of 'Daring to Defy'.

Quakers in Wales and Breaking Barriers for the use of 'Imprisoned for his Conscience.'

The National Library of Wales' (NLW) for the Welsh Newspapers on Line facility, a treasure trove of information for this book.

The South Wales Miners' Library for research facilities and guidance.

The Welsh Centre for International Affairs' Wales for Peace Project for asking the question: 'In the 100 years since the First World War, how has Wales contributed to the search for peace?'

West Glamorgan Archives for the initiative and professionalism of everyone in that organisation.

Finally, my partner, *Dr Sylvia Duffy,* for her invaluable input on cultural perspectives and patience throughout the whole process.

Index of Port Talbot conscientious objectors and key supporters

The supporters are presented in **bold** type.

Anderson-Fenn, Mrs *168*
Anderson, William Crawford *169*
Bamford, John *99*
Bamford, Sidney *101*
Berryman, Percy Albert *63*
Branch, Joe *147*
Brown, John *127*
Davies, David (Denbigh) *64*
Davies, David (Cwmafan) *108*
Davies, Henry *149*
Davies, James *102*
Davies Joseph M. *64*
Davies, Leyshon *65*
Davies, Percy Warren *128*
Davies, Robert J. *66*
Edwards, Dan *110*
Emanuel, Lemuel *113*
Evans, Albert Rankin *67*
Evans, David John *132*
Evans, Isaac John *67*
Evans Robert *68*
Ford, Sidney John *104*
Gill, Nicholas Arthur *69*
Grane, William *70*
Grove, William *105*
Heycock, Edward *70*
Heycock, John *71*
Hopkins, Ivor J. *72*
Hughes, Robert Evan *73*
Hughes, Thomas Henry *74*
Jenkins, William James *75*
Jones, David John *56*
Jones, Evan K. *78*
Jones, John *80*
Jones, John E. *80*
Jones, John Selwyn *121*
Jones, Lewis Emlyn *81*
Jones, Rees *79*
Jones, Robert *80*
Jones, S. *129*
Jones, Vaughan *82*
Jones, William Ivor *82*
Lewis, Frederick James *105*
Lewis, William (Gwilym) *83*

Llewelyn, Joseph *83*
Mainwaring, Richard *84*
Mainwaring, Tal *153*
Mainwaring, Thomas A. *85*
Mainwaring, William J. *86*
Michael, Daniel Rees *106*
Miles, Thomas John *87*
Mills, John George *130*
Morgan, Aneurin *114*
Morris, Dan *121*
Morris, Ebenezer *130*
Morris, John *159*
Mort, Evan David *124*
Mullington, Arthur *87*
Nicholas, Rev T. E. *171*
Older, David William *89*
Pallister, Minnie *173*
Phillips, Daniel H. *89*
Phillips, David John *89*
Phillips, Philip *131*
Powell, Thomas David *57*
Price, James *186*
Rankin, Albert Owen *90*
Rees, George *94*
Rees, Idwal Gwynne *57*
Rees, William (Willie) *58*
Russell, Bertrand *175*
Samuel, Daniel *133*
Scott, Christopher R. *126*
Snowden, Philip *179*
Stephens, David John *106*
Studt, John *132*
Thomas, John Penry *59*
Thomas, William Arthur *60*
Wallhead, Richard C. *181*
Watters, Daniel *160*
Waters, Lancelot Thomas *95*
Wellington, John *97*
Williams, Llewelyn, KC *185*
Williams Robert (Bob) *183*
Williams, Thomas Henry *116*
Williams, William *133*
Woolcock, John (Jack) *118*